Respecting the
Wicked Child

RESPECTING THE

WICKED CHILD

A Philosophy
of Secular
Jewish Identity
and Education

MITCHELL SILVER

UNIVERSITY OF MASSACHUSETTS PRESS
Amherst

Designed by Dennis Anderson
Printed and bound by BookCrafters, Inc.

Library of Congress Cataloging-in-Publication Data

Silver, Mitchell.
Respecting the wicked child : a philosophy of secular Jewish
identity and education / Mitchell Silver.
p.   cm.
Includes bibliographical references and index.
ISBN 1-55849-179-1 (cloth : alk. paper). — ISBN 1-55849-180-5
(paper : alk. paper)
1. Humanistic Judaism.   2. Secularism.   3. Judaism — 20th century.
4. Jews — Identity.   5. Philosophy, Jewish.   I. Title.
BM197.8.S55   1998
296.8'34–dc21   98-22125
CIP

British Library Cataloguing in Publication data are available.

This book is published with the support and cooperation of the
University of Massachusetts Boston.

For May
and Irv

Contents

Preface

Gradually it has become clear to me what every great philosophy
so far has been: namely, the personal confession of its author and a kind of
involuntary and unconscious memoir; also that the moral (or immoral)
intentions in every philosophy constituted the real germ of life from
which the whole plant had grown.

NIETZSCHE, *Beyond Good and Evil*

YOU ARE MODERN, secular, and
thoroughly liberal — a child of the Enlightenment. So why be a Jew?
And how can you be a Jew and make your children Jews, without be-
traying your Enlightenment heritage? Such are the themes of this book.

I come to this project out of personal and professional need. I cannot
remember not knowing I was Jewish. I always felt that this was a very
important fact about me. But it was not clear why it was important.
My parents were not religious, but their irreligion was not a matter of
high, or even low, principle. They just did not take it seriously. I was
sent to Hebrew school, where I learned very little Hebrew and not
much of anything else, either — perhaps only a superficial acquaintance
with some customs that still maintained a hold on American Jewry of
the 1950s and 1960s. It was plain that my parents were not very clear
about why they were sending me to Hebrew school and that they were
not terribly concerned with what I was taught there.

My maternal grandparents were Yiddish-speaking immigrants, but
whatever significance was laid on that had to do with their newness to
America. There was no conscious desire to preserve the old ways they
had brought with them. Although there was a strong sense of ethnic
identity, there was scarcely a concept of Jewish *culture* in the house.
Jewish consciousness was manifested through barely articulated nostalgia, chauvinism, and paranoia. By the time I was ten, actual Jewish

practice of any sort struck me as "square." Three years later I was bar mitzvahed, and I would not have been shocked if that had been the last Jewish thing I ever did. In college most of my friends were Jewish, and none of them ever did anything explicitly Jewish in the four years I was there. But, however alienated I felt from Jewish practice, I never felt estranged from my Jewish identity. *Doing* anything Jewish seemed archaic, provincial, and unreasonable. But my identity as a Jew, although it may have waned a bit at times, was never in question. Still, under those conditions, it was puzzling what that identity amounted to.

With the birth of my children, the puzzle became a practical problem. I found that I wanted my Jewish identity transmitted to my children, but without understanding what my identity amounted to, I saw no likely means of transmission. I could not reproduce the Jewish milieu of my upbringing, and I would not have wanted to even if I could. The old country grandparents were gone, along with the nostalgia and prejudices that were natural to their children's homes. Bad Hebrew schools still existed, but I had lost the innocence that allowed my parents to send me to one of them.

For the religious, or those who can act in good conscience as though they are religious, however difficult it may be, the means of passing on a Jewish identity are not obscure. Judaism abounds with practices, and a modicum of religious observance provides enough family activities to make a strong impression on a childhood. But we of little (or no) faith, who are also fussy about acting in ways not in accordance with our basic convictions, have a problem. How do we make our children feel Jewish when we reject, or are indifferent to, Jewish practice?

For several years I have been the director of a secular Jewish Sunday school (a Workmen's Circle *Shule*), and my job has been largely to help create an institutional solution to this problem. Upon becoming director, I quickly confirmed what I had long suspected: My personal problem was widely shared. There are many people who what to do something, they know not what, for their children's Jewish education. Because our *shule* is advertised as secular and progressive, parents hope that by enrolling their children they will be doing this Jewish "something," without feeling hypocritical about doing it. But these parents seldom have very or any specific ideas about what they expect or hope will be done at the school. Usually they have some vague notions about Jewish values and ethics and a fuzzy desire to have their children learn a smattering of holiday customs. Some hope we will re-create in their children the nostalgic attachment that they, the parents, feel for the immigrant generation's folkways. A few expect "Judaism" without halacha (the traditional Jewish law) or God (the traditional focus of Jewish worship). Most have almost no idea what they expect but a strong sense of what they do not want. In short, I have found, within many American Jews, a substantial unsatisfied desire, whose object is obscure.

My professional encounter with this issue predates my school direc-torship and the birth of my children. Twenty years ago I started to work at Camp Kinderland, a "secular, progressive, Jewish" children's summer camp. This camp is heir to a tradition that confidently claimed to have solved the problem of being a Jew without Judaism. What was the solution? In a word: Yiddish. The Yiddish language was to be the key to a strong ethnic (its proponents would say *national*) identity without religion.

I say more of this socialist Yiddishist tradition in chapters 2 and 7. Here I only point out the obvious: Although the Yiddishists have had some remarkable achievements, their strategy does not and cannot serve as the basis for a contemporary secular Jewish identity. Camp Kinderland, where I still work most summers, is a vibrant, healthy institution. Its politics have gone from an orthodox Soviet-oriented communism to a principled, if nebulous (but after all, its a kids' camp, not a political party), liberal-progressivism concerned with economic justice and human rights. The camp's ideology has adapted in response to the evolution of the political thought of its constituents, the changes in their lives, and the unfolding of history. Feminist, environmentalist, and gay-liberationist perspectives have been integrated into the camp's political curriculum. But what of its ethnic, "national" commitments? It is ironic that Camp Kinderland, whose ideology was for so long more open-minded and flexible on "the national question" than it was about its political loyalties, now has a vigorous political curriculum and a near moribund Jewish one. The sickly state of the camp's Jewish identity is not due to a lack of good nationalist intentions. The Yiddish-ist fields are worked as much as the circumstances allow. But they don't allow much. The children don't hear Yiddish at home. Their parents, by and large, don't understand any Yiddish. Indeed, most of their grandparents don't speak it. The children are almost as removed from the cultural context of the language and its literature as would be any randomly selected native-born American child. The classic Peretz story, "If Not Higher," with its references to *slichos*, Litvaks, wonder-working rabbis, morning prayers, and so forth requires as much gloss for Kinderland's campers as it would for their Gentile classmates.

Camp Kinderland's attempt to remain Jewish solely on a Yiddishist basis has resulted in the diminution of its Jewishness. But it had no other basis, or at least none that would not seem a betrayal of its secularism. Neither the old Yiddishism nor a turn to religiosity felt authentic. The former had little to do with contemporary Kinderlanders' lives, the latter nothing to do with their beliefs. But if not on religion and not on language, on what could a Jewish identity be founded? For various reasons Zionism, the answer for some secularists (see chapters 2 and 6), is not an option for Kinderlanders and is not an adequate answer for secular American Jews in general (see chapters 2, 4, 6, and 7).

In recent years I have become the camp's "cultural director," with primary responsibility for formulating Kinderland's Jewish programming. Here my job has been to take a well-defined, unambivalent, detailed tradition of secular Jewish identity, *which was no longer alive or resurrectable,* and transmogrify it into living, meaningful, contemporary programming. This was both more and less problematic than my *shule* task. Less problematic, because there was a definite tradition to call upon and reshape, a tradition which commanded the theoretical allegiance of the institution and many of its members. More problematic, because the dead tradition set precedents that discouraged practices it did not endorse. While a strong model can guide development, it can also inhibit innovation. At times (although with increasingly less frequency) suggestions for new Jewish programming at camp are met with the response, "that's not *our* tradition," or "that's not secularism." At *shule* there is seldom an objection to what we are doing, but often a concern that we should be doing a not fully specified something more.

So I am the inheritor of multiple impulses toward Jewish secularism and multiple assignments for realizing it. From my childhood I got a strong sense of being Jewish; it was rooted in family memories, Mel Brooks and Allen Sherman routines, and Borscht Belt anecdotes — coupled with a thin formal religiosity that was strongly, although unselfconsciously, de facto secular. As *shule* director I am charged with leading a school that does something meaningfully Jewish, but not religious, for children who are from families that, by and large, have no other Jewish dimensions in their lives. My camp assignment is to find a viable successor to Yiddishist secularism that will remain true to the Yiddishist secular spirit.

Two other biographical elements, though not directly Jewish, are significant. I passed a standard New Left young adulthood that created enduring political values and commitments. In this I am typical of the parents of the children at the *shule* and Camp Kinderland. I have also spent many years studying philosophy, and I find myself, not only more firmly committed to the political values I first forged in the sixties, but also, after weighing, as best I can, all the subtleties of complex and sophisticated analyses, consistently rejecting belief in any transcendence or supernaturalism.

I have given this personal account because what Nietzsche found in all great philosophy is also true of some considerably more modest works such as the present one. This book is confessional philosophy. Its wellsprings are the author's history, prejudices, and inclinations. Its manifest content is a rationalization of its biographical sources. In other words, this book is an exercise in self-justification, but one, I hope, that has application, and therefore use and interest, to other selves seeking justification.

There is a double sense in which this is a book of self-justification. First, the thing that is justified is a self, or a type of self (in this case the type I belong to). Second, the justification is meant to assuage that same self that is being justified. The book is not an attempt to justify that self before God (especially not God) or humankind. It is an attempt to convince me (the self in question) and those like me — liberal, secular, cosmopolitan, highly (but not wholly) assimilated Jews — that central aspects of our lives are coherent and valuable, or at least can be made so.

For those like me, our most naturally inhabited self, that is the commitments, principles, values, and attitudes that come most easily and are worn most comfortably, is built out of our Enlightenment heritage. For all of the fashionable anti-Enlightenment critiques current, "Enlightenment values" still best describes our moral posture. Our devotion to the "rights of man," and the "scientific spirit," is profound. Our commitment to universal human equality is primary. And yet for all our cosmopolitan liberalism, few of us are emotionally prepared to abandon the ancient tribal loyalty. Perhaps this is only an emotional condition, unsupported by the rational dictates of prudence or morality. Indeed, perhaps it is an emotional condition at odds with a rational life and traditional liberal values. But in what follows I try to show that this is not the case. I argue (for philosophers seek justification through argument) that there is no necessary conflict between modern liberalism and a Jewish identity. I describe how they can be harmonized. I try to turn apparent conflict into beneficial complement. I offer a rationale for, and a vision of, an American Jewish life uncompromising in its fundamental modern liberalism but satisfying and substantively Jewish.

I make no claims of comparative worth. I say nothing here to the religious, the illiberal, or the comfortably and completely assimilated. For all I say in this book, those ways may be as commendable as the one I recommend. But I cannot believe in God, won't abandon the liberal emancipation project, and want to remain a Jew. There is no great trick to being an atheist liberal Jew unreflectively. It is a commonplace collection of stances. But their reflective cohabitation is a more difficult domestic arrangement. For me, intellectual *shalom bayes* (household peace) is worth a book. Moreover, I believe that the rational ordering and reconciliation of beliefs and desires, besides being intrinsically satisfying and anxiety allaying, can deepen, broaden, and direct the beliefs and desires. By rationally undergirding and weaving together our liberal, secular, *and* Jewish inclinations, we give each element additional weight, depth, and life.

Numerous philosophical issues are lurking behind the central concerns of this project. I have tried to keep them from cluttering the text. The philosophical bric-a-brac I managed to purge from the text is, however, stored in footnotes. Readers who find them tedious digressions are thereby easily enabled to avoid them. Some readers may regret that they still have to maneuver around much philosophical housekeeping that has not been exiled to the bottom of the page. I apologize to those who are interested in the subject but bored or befuddled by what may strike them as esoteric worries and curiosities. I hope they find a way of reading around these patches. But, for me, these issues are philosophical, and honesty demanded at least a nod in the direction of philosophical rigor. If anything, I have a bad conscience about all of the crucially relevant philosophy that has not found its way even into the footnotes.

My picture of Secular Jewish life is envisioned as an educational program. Although my primary interest is in describing and justifying a type of cultural identity, almost all the practical and concrete questions of its creation, viability, and worth are addressed by exploring the means of its transmission. What it means to be a Secular Jew is often best answered and, in some aspects, only answered, by articulating what Secular Jews teach their children. To a certain extent, casting the discussion as the construction and justification of a Secular Jewish curriculum is only a device for compelling specificity about Secular Jewish identity. But this curriculum is also intended as a realistic and practical guide, though hardly definitive, to developing the content of a Secular Jewish school.

This book is an exercise in preaching to the choir in a congregation of nonreligious, left-leaning baby boomers perplexed by the meaning of their Jewish identity but interested in making their children feel as Jewish as they do. Although I assume throughout that the choir consists of congregants already convinced of church doctrine, I believe its members still stand in need of a sermon attempting to analyze, clarify, organize, and justify the creed. The sermon consists of two parts. The first part, chapters 1 through 4, is concerned with the philosophical bases and fundamental components of Secular Judaism.[1] Chapter 1 tries to motivate the project, chapter 2 provides its historical context, and chapters 3 and 4 explore its connection to spirituality and progressive politics. The second part — chapters 5, 6, and 7 — focuses on philosophical topics in Secular Jewish education. Chapter 5 grapples with the Holocaust as an educational issue, and chapter 6 deals with Israel in similar terms. Chapter 7 tries to draw everything together into an integrated and somewhat more concrete account of Secular Jewish identity and education. There are issues raised earlier in the book that do not receive a full accounting until this final chapter. So, for instance,

---

1. When capitalized, "Secular Judaism" refers to the specific vision of a nonreligious way of being Jewish that is described in this book. Similarly "Secular Jews" are its intentional adherents. Uncapitalized, "secular Jews" refers to all nonreligious Jews. The Secular Jews are drawn from the pool of secular Jews.

in chapter 1, where I give the basic arguments for its not being irrational or illiberal to foster one's Jewish identity, I leave out the role of the subjective rationality of love in explaining and justifying particular attachments. That point, along with others that are related to topics discussed in chapters 1 through 6, are best treated together and appear in chapter 7, a chapter that serves as a sort of peroration to my sermon. The preaching is not meant to recruit congregants from people who have no inclination to join, although I confess to a hope that a latent desire in people listening through the window may be aroused.

Although the book is brief, I have incurred many debts of gratitude in its writing. Informal luncheons at the University of Massachusetts Boston's Department of Philosophy have been a congenial venue in which to try out some of the ideas developed in this book. I want to thank my colleagues there, not only for the luncheon discussions, but for the general congeniality that pervades all the department's activities. I have been fortunate in that my philosophical life has been spent mostly at the University of Massachusetts Boston and the University of Connecticut. The latter, where I trained, showed me that philosophy can be a cheerful and cooperative enterprise, in the words of A. N. Whitehead, a "survey of the possibilities." The leadership of Jerry Shaffer and Joel Kupperman did much to set that good-humored, benevolent tone. Larry Foster, the chair, along with the rest of the philosophy faculty at the University of Massachusetts Boston, has so continued to engender the harmonious feelings of my graduate school days that I wonder how academic departments have earned the reputation of being mean-spirited, competitive, and petty. Neither department could have been more supportive or magnanimous.

Teddy Auerbach, Henry Feingold, Ora Gladstone, Ellen Grabiner, Amy Herrick, Cheryl Klausner, Nelson Lande, Judee Rosenbaum, Steve Vogel, and Alan Zaslavsky read, and made helpful comments on, early drafts of the manuscript. The careful readings and challenging questions of Larry Blum, Dan Willbach, David Goldberg, Art Goldhammer, and anonymous readers for the University of Massachusetts Press forced me to come to grips (or at least consciously not come to grips) with a number of crucial issues for my view of Secular Judaism. I am also grateful for the help I received from Paul Wright, Catlin Murphy, Pam Wilkinson, and Marsha Kunin of the University of Massachusetts Press.

It is with colleagues and friends at *shule* and camp that I have first grappled with some of the issues addressed in this book. At *shule,* Karen Klein, Cookie Avrin, Carol Axelrod, Mike Felsen, Mike Katz, Steve Vogel, Jenny Silverman, Bob Taube, and Alan Zaslavsky have all been key coworkers in the attempt to build a Secular Jewish school. Alice Shecter-Grunfeld, Judee Rosenbaum, Ira Palansky, Elsie Suller, Rachel Wyatt, Maddy Simon, and Valerie Coleman have been dear friends and stalwart comrades at camp. But at both *shule* and camp, it is really the entire communities that sustain the work and contributed to my understanding of the problems and promise of Secular Judaism.

For their interest in this project I wish especially to thank my Joels — Marks and Greifinger — my great interlocutors. Joel Marks brings to philosophical discussions an enthusiasm, seriousness, originality, and daring that is always an inspiration. Joel Greifinger's penetrating intelligence, social insight, psychological acuity, and intellectual openness are constant spurs to more depth and honesty. Both Joels do philosophy with abundant humor, and they read and discussed a number of drafts of this book with great generosity of time and spirit.

Ira Levine has promised to buy this book and Ella Taylor promised to provide a photograph of herself for the book jacket. As of this writing it is unclear if they will keep their promises. If they do, I wish to thank them both for its financial success.

A travel grant from the University of Massachusetts provided some direct support for research on chapter 6. Indirect support came via a Melton Fellowship to my wife, Ora Gladstone, for her own research, thereby enabling to spend time in Israel. Besides getting the money for us to spend a year in Israel, Ora has been my main instructor and exemplar for incorporating Jewish identity as a joyful, central part of life. For that, among other things, I am very grateful to her.

Respecting the
Wicked Child

CHAPTER ONE

Why Bother?

MOST JEWS are familiar with the parable of the four sons in the Passover Haggadah. Three are characterized in terms of the wisdom of their questions: There is a wise son, a simple son, and a son too ignorant to formulate a question. These labels emphasize the intellectual properties of the questioners. But the fourth son is given a moral description. He is the wicked son. His sin is the expression of alienation from the tradition. The other sons ask how to celebrate the seder properly or what it is all about. The wicked son asks, "What has it to do with me?"

Among contemporary Jews there are many wicked children, and they merit answers that amount to more than the traditional scornful dismissal. This chapter is an attempt to address one large group of alienated Jews from a perspective they already have: secularist. It is unlikely that any arguments can create a Jewish identity or commitment where none exists. But a confused identity and weak commitment might be clarified, strengthened, and rationalized by certain considerations. While the remainder of this book discusses issues within secular Jewish education, this chapter tries to motivate a concern for such education.

Why bother getting a secular Jewish education or, more to the point, giving your children one? The reasons I will provide are neither general nor conclusive. They are not general because they do not apply to those who are "religious"[1] or those who feel absolutely no connection to the Jewish people. They are not conclusive because there may be weighty, unrefuted, counterbalancing reasons to drop one's Jewish identity. But

---

1. It is perhaps more accurate to say that there are other reasons for being Jewish that are the dominating ones for religious people.

they are reasons that support and add substance to an already existing inclination seeking justifications.

Portrait of a Wicked Child

I begin with a portrait of a typical contemporary "wicked" child, now in fact an adult with some children of her own. Her grandparents or great-grandparents immigrated to America from Eastern Europe, and she heard some Yiddish during childhood. She was sent to a few years of Hebrew school, where she learned some Bible stories, a few holiday traditions, and some Hebrew. She hated it and remembers almost nothing. She speaks no Hebrew and knows only a couple of Yiddish expressions, and these are pretty much the same ones that the average television-watching Gentile American is coming to know. Similarly, while she believes she has a special attachment to Jewish foods, her daily diet is standard, urban, middle-class American. She eats more tuna than herring, more yogurt than sour cream, more tofu than cabbage. If she eats a lot of bagels, well, so do her non-Jewish neighbors. There was little synagogue attendance in her youth and for years only a friend's or relative's wedding or bar/bat mitzvah gets her to shul. Agnostic or atheist, she believes that the Bible is a wholly human document. Its laws and recommendations are without any supernatural authority, its metaphysical explanations, myths of more or less charm, its narrative accounts, legends of varying historical accuracy. She is too dimly aware of other traditional Jewish texts to have any opinion about them beyond the belief that they are of no relevance to her life. What she knows of Jewish laws and customs — Sabbath observance, kosher laws, *mikvah* ritual — strike her as burdensome and silly and perhaps even morally objectionable. Still she is a Jew. She would not deny it or its importance. Furthermore, it is important to her that her children feel that they are Jews. While she might bristle and would dispense with the ritual, in the end she would certainly have her sons circumcised. And although she is not sure how or why it happened, most of her friends are Jewish.

Such a person finds in herself a gut desire to instill a Jewish identity in her children but has difficulty finding reasons for doing so. Without reasons, the will to enact her desire is weakened, and the way to enact her desire seems a muddle.[2] This muddled way further undermines her will. When there is no way, it is hard to maintain a will.

Enlightenment Loyalties
Enlightened Assimilation: Only a Social Democrat!

Not only is it hard for the secularist to find reasons to maintain Jewish identity, it is also hard to *overcome* reasons *against* maintaining a Jewish identity. The most powerful arguments for assimilation stem from the liberal Enlightenment vision of a universal common humanity. On this view all that is significantly human is, or ought to be, universal. We all partake of reason, share basic emotions, and have irreducible needs. We all have rights and deserve equal respect. Moral progress consists of recognizing and consistently applying these truths. This involves constant widening of the circle of people treated as complete equals and as subjects of concern. While there is nothing in this attitude that is logically incompatible with having a particular ethnic or religious identity, it has historically tended to assimilationist positions. If our similarities are of crucial moral importance, how important can our differences be? Won't emphasizing the particularities obscure the commonalities? And, as a matter of historical fact, haven't ethnic and religious differences impeded the realization of an Enlightenment morality of universal rights and human equality? Indeed hasn't ethnic consciousness contributed to history's worst brutalities and oppressions? Is it not today the motor driving war and massacre?

The classic Enlightenment liberal might allow that the answer to these questions is more complicated than the questions' rhetorical nature suggests. The roots of oppression, moral callousness, and bloody-mindedness may involve economic, sexual, biological, and psychologi-

---

2. Of course the desire is a muddle too. It is not simply that we have a sharp, clear, but nonrationally motivated desire. The desire is of mixed and murky origins. To a limited extent, my project of rationalizing the desire throws light on those origins, for I suspect the desire often grows from *reasons* of which we are dimly aware. But the desire typically will also stem from nonrational psychological processes. These are of great interest, but not of direct pertinence, to this inquiry. Whatever its origins, I'm concerned to show that the desire to remain Jewish, and have your children identify as Jews, is a desire that can be given a rational and moral foundation.

cal factors only tangentially related to ethnic/religious identity. But at the very least ethnic/religious identification does not seem to have helped matters. Even in the view of those who find the fundamental moral flaws in human society to reside in other structures, our ethnic/religious identities aggravate the problem by obscuring its real nature. The best example of this view is the classic Marxist position: Nationalism creates in workers an (unreciprocated) identification with their bourgeoisie and a division from the workers of other countries. Marxist strategy and morality calls for internationalism. The workers have no homeland. Attaching importance to differences other than class differences distracts workers from the real struggle, whose goal is to do away with that class difference.

There are differences between Marxist and classical Enlightenment morality, but they share a vision of equality and universalism that fosters an internationalist outlook. When Trotsky was asked if he thought of himself as a Russian or as a Jew, he answered that he was a Social Democrat and only that. One need not be a Marxist to feel the moral lure of rejecting ethnic, religious, or national identifications in favor of universal human solidarity.[3]

Marxism also shares with other Enlightenment ideologies a devotion to reason and science. Here, too, ethnic particularities, especially religiously based ones, are thought retrograde. Reason and science are ways, or rather, in tandem, are the way everyone has equal access to reliable knowledge. Religion supports superstition. Folk traditions preserve prejudices. It is practically and morally good to have this hodgepodge of beliefs replaced by knowledge — universally justifiable true beliefs. Education, therefore, should be rationalist. We should teach our children what science tells us is true of the world and how reason tells us to discover new truths. Religious and folk beliefs are intellectual obscurantism, just as religious and folk loyalty are moral obscurantism. There are no national sciences, no ways of knowing, valid only for certain peoples.

In general the Enlightenment weltanschauung, whether Comte's Religion of Reason or Marx's Scientific Socialism, placed considerable moral weight on the universally valid epistemological method. My

---

3. Something like this position is argued by Martha Nussbaum (1994).

quarrel is neither with these basic Enlightenment epistemological ideals nor with basic Enlightenment moral ideals. Indeed, reconciling a contemporary American Jewish identity with these fundamental ideals is central to my project. Whatever doubts twentieth-century philosophy has cast on Enlightenment philosophy, and substantial doubts have been cast from many directions — from Quineans, from the Frankfurt School, from the host of postmodern neorelativisms — still, my loyalty to the basic Enlightenment world view remains untouched.[4] But more important, these twentieth century philosophical developments have left the gut Enlightenment commitments of most secular American Jews untouched. My dispute with the Enlightenment is merely with one common, I believe mistaken, interpretation of those ideals, an interpretation that condemns all ethnic particularism: Enlightenment Universalism.

Enlightenment Universalism: The Smorgasbord Cultural Ideal

Of course human life requires particular cultural forms.[5] However universal our deep grammar may be, we need particular grammars and particular vocabularies to speak; however common our nutritional

---

4. Because this book is, in large part, an argument for the compatibility of the Enlightenment ethos and ethnic particularism, and the value of their coupling, a reader might feel she has a right to expect a defense of both elements. But, in spite of the considerable recent fire directed at the Enlightenment, I take its fundamental desirability as a given. This is not because I believe critiques of the Enlightenment ethos are obviously wrongheaded and not worth refuting. On the contrary, I think their refutation is a large undertaking meriting a separate volume. I feel justified in not doing it in this volume because the academic attempts to undermine Enlightenment values have not (yet?) destabilized their role in most secularist Jews' hearts or daily-life minds. Unlike their Jewish loyalties, Enlightenment loyalties have not become a practical and moral problem.

5. Here and throughout I will use the term *culture* innocently to refer to a set of patterns through which a group of humans live their lives. How we individuate these sets, how we determine their members, and how we identify the groups and *their* members that live through these sets of patterns are all problems that should make us wary of the concept. A case could be made that there is no such thing as a culture, or more modestly, that the concept is either too vague or tacitly incorporates too many myths to be usefully employed. I concede the premises. I do think "a culture" is a multi-problematical concept, vague in many dimensions and velcro for social myths. But, although I shall not argue it here, I deny that its problems vitiate its usefulness. In the end we still need a term to refer to the commonalities between certain people that most generally characterizes how they live. I hope that my innocent use of the term remains innocent in both senses, and never trades in on its vagueness or mythical connotations to carry a point. For interesting discussions of the concept of *culture*, see the work of Clifford Geertz (1973).

needs, we require some specific ways of preparing and eating food. But although we cannot avoid being cultural beings, an extremist Enlightenment liberal might deny the necessity or desirability of our being separate cultural beings. I call this ideal Enlightenment Universalism. It aspires to a universal culture that might be an amalgam of previous cultures, preserving and developing the best elements of each. To those who would argue that cultures form coherent wholes whose parts lose value when torn from context and pasted onto a cultural collage, the Enlightenment Universalist partisan replies that cultural purity is as problematic as racial or ethnic purity. Indeed, some maintain that belief in cultural superiority, or even separatism, merits the epithet *racism* as surely as analogous beliefs in the biological sphere. Why should the blending of our cultural inheritances not be as acceptable as the blending of our biological inheritances? In addition to being fully egalitarian and integrationist, this vision of cultural homogeneity has the virtue of removing many sources of conflict and oppression. So says the Enlightenment Universalist.

A less extreme position, which we can term modified Enlightenment Universalism, recognizes the value of cultural diversity but believes it can be maintained without separate cultural groups. In this view the world should present a cultural smorgasbord from which individuals freely choose the most appealing elements. In other words, instead of one music tradition, which blends the best of jazz, gamalan, reggae, salsa, European classical, and so on (the extreme Universalist position), the various musical traditions continue to lead separate existences, but they are not attached to separate ethnic or regional groups. Rather, they are practiced and appreciated by individuals who freely choose to practice them. Culture is not imposed by an accident of birth, it is chosen in accordance with personal tastes and values. Those cultural forms that must be introduced before individual choice is possible, such as a child's initial language or diet, or those cultural forms that must be standardized to function, such as modes of transportation or, again, language, should be chosen by the smallest feasible unit, be that family, school, or neighborhood. In some cases the smallest feasible unit may be the entire world. Perhaps we will all have to learn and use Windows 98. But the ideal is to have a world in which the greatest possible variety of cultural forms is open to each individual. It is an ideal inspired by devotion to the value of individual freedom.

In sum, ethnic and religious consciousness appear to be in tension with universal justice, reason, and individual freedom. Those of us committed to these classic Enlightenment values must think twice before indulging any gut desire to make our children feel like Jews.

Reply to Enlightenment Universalism: The Costs of Universalism and the Realization of Enlightenment Ideals without It

Enlightenment Universalists lodge the intertwined charges of racism and warmongering against ethnic/cultural particularism. Again, this is a caricature of the Enlightenment Universalist position. Universalists concede the naturalness and inevitability of cultural groupings and even the value of cultural diversity and "group cultural rights."[6] But these are concessions to realities and values that run counter to the Enlightenment Universalist's ideal world.[7] The Universalist still wishes to see the realities altered as much as possible and the values degraded as much as possible, for she sees them in tension with the quintessential Enlightenment liberal vision. I do not deny that this tension exists. But while the Enlightenment Universalist sees a threatening tension, I believe it is possible to completely defuse the tension and have a world of diverse cultural communities that still realizes the fundamental Enlightenment liberal values. Before explaining how that world can be structured, I will discuss the problems of Enlightenment Universalism.

An unsegmented universal culture, even were it to contain the same inventory of "items" that now exists in the various separate cultures, would represent a great aesthetic loss. Not only would uprooted individual artifacts be devalued, but the value inherent to the whole would also be totally lost. It would be as if we could only listen to Verdi's arias in alphabetical order. Outside their dramatic setting and proper relation to other arias (and recitatives), each aria is diminished, but, in addition, we lose completely the value of the operas as artistic objects. A well-wrought work of art has a beauty beyond the beauty of its parts. And so it is with human cultures. They cannot be indifferently

---

6. See Kymlicka 1989.
7. Of course modern nationalism is also a child of the Enlightenment, and indeed till the late eighteenth century was part of its *liberalism*. But it is not the strand of Enlightenment liberalism that has ongoing influence on the "wicked children" of contemporary Jewry.

mixed and heaped without a great falling off. This is not a racist call for purity but an aesthetic call for integrity. This distinction will be elaborated in chapter 7's discussion of intermarriage. But for now we note that cultural integrity in no way precludes the absorption of new elements or the evolution of old ones. Cultural life is not static, but it is more than a collection of artifacts.

More than just aesthetic value is lost when individuated cultures are lost. There is also moral loss. People are deeply attached to their cultures. It is where they are at home, where they find meaning. It is an object of their loyalty, their love, and their hopes. They revere it as they do a parent. They take pride in it as they do a child. People so much see themselves within their culture, that the destruction of a culture is in some ways the destruction of the people who inhabit that culture. In addition to the harm done an individual when she is personally deprived of her culture, there is the harm done to her by the imminent death of her culture, even if she does not personally experience that death. To have one's culture become extinct is a little like being sterile. But it is actually the much more significant harm of spiritual, rather than genetic, discontinuity. People are seriously harmed when cultures are lost. This is a moral loss. Together with the aesthetic loss, it provides strong grounds for maintaining whole, coherent cultures and not just valuable elements from all cultures.[8]

Moreover, since one's culture is the largest social context for personal formation, it cannot be offered, at least not initially and perhaps not ever, as one option among others. It is more that which does the choosing than that which is chosen. One cannot expose a child to an array of coherent human cultures and ask her to choose her favorite. The existence of particular cultures depends on the existence of parents willing and able to raise their children in them. So an Enlightenment Universalism that seeks to retain particular cultures only as completely

---

8. Larry Blum wonders if there might be a value carried by cultures that is neither aesthetic nor moral (personal communication). For me the answer is no. I take these two categories to exhaust the realm of value. I can conceive of no nonmoral value that I would not term *aesthetic*. But there are certainly possible subcategorizations within the moral and the aesthetic. Someone might want to reserve the term *aesthetic* for the type of value (if it is a single type) embodied in art or nature (or in the appreciative experience of art or nature). Maybe a good meal, good sex, and good basketball carry different kinds of nonmoral (as well as moral) values, but they strike me as broadly aesthetic. I find the basic bifurcation of value into the *moral* and the *aesthetic* the most useful initial approach to discussions of value.

freely chosen options for individuals is tantamount to an Enlightenment Universalism that envisions the abolition of particular cultures in favor of a universal one. And this, I have argued, entails aesthetic and moral losses.

In rejecting the "smorgasbord" ideal of culture, I do not mean to deny the possibility or desirability of selecting from a broad array of cultural goods. Nor do I disparage the value of customizing cultural pursuits to individual inclinations. I only claim that there are limits to cultural freedom beyond which it either ceases to be a genuine freedom or ceases to be a valuable freedom. It is not a genuine freedom if it leaves a child culturally shaped by random forces. The child is still constrained to choose from *a* cultural perspective. It is no less restrictive than some other (but still liberal) cultural perspectives, for being accidental. And it is not a valuable freedom if it leaves the child free to pick "the best" or the most "personally meaningful" from all of world culture at the expense of experiencing the coherence and value of any one culture. Even assuming that the "personal culture" built for and by a child had a coherence and beauty of its own, its wholly personal nature would diminish much of the value to be had from cultural life. The recommendation to cultivate one's own garden does not discourage a wide survey of all the pleasing flora that might grow there. But there must be a connected soil to root them in. Otherwise you have a collection of potted plants and no real garden at all.

There might be a reluctance to give up Enlightenment Universalism by those who see it as integral to the more fundamental Enlightenment ideals of reason, fraternity, freedom, and equality. One might agree that there are aesthetic and moral losses in the demise of particular cultures but still believe that these losses are outweighed by the ability to realize the fundamental Enlightenment values.

I think it is true historically that cultural differences and the existence of "separate and distinct" societies have often promoted inequality, superstition, oppression, and hostility. But I believe this connection between the existence of particular cultures and conservative or reactionary values (i.e., non-Enlightenment values) is an historical contingency. It is a connection that can be undone. A world of particular cultures and enlightened liberal values is possible. While I have no detailed blueprint for bringing that world about, I can broadly suggest conditions conducive to its existence.

The problem is to find conditions that simultaneously promote Enlightenment values and that maintain the existence of particular cultures. Substantial headway is made once we realize that the maintenance of, and respect for, particular cultures does not require that our respect be unqualified. We can work for a world of particular cultures, none of which has certain features and all of which have other features. There are an infinite number of nonsexist, nonracist, egalitarian possible cultures. An advocate of cultural pluralism need have no commitment to moral relativism. And her nonrelativist values can be Enlightenment ones as easily as any others. Moreover the existence of multiple particular cultures does not require that any of them reject the ideal of universally valid scientific knowledge. Each culture may have ways of supplementing this universal knowledge with its own ways of knowing, its own insights and concepts. But its members could still partake of a universal knowledge, a knowledge that, along with shared values, regulates intercultural relations.[9]

Nor need cultural difference give rise to intercultural fear, hostility, or contempt. Although few in number, historical examples of intercultural harmony and respect prove the possibility of such harmony. The various Swiss ethnicities have not been at each others' throats for quite some time now. We may not fully know all the conditions that create it, but it is probable that nonexploitive economic relations are necessary; also, some knowledge of the other culture is helpful. A vision of secular Jewish culture should incorporate these features. More of this in chapters 4 and 7.

Why Be Jewish?

Suppose we agree that maintaining particular cultures is valuable and not incompatible with fundamental Enlightenment values. Still we have no specific reason to be *secular Jews*. It is good to be something, but is it good to be *this* something? The question is especially acute for the Wicked Child profiled above, who arguably already has a serviceable culture; she is an American. Choosing to be a secular Jew is not a

---

9. Cf. Rawls's overlapping consensus (Rawls 1993).

choice for maintaining a whole way of life but a choice to supplement or further refine a way of life that has not yet been shown to need supplements. What reasons can we give her for identifying with and, more to the point, educating her children as secular Jews.

Although I give secularism (i.e., principled irreligion) some attention in chapter 7 (for some defense of it must appear in a book pleading the value of a secular Jewish identity), for the most part, I do not deal with this part of the question. Whether, having chosen to be Jewish, it is better to be religious or secular, is a question beyond the scope of this book. In chapter 3 I explore the possible relationship between secularity, religion, and spirituality, and much of the book can be taken as an argument that being a *secular* Jew is a feasible cultural identity; but for now I simply want to give nonreligious reasons for the Wicked Child to retain some sort of Jewish identity. As I said earlier, I do not think there are conclusive reasons. Ultimately the reasons I give only shore up (indeed they themselves, in part, grow out of) the emotional attachment to being Jewish. They can have little or no force to someone who, for whatever reason, does not feel Jewish at all. But if there is a feeling there, there are some things to be said for it.

The Blood of the Martyrs

I begin with a family of considerations I call "the blood of the martyrs" arguments. The most common and powerful one relates to the Holocaust. The Nazis' goal was to exterminate the Jewish people. Their success in destroying the Yiddish-Jewish world of Eastern Europe as a living culture was almost complete. The murderers made substantial progress in the physical destruction of the Jewish people. Still, the Jewish people survived the Nazis. Jews did not disappear. But if Jews ever were to disappear, Hitler's dream of a Jew-free world would be realized. To deny Hitler this "posthumous victory,"[10] Jews are obliged to continue to exist as Jews. Even if there were no positive reasons, spiting Hitler might be sufficient grounds for maintaining a Jewish identity. Indeed, as long as there are anti-Semites, it seems dishonor-

---

10. The term is Emil Fackenheim's (1970).

able and cowardly to stop being Jewish. There is some good in frustrating an evil. In addition, there is some good in affirming solidarity with any group of human beings who are unjustly persecuted and despised.

It may be argued that Hitler would best be spited by fighting irrational obsessions with ethnicity, in which case cultivating one's Jewish identity may seem an endorsement rather than a rejection of Hitlerism.[11] But Hitler worshipped "race," not ethnicity. Not every basis of group identity has equivalent moral connotations. Racial consciousness is noxious in a way that ethnic consciousness need not be. Further, a central aim of this book is to show that a secular Jewish identity can be rational and can include wider human solidarities; that is, it need not be irrational or obsessional. But even if ethnic consciousness were viewed as an item in Hitler's agenda broadly conceived, its rejection would only spite bigots, in general, but would not offer a specific reproach to anti-Semites. Hitler hated Jews more than he hated liberals, and Jewish continuity spites Hitlerism more specifically than does broad-minded tolerance. Of course, combining Jewish identity with a broad-minded tolerance is the best rebuke of all.

Anti-Semitism affords grounds for maintaining Jewish identity beyond spiting anti-Semites. Since anti-Semites won't let you forget that you are a Jew, since they hate you and heap calumny on you for being a Jew, you should acknowledge and have knowledge of being a Jew, lest you understand your social identity solely through the attitudes and beliefs of those who hate it.[12] If the existence of anti-Semitism means there is no escape from being Jewish, is it not wise to explore and understand your place of social interment?

There is a more uplifting blood of the martyrs argument. For thousands of years Jews have been scorned, robbed, humiliated, ostracized, oppressed, tortured, murdered, and expelled for being Jewish. Until Hitler they had the option, as a group and as individuals, of abandoning Judaism and, if not completely ending their travails, at least greatly

---

11. This line of thought was suggested by an anonymous reader for the University of Massachusetts Press.

12. I was reminded of this Sartrean point by Joel Greifinger. Sara Bershtel and Allen (1992) Graubard correctly point out that consciousness of anti-Semitism may lead to acts (like keeping a valid passport on hand) that have no especially Jewish content. I agree, but my point here is that it could motivate maintenance of a positive Jewish identity.

mitigating them.[13] And while there were many apostates, there were many who stayed Jews. The suffering they endured in their devotion to the Jewish people seems to call for some devotion from us.[14]

Treasures of the Legacy

Beyond the blood of the martyrs, there are the treasures of the legacy. Few Wicked Children are aware of the depth and breadth of Jewish civilization. It contains traditions rich in music, poetry, folktales, philosophy, theology, mysticism, liturgies, sacred objects, ornaments, rituals, homilies, myths, legends, and law. For drama and variety Jewish history is not easily matched. Earlier I made the general point that particular cultures have aesthetic and moral value and therefore merit preservation. Now I make the specific claim that Jewish culture is of great value and merits preservation. But it will not be preserved by the Chinese or Hopi or Quebecois. It will be preserved by Jews or not at all. So Jews are under some obligation to do some preserving.[15] But this

---

13. There is some controversy over whether Spanish Jewry could really escape anti-Semitism through conversion. It has been recently argued that even after becoming sincere New Christians, former Jews were subject to something akin to modern, racist anti-Semitism. See Netanyahu 1995.

14. The saga of Jewish suffering can, with equal logic, give rise to a call to abandon Jewish identity. Lionel Rubinoff (1993) quotes Norman Podhoretz and a character in Pasternak's *Dr. Zhivago,* giving voice to such views. Podhoretz asks, "Will this madness in which we are all caught up never find a resting place? Is there never to be an end to it? In thinking about the Jews, I have wondered whether their survival as a distinct group was worth one single hair on the head of an infant. Did the Jews have to survive so that six million innocent people should one day be burned in the ovens of Auschwitz?" Mischa Gordon in *Dr. Zhivago:* "Their national idea has forced them century after century to be a people and nothing but a people. . . . But in whose interest is this voluntary martyrdom? Who stands to gain by keeping it going? So that all these innocent old men and women and children all these clever, kind humane people should go on being mocked and beaten up throughout the centuries? . . . Why don't the intellectual leaders of the Jewish people ever get beyond facile Weltshmertz and irony? Why don't they . . . dismiss this army which is forever . . . being massacred nobody knows for what? Why don't they say to them: 'That's enough, stop now. Don't hold on to your identity. Don't all get together in a crowd. Disperse. Be with all the rest.'?" These positions only make sense from a secularist perspective, since a religious Jew has a ready answer to the question, "Why remain Jews?" It is interesting that neither Podhoretz nor Pasternak ultimately opts to end anti-Semitism through total assimilation, although Pasternak came as close as he could without converting.

15. Of course Hopis have a prima facie analagous duty to preserve Hopi culture. Eddy Zemach (1993) makes the case for Jews having an obligation to be the "custodians" of Jewish culture. Zemach sees a stronger obligation than I do. His extends to all Jews, rather

is a duty that should prove far more enriching than arduous. The most straightforward reason to be a Jew is also one of the strongest; *es iz gut tsu zayn a Yid*, "it is good to be a Jew."

It is especially good for those seeking resources for a life devoted to social justice and ethical acts. It is certainly chauvinistic and probably historically naive to claim that the Jewish culture is *the* progressive tradition par excellence. One does not have to search too long or too hard to find reactionary themes in Jewish tradition. But there is no gainsaying the strong social justice element. Those of us wishing to strengthen our social and moral commitments and pass these commitments on to our children will find that Jewish tradition affords rich resources for doing so. In chapter 4 I discuss these in more detail.

The Inadequacies of American Culture

My mother once described a couple as follows: "He's Italian and she's Elizabeth." I took her to mean that Elizabeth had no ethnic identity beyond being American. Ethnically speaking there was nothing to be said about this woman. She was simply Elizabeth. Her American ethnicity was not worth mentioning, in part because it is common (in America) and in part because it lacks a certain substance. For many, unsupplemented American culture is significantly incomplete. There are a number of reasons for this sentiment. One is that an additional ethnic identity is so widespread in America that its absence is felt as a deprivation. But not all of the reasons are so empty. There are reasons for desiring a cultural supplement even if no one else had one.

America has a national language, a history, sports, holidays, a cuisine, political institutions, and modes of daily life that, while not as uniform as in some other nations, are still characteristically American.[16] Moreover, in arts and entertainment, America is the primary source for whatever might pass as world culture. American music, television, and film dominate the international market. So how is America culturally deficient? It is deficient in its provision of a person-

---

than just those who choose to continue to identify as Jews and to have their children so identify. Zemach also seems to believe that an American Jewish culture cannot contribute much to preserving Jewish civilization.

16. In fact, there is probably more cultural uniformity in America than there is in most nations.

ally sustaining ideology and a sense of a *meaningful* common life. America, of course, is not without strong ideological commitments. But they comprise a sort of anti-ideology ideology. The emphasis on individualism, freedom, anti-statism, and self-interest as the basis of economic life allows individuals to decide for themselves what makes life worth living and to create for themselves those (different) worthwhile lives. This is America's fundamental liberalism, and I am not criticizing it. Indeed much of this book is about reconciling a form of Jewish life with this liberalism, since I take this liberalism, and the freedom it offers, to be among the highest goods. But this freedom must be used somehow. Freedom is not an ultimate goal but a means for selecting and pursuing other goals. Of course people can devote themselves to the advancing and securing of American liberalism. American Civil Liberties Union and League of Women Voters activists do find the pursuit of common American purposes personally sustaining. But for most Americans, American liberalism is a background condition of the good life, not the substantive goal in its pursuit. Americans whose Americaness goes unsupplemented usually fill up their lives with consumerism. Indeed even "culturally supplemented" Americans, to the extent that they partake in mainstream American life, are ensnared by consumerism. Not because consumerism is peculiarly American. It flourishes in all developed nations and is aspired to in developing ones. But in the absence of other culturally given goals, consumerism becomes the sole end of life. If consumerism seems especially American, it is because, more than most other cultures, American culture endorses no competing goal.

Granted, this "unsupplemented" American culture I am describing is an abstract caricature. It is not American culture as anyone actually lives it. Most Americans do have some ethnic identification, and all Americans are the inheritors of multiple ethnic traditions that indeed constitute American culture. Pizza, frankfurters, and bagels are American foods, and gospel, jazz, and bluegrass are American music. To deprive American culture of its Italian, German, Jewish, African, and Celtic (to name but a few) ingredients, and then declare it unnourishing, seems hardly fair. Moreover, a crucial component of American culture is Christianity. Christmas and Easter, baptisms and hymns, are not ruffles that some Americans have tacked on to their ready-to-wear, unadorned, secular American costume. To de-ethnicize and de-

Christianize American culture and pronounce it inadequate is like declaring sex without playfulness, fantasy, and affection dull. Neither sex nor American culture are themselves deprived of these elements.

But the inadequacies of my admittedly abstract caricature of American culture — what I have been calling unsupplemented Americanism — are relevant because unsupplemented Americanism is the Wicked Child's theoretical alternative to leading some kind of Jewish life. This is because the Wicked Child has presumably ruled out, as components of her life, recognizably Christian traditions, traditions that are central to "standard" American, as well as most ethnic-American, culture. In chapter 7 I discuss the complexities of intermarriage, and I qualify the Wicked Child's refusal to Christianize her life. But for now I assume that the Wicked Child is weighing the virtues of an American-Jewish life against those of a nonethnic, non-Christian Americanism. It is this unsupplemented, stripped down Americanism that is so wanting. If it is not the Americanism of most Americans, it is because they are Christians or at least have no problem inhabiting the cultural residue of Christian civilization. But if this *is* a problem for you, and, by hypothesis, it is a problem for the Wicked Child, the alternative to Jewish life is likely to be little more than the cutting edge consumerism of modern societies. The non-Christian ethnic contributions to our common American life do not add up to a sustaining communal vision of the good life and our civic American liberalism is no substitute for such a vision.

Of course Christian traditions and ethnicity are not the only source of meaning, and consumerism is not the inevitable alternative to un-supplemented Americanism. People devote themselves to family, art, and politics. The poor sometimes cannot devote themselves to anything but getting by. But these goals tend to be narrow in one way or another. Either they do not link us sufficiently with others or they do not provide an outlet for the full range of our capacities. Many require a specialized skill or interest. Not everyone can be a flutist or can work up a passionate concern for the rain forest. Efforts on behalf of your family's well-being seldom involve singing or public speaking. Getting by can be done without company. Of course there may exist unsupplemented Americans who shape a meaningful, nonconsumerist life through an eclectic selection of goals and activities, through good work, family, friends, chorus, poetry groups. NOW, and block associations, for example. But these are rare individuals, and even they have no natural way, no way that is communal and integrated with daily life, to pass purposefulness on to their children. Moreover these non-consumerist, unsupplemented Americans often want forms to celebrate important events or to imbue them with solemnity. Consumerism is forever lurking as the common denominator in American life. You can buy your music, diving lessons, birthday parties, weddings, and funerals. You can contribute to the Red Cross and to the Republicans. You can take courses at the New School. If the business of America was business, now the custom of America is to be a customer. We all live in Shopper's World, and for some of us it is the only world we live in, for America per se, allows, but does not provide, other communal goals.

This lack of common goals is related to an absence of a common community. Americans may join associations for limited common purposes — PTAs, bowling leagues, charitable organizations — but qua Americans, they are not part of a community that shares overarching goals. The American people share overarching principles that I, as a good liberal, believe are enough to form sound common political institutions. But it is not enough to form a satisfying human community. Perhaps this is why Americans are more vulnerable to isolation and anomie. It is also one of the reasons why Americans are such good churchgoers. Institutionalized religious faith provides the kind of community that the national identity cannot: a community of overarching purpose. But this kind of community, most commonly found in a church, is not restricted to religious organizations. Some political groupings and philosophical groupings can serve. The key is that the members share purposes and values that they consider central to their lives and to their most important projects. Ethnic identities do not necessarily do this (indeed I am arguing that being an American, tout court, does not do this at all),[17] but an ethnic identity can, at least in part, create such a community. For an ethnic community may contain cultural resources replete with values and worthwhile purposes. Moreover this ethnic/cultural identity has the advantage, over other overarching communities, of having its values and purposes packaged in story, song, ceremony, art, and all the accoutrements of culture that

17. Unless one devotes one's life to fostering "Americanism." But, as I have said above, such dedication is not normally part of ethnic American identity.

command their own independent loyalty. It makes it a community more easily passed on to children, for the values and purposes are interwoven into a way of life. One's deepest commitments are not easily detachable from the habits, rhythm, and feel of life. They are rehearsed in holidays, funerals, marriages, and folktales.

This book claims that a secular Jewish identity can embody such a culture and create such a community. I do not say that it can do it better than other ethnic or religious identities. Only that it can do it and that unsupplemented Americanism cannot. For most Wicked Children a secular Jewish identity is the one that is most natural and attractive. It is where, as the overused but underanalyzed phrase puts it, their roots lie.

Roots

It has become a commonplace that it is good to know your "roots." But what does knowing about your roots amount to, and why is it good? Let's take these questions in order.

Broadly speaking, *roots* is used as a metaphor for *origins*. The injunction to know your roots is an injunction to know your origins. There are different types of origins. They include the Big Bang and the evolution of apes into humans, as well as ethnic and familial origins. Familiarity with the first would require some knowledge of physics and biology. This would then provide a person with some generic knowledge of her origins. Of course this would not allow her to trace the particular atoms of which she is presently composed or the specific monkey from which she is descended. With these matters there is little curiosity, however, for that degree of specificity. But regarding ethnic and family roots, general knowledge is insufficient. Anthropological knowledge about the origins of human culture or kinship systems is not enough; she wants to know about *her* ethnic group and *her* family.

In each of these categories her origins are multiple. Families and ethnic groups are mixtures with more or less interbreeding. Our Wicked Child, for instance, may have Cohen, Seigal, Gold, Levine (and, increasingly, Wong, Rodriguez, O'Brien, and Johnson — but we shall look at that complexity in chapter 7) as elements in her family background. She also has an ethnic identity that *at least* includes an American as well as Jewish component. As an American, the full American story is relevant to her. No matter that her family did not enter the

American story until 1906. She has now become a character in, and a character formed by, a story that includes Iroquois and Puritans, the African slave trade and the Alamo, the Civil War and Reconstruction. Some of her origins are in these events, and they may in part explain her attitudes toward race. But her story is also a Jewish one, and her origins must also be sought in the expulsion from Spain and in talmudic disputes.

But what is the value of all this knowledge of origins? Knowledge of one's origins is valuable because self-knowledge is valuable. "Know thyself" is an ancient recommendation that finds echoes in the wisdom of many traditions, including many contemporary psychotherapies. Self-knowledge is a key to contentment because it makes possible self-acceptance, self-understanding, and self-control. It discovers possibilities and unlocks effectiveness. Knowledge of origins is the core of self-knowledge. We are not abstract, timeless entities. Nor are we static entities. There is no distinction between what we are and how we came to be. We are historical creations and there is no self-understanding without knowing the history. We separate our histories into natural history and social history, and these in turn get subdivided. But the divisions are artificial heuristic devices. Our genes, our jobs, our elementary school record, our mothers' tastes and fathers' neuroses, our great grandmothers' convictions, the Federalist papers, the Crusades, and the Big Bang are all a more or less central, a more or less recent part of the story that must be told in order to explain who we are.[18] The whole story will forever elude us, but the fuller the story, the fuller the explanation, the richer the self-knowledge.

The requirement that self-understanding be a historical understanding is especially true when it comes to understanding values and purposes. The goodness of things and the worthwhileness of goals only make sense in a narrative context.[19] Minor values and purposes can be understood with small stories. "This knife is valuable because I am trying to cut bread, and I am trying to cut bread so that I can make a sandwich." But the values and purposes that guide a life require a

---

18. I overstate the case a bit. I do not want to deny that there may be useful structural understandings of certain aspects of people. But I believe that the "higher" human attributes, most of our conscious psychology and culture, can best be understood in a narrative.

19. See MacIntyre 1984.

longer, more elaborate story. Knowledge of roots provides that story, but it does more than that. It ties the story to personal experience. Your values and purposes are not arbitrary. They emerge from the same story that accounts for you as a whole. They are of a piece with the rest of your self-understanding. They are reinforced by memories and in harmony with attitudes. Moreover they are tied to purposes beyond those you can immediately achieve. Your goals are part of a larger project. (In chapter 3, where I discuss spirituality, I explore this theme further.)

The understanding of your character and values that comes from knowledge of origins results in your being rooted. It is not simply a matter of knowing where you come from; you also feel *connected* to where you come from. You do not view yourself as an arbitrary or accidental creation indifferently located in space or time. Whether or not you feel good about your home, having a home has advantages over being homeless. With roots you are securely tied to a place in the world. There is a soil to nourish you, to help you grow. You will not easily be tossed about by every passing breeze. Indeed if the roots are deep and strong, you may be able to hold your place in a storm. You may lose the type of freedom and psychological mobility that comes with rootless cosmopolitanism. But perhaps *that* freedom is just another name for alienation. In any event, rootedness doesn't preclude growth and change. History is necessarily about change, and a place in history gives one a place to change from and a reason to change. It provides a perspective from which to evaluate the change. This rootedness is the opposite of the Existentialist picture of the radically free person set adrift in a meaningless, absurd (i.e., purposeless and valueless) world, free to create whatever meanings and values she chooses, free to totally remake herself. Rather than describing the human condition, Existentialism describes the completely unrooted human condition, the human being who either has no stories to tell of herself or finds every story equally plausible.

Many modern liberal Judaisms and Jewishly inspired movements have floundered, in part, because of insufficient attention to their origins. This failure to tend to and cultivate their roots left Yiddishists vulnerable, Ethical Culturists marginalized, and Reform Jews, if they wished to stay alive, forced to replant themselves in Jewishly richer soil. A lesson of their history, a history we will review in the next chapter, is that a group identity that hopes to endure can ill afford to dispense with too much of the identity from which it has been shaped.

Avoiding Other Cultures

Earlier I argued that one reason to be culturally supplemented is to avoid consumerism as a summum bonum. For nonreligious "plain" Americans, consumerism is the likely source of value and purposes. But it is quite possible that people offered nothing more than the consumerism of unadorned Americanism will seek out supplements of their own. At the very least their consumerism will probably take on the trappings of the majority culture. Above I spoke of unsupplemented Americanism as the Wicked Child's *theoretical* alternative to Jewish ethnicity. But the practical alternative is likely a more standard Americanism: Christianity. A culturally unsupplemented American child may not necessarily seek Jesus as her personal savior, but she is sure going to want a Christmas tree with gifts under it on 25 December. And since the tree with gifts does not make fat what I have claimed is a thin American culture, she well may seek Jesus after all.

Recently I heard an hour-long piece on National Public Radio, an account of a "secular" correspondent's experience investigating the attempt of Colorado Spring's Christian community to systematically pray for all those in the city they deemed in need of prayer. I missed the beginning of the report, so I didn't hear the reporter's name and didn't have that as a possible clue to her identity. Nonetheless, I muttered to myself that she was probably an atheist Jew. Sure enough, a few minutes into the report, the reporter described herself as coming from a "nonpracticing Jewish home." The remainder of the story was as much about the enormous attraction the Colorado Spring Christians and their "Prayer Walks" had for this atheist Jew as it was about the nature of their faith or the sociological interest there was in the combination of their premodern beliefs and cutting edge organizational techniques. What struck me was how tempted this fellow atheist Jew was by the quest for Jesus, even when that quest was embodied in what I thought was a flagrantly meshuggener form.[20]

---

20. Broadcast on WBUR Boston, 28 September 1997.

Now I am not here arguing that there is anything objectively wrong in seeking Jesus or that Christianity is inferior to any other religion or ideological commitment. Nor do I want to claim that Irish American, or Korean American or African American, or any ethnic cultural supplement will be less satisfying than Jewish American. But for most people born as American Jews, it would be difficult to adopt a full-bodied identity in one of these cultures. (Indeed, however tempted, in the end, for undisclosed reasons, the reporter could not bring herself to Jesus.) Even if they did tempt her, since these cultures would not specifically explain her origins, they could not provide as strong a sense of roots to the American Jew as a Jewish ethnic identity could. There also is a good chance that the "cultural" supplement will be sought in more recently formed communities like the Church of Scientology or the Unification Church. Still, I am not even arguing that these so called cults, are objectively inferior to secular Jewishness. But *for the Wicked Child,* it would be undesirable to have *her* children "become" Christian or Krishna. And while it is unlikely that she will try to make herself into an Italian American, if somehow this could be successfully brought off, the Wicked Child would find that this, too, would not be the identity she would want for her children. For, although partially alienated from her Jewish identity (which is indeed why she would not feel much better about her kid becoming a Lubavitcher), the Wicked Child retains a deep attachment to being Jewish and wants her child to be Jewish. But without provision of a Jewish identity, not only will the child not be Jewish, or not Jewish in a satisfying way, the child might become something else. And if the Wicked Child thinks she feels alienated from her Jewish identity, wait until she sees how she feels about her daughter's Earth Goddess Pathway of life.

Again you might be tempted to hope that you and your children will realize the Enlightenment smorgasbord ideal. Why can't our music be blues, our food Szechuan, our folktales Grimm, our politics Fabian, our morality Utilitarian, and our metaphysics Platonic. Isn't this, or some such combo, the alternative "culture" I might pass on to my children or that my children might select for themselves? Aren't the "cults as sole alternative" being used as a bogeyman to frighten Wicked Children into acting on their atavistic loyalty to Jewish identity?

My first reply is that any individual American secular Jew's music can be blues and her food Szechuan. Rejection of the Enlightenment Universalist cultural ideal does not mean rejection of the belief that all cultures have potential value that can be appreciated by all people. Indeed, although unsupplemented American cultural identity contains next to nothing, the sum of its "supplements" is a cornucopia. As Americans we have as part of our legacy the cultural creations of all groups who have made these creations a part of American life. All humans are potential heirs to gospel music, but Americans are more direct legatees.

Still, no selection from world culture or the de-Christianized American supplements amounts to a coherent culture or fully replaces one. Perhaps someday the secular American supplements will fuse into a culture that could ground a full ethnic identity and meaningful life. If and when that happens, the Wicked Child will have less reason to be a secular Jew and to educate her children as such. But she will not be without reasons. One reason that will remain for retaining a secular Jewish identity is that this identity will always be required for the self-knowledge that explains and "roots" her.

Summary

Why maintain and attempt to pass on a Jewish identity? Because human cultures are valuable; because Jewish culture is valuable; because only Jews will maintain Jewish culture; because people have suffered to maintain Jewish culture; because Jew-haters want to see the death of Jewish culture; because you cannot help living in some culture, and a Jewish American one will feel most natural (unless American consumerism does, but that will leave you isolated and alienated; because Jewish culture can provide you with a place in a community and history, and it can give substance to many of your ingrained attitudes and habits; because Jewish culture can ground your progressive politics and moral commitments; because it gives you something that you like to give to your children, making them less likely to seek what you do not like; because it does not prevent you from appropriating anything that is of value or appealing to you from all of human culture (indeed, the secular Jewish culture described in this book positively encourages, nay enjoins you, to appreciate the riches and integrity of other cultures); finally, because it in no way prevents you from being a tolerant, rational, good citizen of the world who treats all humans as equals and with respect.

All of this together does not make it irrational or even unwise for a person born a Jew to abandon the identity or let it wither. But I hope it shows that *if you do feel an attachment to your people,* acting on it is not silly. Although I do not recommend that this chapter replace the customary seder midrash of the four sons, I think it is a more respectful reply to the Wicked Child's question than the traditional contemptuous dismissal.

CHAPTER TWO

The Historical Background

CONSCIOUSLY refashioning Judaism and Jewish education has become a modern tradition. In that sense this book's project is in the mainstream. But an overview of the rest of the river is useful for assessing how this project does and does not flow in new paths. In this chapter I provide some historical context for a philosophy of contemporary secular Jewish identity and education. As a sketch of over two hundred years of turbulence and creativity in Jewish thought, it does not avoid some simplification, and there are many subtleties that go unmentioned. In addition, some of my interpretations may be idiosyncratic. Still the basic narrative should help orient the reader unfamiliar with the outlines of the history of modern Jewish ideology. Those acquainted with the evolution of postemancipation Jewish ideologies might find this primer an unnecessary interruption in my discussion of an American secular Judaism. But a retelling of the story in light of the issues at hand gives the proper context to my project, even for those already familiar with the story. For others, to whom the story is new, the retelling is an indispensable stage setter. I move rapidly and with broad strokes through the story of the origins of modern religious Judaisms and Zionism. The Yiddishist secularist part of this history is generally less familiar and of more immediate relevance to my project, so it gets a more detailed review.

Religious Movements
Traditional Judaism

All modern Jewish movements find their origins in the Haskalah, the Jewish Enlightenment of the eighteenth and nineteenth centuries. Before the Haskalah you were either a traditional Jew or you left the Jewish people to become part of the Christian majority.[1] While local conditions varied, in general, pre-Haskalah Jewry led a life apart from its Gentile neighbors. In Western Europe Jews lived in ghettos (or at least in their own separate areas), in Eastern Europe in shtetls. This independent social life did not preclude commercial relations, but in almost all other respects Jews and Gentiles belonged to separate communities. "I will buy with you, sell with you, talk with you, walk with you," Shakespeare's Shylock says, but "I will not eat with you, drink with you, nor pray with you." Although Shakespeare portrays Shylock as the stand-offish one, the truth is that Jews were prohibited from joining the larger society. Law and custom kept Jews in distinct communities in the European lands of their birth. It was not a separate but equal arrangement. Jews were saddled with a myriad of economic, social, and political disabilities, and they periodically suffered expulsion and massacre.

While no doubt the Jews hated the oppression, Shakespeare was right that the separateness was not by and large objectionable to traditional Jewry. For centuries Jews were attached to a way of life that was very different from that of their neighbors. Jewish life was strictly and minutely guided by Jewish law. There was hardly any facet of life that was not regulated. How to eat, how to sleep, how to dress, how to talk — not to mention how to marry, how to give birth, how to die, how to be buried, and how to pray — were all done in a specifically Jewish way. Jewish law touched on every aspect of life, and the ideal life and community was devoted to the fulfillment of the law. To that end, study and interpretation of the law, the Torah, was a central activity of the traditional Jewish community.[2] While not everyone could be a genuine Torah scholar, each male was enjoined to be as much of a Torah scholar as he could be, and all people, male and female, were expected

---

1. I am speaking here of the Ashkenazic Jews of Europe. By the nineteenth century they were the vast majority of the world's Jews, and it is from them that modern Jewish movements arose.

2. The Torah consists of the first five books of the Bible. But the term is also used to refer to all the Jewish commentaries and elaborations on these first five books — especially that vast compendium collected and written in Palestine and Babylonia (approximately 200 B.C. to A.D. 500) known as the Talmud. So when I speak of a Torah scholar I speak of someone learned not only in the Pentateuch, but also in the Talmud, subsequent commentaries on the Talmud, commentaries on those commentaries, and "responsa" — letters from scholars giving rulings on legal questions submitted to them. It is a voluminous literature.

to shape their lives according to the legal rulings of the Torah scholars. These scholars, the rabbis, along with prominent lay persons, governed the internal affairs of the community. State authorities tended to treat the Jews as a corporate entity and, when not restricting or exploiting the community as a whole, left it to manage its own life. That life revolved around the synagogue, which served as a study hall, community assembly hall, and house of worship; the home, which was the locus of much Jewish ritual; the *mikvah*, the ritual bathhouse; and the market/workplace, the only place where the traditional Jew might have dealings with a non-Jew. Life was lived to the rhythm of the Jewish calendar and daily Jewish rituals.

The alternative to this highly structured community was not autonomous individuality. The alternative was membership in the Christian community, with its own norms that were just as rigid, if considerably less detailed, than Jewish ones. Conversion would free you from persecution, but it held little other appeal for most Jews. It meant religious, family, and community betrayal. It was tantamount to expatriation, for it entailed a new language, new foods, new habits, and an entirely new circle of personal relations. And it meant doing all this to join a community whose culture had no obvious advantages. For a long time, membership in Christian Europe had no aesthetic, intellectual, moral, or even material lure for Jews. Baptism might save your skin, but it did not offer a better life (and, of course, for the believing Jew it had some negative spiritual implications). While Jews could do without the ruinous taxations, occupational exclusions, living space restrictions, expulsions, slanders, murders, and tortures — the enforced social separateness was not unwelcome. It strengthened and facilitated community life and solidarity. Jews were content to live with Jews, living, as best they could, a totally Torah-dominated life.

Then came the Renaissance followed by the Enlightenment, and the world beyond the ghetto became more welcoming and attractive. For the first time in a long time, the non-Jewish world had something worth having,[3] and there was the glimmer of hope that Jews could have it while remaining Jews. The Jewish incarnation of the Enlightenment, the Haskalah, was the result.

---

3. I speak from the Jewish perspective. I do not mean to deny the cultural riches of medieval Europe.

The Haskalah begins in Western Europe, and it is there that it gives rise to the first modern Jewish movements. There is no late eighteenth- to early nineteenth-century Haskalah in Eastern Europe largely because there is no general late eighteenth- to early nineteenth-century Enlightenment there. It is one thing to join the burghers of Frankfurt, to read Schiller and listen to Haydn, or to become a citizen of Republican France, a devotee of *liberté, égalité, et fraternité*. That is real competition for the ghetto and Rashi. But the illiterate, impoverished peasantry of the czarist empire, itself horribly oppressed, was not a club to which shtetl Jews eagerly sought membership. And it would be a while before an enticing Eastern European bourgeoisie emerged. When the Haskalah is finally felt among the Jews of Eastern Europe, it is under circumstances that give rise to very different modernist movements than those that emerged in the West. But it is these Eastern European movements that are the most immediate and influential forebears of the secular Jewish philosophy developed in this book. Later in the chapter I will turn to them. But first we will survey ideological developments among the Jews in Western Europe and its offshoot, the United States.

Mendelssohn

The emergence of the Jews from their isolation is most closely associated with the life of Moses Mendelssohn (1729–86). Prior to Mendelssohn a handful of Jews had acquired a secular education at German universities, but they had had no dramatic impact on the lives of traditional Jews in the ghettoes. With Mendelssohn we have the real beginning of the discussion among Jews: "How should we react to the modern world?"

By the eighteenth century a few Jews had permission to live in Berlin (and other German cities) because they were economically useful to the rulers. These Jews were called Shutzjuden (protected Jews). Initially Mendelssohn was allowed to live, study, and work in Berlin because of his association with a Shutzjude. Eventually he obtained this status for himself.[4] Mendelssohn had received a traditional Jewish education

---

4. Rudavsky 1967.

from his father, Menachem Mendel, and his rabbi, David Fraenkel. When the latter was appointed rabbi of Berlin, Mendelssohn followed him there to continue his Jewish studies, but while there he also obtained a thorough secular education.

Mendelssohn's first writings in German were secular philosophical works on aesthetics and metaphysics. When he turned to the nonsectarian rationalist philosophy of religion, Christian clerics, inclined to see Christianity as the embodiment of rational religion, challenged Mendelssohn to defend his Judaism. Mendelssohn was disinclined to do it. He had never made any claims of superiority for Judaism, and he was against engaging in religious polemics for principled and practical reasons (Mendelssohn noted that Jews were an oppressed minority in Germany). Still, he reluctantly took up the challenge, arguing that adherence to Judaism was rational for the Jews. Thereafter, much of Mendelssohn's work concerned Jewish issues. He translated the Pentateuch and the Psalms into German, and he wrote biblical commentaries in Hebrew. He argued for the improvement of the civic status of Jews, and he intervened on behalf of Jewish communities with various governments. But of most interest to us here are his attempts to modify Jewish custom.

A loyal, learned, and observant Jew, Mendelssohn denied having an interest in changing any Jewish law or practices rooted in the law. He considered Judaism to be "revealed legislation." Jews were divinely commanded and obliged to observe the law. But they were not obliged to have any particular religious beliefs. Judaism was not revealed dogma. Jews were free to believe what they would. Hence Mendelssohn did not view his rationalist interpretation of Jewish practice as an innovation in the religion. But his rationalism did lead to a call for changes in certain Jewish practices that Mendelssohn deemed irrational and unrelated to the law. He thought these practices were based in superstition and degeneracy, the fruit of isolation and oppression. He anticipated two outcomes from the changes: 1) Judaism would more clearly emerge as the rational and dignified religion it essentially was, thereby uplifting the Jewish character, and 2) Jews would ultimately be more acceptable as fellow countrymen to the Gentiles. This second outcome would be a result of the first, combined with the increasing rationalization and liberalization of Christian society itself.

The religious communities were to live together in mutual respect, sharing a rational, secular national and civic life.[5]

Mendelssohn's program for the Jews was aimed at making them fit for participation in this common national life. They were to abandon Yiddish and learn German. Jewish education should include secular subjects that would prepare Jews for commerce and citizenship. The Jewish community should relinquish any claims to juridical authority over its members. Religious life must be voluntary. All compulsion should be exercised by the state, and the state should stand aloof from religion.[6] Mendelssohn was also interested in a revival of Hebrew language knowledge. He used Hebrew as a means to introduce Talmudic students to secular learning, but he also felt that the Jewish people and their religion would benefit from a better understanding of their ancient national tongue. Although he did not develop it with complete consistency, it was Mendelssohn who introduced the idea that one could be a Jew *and* a German. For the Jews to obtain this status, Mendelssohn thought that only some halachically allowable tinkering with customs was needed. But to realize Mendelssohn's vision of a Germanized Jewry, some of his successors thought that more radical changes would be necessary.

Reform Judaism

The movement for reform in Judaism can be understood as having two motives and an overarching rationale. On the one hand the reformers wanted to remove those aspects of Judaism that Christians found objectionable.[7] On the other hand they wanted to increase the appeal of Judaism for Jews attracted to modernity, Jews who were rushing to the baptismal font in growing numbers. They reasoned that society would be quick to grant civic emancipation to a modernized Judaism and that with emancipation and modernization Jews would have no reason to leave the fold. These were the basic motives. The overarching rationale

---

5. Jospe and Yahil 1972.

6. Except that Mendelssohn felt the state could demand conformity to the universal truths of religion revealed by reason.

7. With hindsight it is much easier to see that the entire religion (and as it turns out, the Jewish people's existence itself) was found objectionable.

for reform was the belief that Judaism should be shorn of its inessential, historically accidental, irrational accretions. Thus purified, it would stand forth in its true nature, a rational faith of ethical monotheism.

The first reformers were wealthy lay people interested in improving the decorum and aesthetic qualities of the worship service.[8] The traditional Jewish service, with its mumbled, chaotic-sounding prayers, its interruptions to discuss community affairs, and its substantial length was not to the taste of an enlightened burgher. Choral singing, organ music, and an abbreviated service were among the first innovations introduced by reformers. These aesthetic reforms were soon followed by ideological ones, as secularly educated rabbis tried to articulate a coherent program of reform.

Reform in Germany was mostly an unorganized movement displaying a wide range of practices and doctrines. At one end was Samuel Holdheim (1806–60), who questioned the covenant of circumcision, countenanced intermarriage, approved sex-mixed pews, dispensed with the wearing of prayer shawls and skullcaps, rejected the dietary laws, and conducted services primarily in German. Abraham Geiger (1810–74), representing another wing of Reform, treated tradition, in general, and Hebrew, in particular, more gingerly. He advocated evolutionary rather than revolutionary changes. But there was an underlying ideological agreement throughout Reform that centered on the following doctrines: Judaism was a religion, not a nationality; Jews' homelands were in their countries of residence, so prayers expressing a longing for Zion were no longer relevant or appropriate; Jews were to pray for the redemption of humanity, not just the redemption of the Jewish people; Judaism was to be a fully rational religion and had to discard messianism and belief in resurrection; rather than a curse, the Diaspora was a means for Judaism to fulfill its mission of exemplifying ethical monotheism to all the world; Jews were a chosen people only in their embrace of that mission.

In the mid-nineteenth century, Reform was losing steam in Germany, but it was being successfully organized, standardized, and Americanized in the United States, where, under the leadership of Isaac

---

8. Petuchowski 1972.

Mayer Wise (1819–1900), it became the dominant form of Judaism. In 1875 a Reform seminary, the Hebrew Union College, was opened in Cincinnati, and in 1885 a conference of Reform Rabbis met in Pittsburgh and adopted a platform that defined American Reform for the next fifty years. The Pittsburgh Platform proclaimed the rational, universal, and ethical nature of Judaism. It confirmed Jewish theism, "the God idea," a belief in immortality, and the importance of the Bible, but it forswore anything that smacked to the Reformers of the miraculous. The platform asserted the Jewish people's right to reject any ritual that did not accord with the modern zeitgeist (and, like Holdheim, it found an awful lot that did not). The platform also declared that Judaism was dedicated to the struggle for social justice, with a general approval of egalitarianism and specific concerns for labor, children, pensioners, and the poor. Also, the Jewish people was "no longer a nation but [it was] a religious community" seeking to promote justice through its belief in, and adherence to, the moral commandments of the one universal God.

Ultimately, even the minimal amount of religious/ethnic particularism countenanced by the Pittsburgh Platform proved distasteful to some Reformers. In 1876 Felix Adler (1851–1933), the son of prominent Reform Rabbi Samuel Adler, founded the Society for Ethical Culture. All attachments to Jewish traditions were abandoned. Ethical Culture was a nontheistic sect devoted to reason and to a universalist, Kantian notion of moral duty. Although its origins were in Reform Judaism, Ethical Culture's doctrinal disaffiliation from Judaism was complete enough to make the sect appeal to some of the more liberal members of Protestant sects, for whom even Unitarianism retained too much theism and Christology. But Ethical Culture remained a marginal phenomenon. It never went beyond a few thousand adherents in New York, where it was founded, and a few thousand more scattered throughout the United States.

Orthodoxy

There were no Orthodox Jews before the Haskalah. While there were some variations of local customs, there was only one brand of Judaism. Individuals may have been more or less pious, but there was no disagreement about the substance of Judaism.[9] It was only with the Enlightenment and the rise of Reform that traditional Jewry had to define its relation to modernity. Reform Jews were claiming that it was now possible to join European civilization *and* remain a Jew, if certain changes were made in Judaism. But of course many Jews refused to deviate from traditional Jewish law. One segment of the Jews who were unwilling to make changes in the law thought that modernity and Judaism were incompatible; these Jews had no desire to join European civilization. They are best termed Traditional Jews. Traditional Jews tried to ignore and isolate themselves from non-Jewish culture. Except for some Hasidic sects, there are really no surviving communities of traditional Jews.[10]

But there was another segment of Jews, also completely opposed to any changes in the law, who believed that strict Torah adherence could accommodate modernity. They constitute Jewish Orthodoxy, which, in its way, is as much a child of Mendelssohn and the Haskalah as Reform is. The basic belief of Orthodoxy, which it shares with Traditional Judaism, is that the Torah is divinely given and eternally valid. Even the authoritative rulings of the future are believed to have been revealed at Sinai.[11] The Orthodox hold that to deny the divine and binding nature of the Torah is to drain Judaism of its substance. The 613 traditional *mitzvot,* commandments, are divinely ordained and obligatory for Jews. No doctrinal concessions are permissible.

This does not, however, mean that Jews must be cut off from modern life and all secular culture. Orthodoxy allows changes in customs, so long as they *are* customs and not laws mandated by the Torah.

---

9. This is not quite literally true. Sephardim had different rituals than Ashkenazim, Hasidim different beliefs and practices than Mitnagdim, and there was always room for different esoteric interpretations of the true meaning of central beliefs and practices. There were some differences concerning appropriate forms. But all of this was taken to be dressing on the same Torah-centered life.

10. The non-Hasidic traditional Jews, the Mitnagdim, have pretty much merged with the Hasidim. In Israel they are known collectively as Haredim. Indeed, over the years the modern Orthodox movement and the antimodernist traditionalists have merged to some extent, and today they are all referred to as *Orthodox.* This contemporary Orthodoxy forms a continuum: from some rigorous antimodernist Hasidic separatists to Orthodox theoretical physicists and psychiatrists who lead lives highly (albeit not completely) integrated with the general culture.

11. Rudavsky 1967, 233.

Samuel Raphael Hirsch (1808–88), the seminal thinker of early Orthodoxy, believed that Jews should receive a secular education; God, after
all, had created nature as well as Torah. Hirsch also sanctioned learning about history and Gentile cultures. He felt that such a secular education would serve to enrich one's knowledge and appreciation of Judaism. Hirsch thought that this secular education should be combined
in the same school with Torah study, for he feared that religious education would lose its status if relegated to an after-school supplement,
and, for Hirsch, Torah study should be the touchstone of all education
for Jews.[12] But as long as Torah study was preeminent, Hirsch encouraged secular education. Yeshiva University today is a model of the Orthodox ideal of education: religious and secular studies housed in the
same institution, which is itself managed in accordance with halacha.

Although many observances, such as obedience to the Sabbath and
dietary laws, would naturally tend to segregate Jews, Hirsch did not
believe that Jews needed to be, or should be, barred from participation
in the wider culture. While the Orthodox never gave up the notion that
Jews constituted a people, Hirsch observed that Jewish law enjoined
obedience to the civic authorities of the land. Like the Reformers, the
Orthodox sought political emancipation and did not see Judaism as a
hindrance to full and loyal political citizenship. Unlike Reformers, the
Orthodox would not give up the ritual longing for Zion. But they
rejected as sacrilegious any human attempt to bring about the return
to Zion; God would bring it about in the messianic age. For the
time being, Orthodox Jews, like Reform Jews, intended to be good
German citizens.

The Science of Judaism and Conservatism

In addition to efforts to adapt Judaism to the modern world, the
Haskalah gave birth to a movement to understand Judaism from a
modern perspective. The *Wissenschaft des Judentums*, the Science of
Judaism, sought to bring modern historical and critical techniques to
the study of Jewish texts and traditional Jewish culture in general. The
motives of the scholars in this movement varied. Some may have been

---

12. Ibid., 241.

disinterested investigators, motivated by scientific curiosity. More, like Abraham Geiger, found support for their Reform agenda in their scholarship. But most, although sympathetic to the Reform vision of Judaism as a mutable organism, felt the Reformers were too cavalier about implementing change. Indeed the Science of Judaism was most closely allied with the Historical School of Judaism, a modernist movement neither as rigid as Orthodoxy nor as radical as Reform.

Zacharia Frankel (1801–75), a leading figure in both the Science of Judaism and the Historical School of Judaism, thought that Judaism should be viewed as the creation of the Jews, not the Jews the creation of Judaism. Judaism had evolved since the Sinaitic revelation and could be expected to continue to do so. Like the Reformers, the Historical School accepted change within Judaism, even changes in the law. But they parted with the Reformers over which particular changes were wise, and even more important, over the manner in which legitimate change could come about. The Reformers, believing that they had discovered the essence of Judaism in the mission to exemplify ethical monotheism, were eager to consciously shape Judaism toward that end. Anything that did not subserve ethical monotheism was dispensable. But the "Historicists" believed that Judaism was the ongoing historical creation of the Jewish people. That history included the divine revelation at Sinai, but it did not end there. Judaism continued to be created throughout Jewish history. Indeed, God reveals Himself through Jewish history.[13] So the traditions are authoritative but not immutable. If the Jewish people as a body choose to adapt or adjust traditions because they no longer serve the people's circumstances or sentiments, such change is permissible. But change should not be initiated from the top by theoretical clerics. Historicists claimed that that process was alien to the spirit of Judaism, which had long abjured a hierarchical priesthood dogmatically defining the faith.[14] To the Historicists, the Reformers were imposing changes on the Jews, whereas the Historicists believed that, if changes were made, the Jews should impose them on Judaism.

---

13. The Hegelian and Romantic influences on the Historicists are not surprising. These were, after all, people getting their secular education in the first half of nineteenth-century Germany.

14. Rudavsky 1967, 213.

The Historical School objected to the substance as well as the manner of the changes current in Reform. They felt that traditions such as kosher laws and Sabbath observance were too valuable and meaningful to most Jews to be abandoned. They especially objected to Reform's inclination to replace Hebrew with secular languages in Jewish worship and ceremony. Judaism was rooted in the historical culture of the Jews, and Hebrew was a primary vehicle of the culture. Continuity with the tradition was what had made Jews, and dropping Hebrew from the religious life of the people would severely rupture that continuity. The Historicists were not averse to the introduction of some secular language into worship, but they didn't want it at the expense of Hebrew's centrality.

The Historical School, like Orthodoxy, was a reaction to Reform. While unwilling to embrace the Orthodox view that Judaism was fixed and impervious to historical change (in large part because their scholarship found this false), the Historicists also believed that Reform's wholesale abandonment of traditions was tantamount to abandoning Judaism itself. The Historical School straddled the line between the headlong rush to "modernize" Judaism and the adamant refusal to allow it to evolve. This approach made for some vagueness. Traditions could change, but exactly which, when, and by whom was unclear; the Jewish people don't convene national assemblies to write prayerbooks. And even if they did, it was not clear that a single generation should radically cut itself off from the past. History, the Historicists said, is the legitimate reformer of Judaism. But history works through human agents and the Historicists were a little murky on just who its authorized agents were. Certainly the Historical School held to the role of the rabbis as the interpreters of Jewish tradition. But the rabbinic interpretation should not be based solely on an ahistorical understanding of the sacred texts. It must also consider the meaning and value of the tradition throughout Jewish history and to contemporary Jewry. To be legitimate, the rabbis' dicta needed the endorsement of the Jewish people and, ultimately, of Jewish history itself.

In Europe the Historical School never really became an independent religious movement; it was more a tendency — in the most moderate wing of Reform and in the most flexible, secularized wing of Orthodoxy. It was in America, under the name of Conservativism, that this ideological tendency acquired organizational and institutional embodiment. To a certain extent its institutional embodiment in America came before its ideological articulation. Sabbato Morais (1823–97), seeking to create a rabbinical seminary more devoted to Jewish laws and traditions than The Hebrew Union College, founded The Jewish Theological Seminary in 1887. Fifteen years later Solomon Schecter (1847–1915), a scholarly European rabbi sympathetic to the Historical School, was invited to be president of the seminary. Schecter recruited a diverse but fundamentally like-minded group of outstanding scholars to the seminary's faculty. They typically were traditionally observant in their personal lives and devoted to objectivity and science in their scholarship, and, while dedicating their lives and work to maintaining tradition, they recognized the need and inevitability of change in Judaism. In 1913 Schecter formed The United Synagogue, an organization of congregations in ideological harmony with the seminary. In 1919 the Rabbinical Assembly, the organization of Conservative rabbis, was founded.

A significant feature of the Conservative movement was its lack of ideological fussiness. Although the preamble to the constitution of The United Synagogue speaks of loyalty to Torah, maintaining tradition, fostering observance, preserving hopes for Israel's restoration, and a host of such phrases that might warm an Orthodox heart, the preamble also states, "It shall be the aim of The United Synagogue of America, while not endorsing the innovations of any of its constituent bodies, to embrace all elements *essentially* [emphasis added] loyal to traditional Judaism and in sympathy with the purposes outlined above."[15] The Conservative movement was tolerant of a wide array of practices. This flexibility does much to account for the dominating position, displacing Reform, that Conservatism came to hold in American Jewish life. The congregational autonomy and diversity that Conservatism fostered was well suited to American democracy. In addition its Orthodox-style service and its tolerance of Reform-style personal observance was especially appealing to the children of the Eastern European immigrants who came in massive numbers between 1882 and 1924. These second-generation American Jews were emotionally attached to the services and ceremonies of their traditionalist parents,

---

15. Quoted in Rudavsky 1967, 329.

but they were not about to have their lives actually limited by the constraints of Orthodoxy.[16] For them the easygoing traditionalism of Conservative practice was a good match.

It was among Conservatives that Jewish nationalism most flourished. Reform dropped Jewish nationalism as anachronistic. Although Orthodoxy was fully committed to the peoplehood of the Jews, Orthodox nationalism was theological; other than obeying God's commands, there was nothing Jews should do to reconstitute national life. Furthermore, in Orthodoxy, Judaism is entirely a function of what God wants, not what Jews do. But Conservative thought made the Jewish people the soul of Judaism. Religious devotion, being less focused on the Torah, was all the more focused on the Jews. The Conservatives were also less bound than the Orthodox by the traditional doctrine that national restoration was a divine task. As a result, Conservatism put much energy into building community institutions and was the religious movement most sympathetic to Zionism. The nationalism of Conservatism did not deny that Jews could be, or were, nationals and full citizens of Diaspora countries. This affirmation of both Jewish and secular national identity was particularly easy to affirm in America, the heartland of Conservative Judaism, where the Gentile part of the nation was transparently constituted by many (melted? mosaiced? multied?) nations. The Zionism of Conservatism affirmed the value and viability of the Diaspora. Still, the glue that held the Conservative movement together had large dollops of nationalism in its ingredients.

The ideological looseness of Conservatism characterized its general membership and their practices more than its leadership and their articulated views. This was especially true of the early leadership. Although there may have been some inconsistencies in Schecter's thought, and although Conservative philosophy had more conceptual reconciliation work to do than did Orthodoxy and Reform, the faculty members of The Jewish Theological Seminary were hardly shallow thinkers indifferent to ideology or mute on the issues. As I noted above, they were a pious group devoted to maintaining traditions. But their relatively tolerant and flexible attitude toward the observances of oth-

---

16. Rudavsky 1967, 330.

ers allowed for a Conservative movement of pluralistic practice, the most common of which was a fairly permissive attitude toward personal observance. One consequence of this ideological fuzziness was great popularity. Another was Reconstructionism.

Reconstructionism

Reconstructionism was a faction within Conservative Judaism that grew into an independent movement. Its theoretical and organizational founder, Mordecai Kaplan (1881–1983), sought to provide a coherent philosophical foundation for Conservative Judaism. He thereby hoped to create a more united, integrated community and an "affirmative" basis for contemporary Jewish identity.

Like the Historical School, the German movement whose ideas inspired the pioneers of Conservatism, Kaplan believed that Judaism was the creation of the Jewish people. But he believed that not only did they create a religion, they created a civilization. Religion was at the core of this civilization, but it also contained the standard paraphernalia of a civilization: language, art, literature, folkways, norms, and so forth. Kaplan advocated the creation of institutions that would allow all Jews to live their lives within Judaism, that is, within Jewish civilization. To that end, he felt that Jewish religious doctrines had to be reconceptualized (as he believed they had been, many times, in the past) to retain a meaningful place in the lives of contemporary Jews. Conservatives wanted to maintain traditions. Kaplan believed that traditions had to be reinterpreted to be maintainable.

Kaplan thought that a supernatural, transcendent God could no longer command sincere belief. Instead he spoke of that power which makes salvation possible. Salvation "means the progressive improvement of the human personality and the establishment of a free, just, and cooperative social order."[17] The power that occasioned salvation was a natural power, and Kaplan believed that all knowledge that made this power accessible was divine revelation. Kaplan's theology is not atheism; there is still a divine object of worship. But it is religion fully rationalized and naturalized.

---

17. Liebman 1972.

Reconstructionism instituted other changes in doctrine. Its 1945 *Sabbath Prayer Book* deleted all references to choseness; the idea of choseness was judged inescapably chauvinist. In the same book passages about a personal messiah and the revelation to Moses on Sinai were also edited out as unbelievable supernaturalism. These changes led the central organization of Orthodox rabbis to excommunicate Kaplan. His colleagues at the Jewish Theological Seminary condemned the excommunication but were also moved to express extreme disagreement with the prayer book.

Although there are some Reconstructionist congregations, Kaplan's influence has mostly been limited to Jewish scholars and teachers. But here his influence has been considerable. These Jewish intellectuals were particularly drawn to his conception of Judaism as a civilization. Here was a fleshing out, in completely nonracist and nonchauvinistic terms, of the Conservative idea of the Jewish people as the heart of Judaism. Moreover, Kaplan outlined a practical program for organizing institutions that would support Jewish civilization. He advocated democratic Jewish councils that would coordinate all the activities of the communities. The councils would attend to the communities' needs and manage their interests. Pluralist and tolerant, encompassing Orthodox and atheist, the councils would be the organizational bases for all Jews to live together Jewishly. Although Kaplan's all-embracing vision has not been realized, he has inspired the proliferation of Jewish community centers that often offer educational, religious, youth, senior, and cultural activities under the same roof.

Kaplan's naturalistic theology was less enthusiastically greeted than his conception of Judaism as a civilization. Even important Kaplan disciples, such as Milton Steinberg, felt that he offered Jews too abstract and rationalized a God to satisfy the religious impulse. Kaplan's God lacked "the poetry and sense of mystery one commonly associates with the idea of the supreme being."[18] And though the movement is theologically undogmatic, Steinberg's more traditional theism is more common in Reconstructionist circles. Among contemporary Reconstructionists, Kaplan's ideas on theological naturalism are the least attended to of his ideas. If anything, the average lay Reconstructionist

---

18. Rudavsky 1967, 364.

is more religiously observant than her Conservative counterpart. What most differentiates today's Reconstructionist congregations from Conservative ones is the continuing effort of the former to consciously find new meanings in the old traditions. Of course, not all Reconstructionist groups are so probing nor all Conservative ones so unreflective. But the general characterization is accurate.

Jewish Secularisms
Simple and Socialist Assimilationism

Although it does not really qualify as a *Jewish* secularism, I begin this section with the most common secularism of the Jews: assimilationism. One of the reasons that Haskalah-era Germany did not have even more Jewish defectors is because, at first, assimilation wasn't a completely secular option. To become a German, you had to do more than stop being a Jew; you had to become a Christian. The many baptisms of early nineteenth-century Jews were not due to a sudden outpouring of evangelical eloquence. There may have been some spiritually motivated conversions, but they were dwarfed by the careerist and socially motivated ones. Still, the requirement that one become a Christian before becoming a German was an impediment to the assimilationist aspirations of many Jews. They were quite prepared to give up the Torah but taking up the cross was quite something else again. In 1799 David Friedlander wrote to the Prussian Ministry of Religion that he and some associates would be happy to become Christian as long as they were permitted not to commit themselves to certain Christian doctrines — such as Jesus' divinity. Their offer was declined.[19] The Prussian ministry did not yet grasp what Friedlander's offer presciently, albeit in farcical form, anticipated: A national identity required no confessional dimension whatsoever. To Friedlander baptism symbolized an abandonment of Judaism, not an initiation into Christianity.

When nation states finally did allow secular assimilation, it became the favored option of many Jews. The (seemingly) simplest way for Jews to fit into the modern secular world was simply to stop being Jews. This would not require any dramatic renunciation and would

---

19. Ibid., 156.

41

not usually get one. The main requisites would be to adopt the majority culture as your sole culture and to pass no Jewish culture on to your children. Some habits and memories might linger, but they would be extinguished in a very few generations. This blending strategy, which I term simple assimilationism, need not even be consciously employed. It is the default option in a modern, liberal, secular society whenever an individual pursues no form of Judaism. It is the de facto option secular Jews who are not Secular Jews opt for. As I argued in chapter 1, I suspect that, in America, this simple assimilationism will lead, in a few generations, to Christianized descendants.

Eastern Europe was not a modern, liberal, or secular society when the winds of the Haskalah reached it. Those Jews of the czarist empire desiring to join modernity found no modernity to join. What they did find was a movement to overthrow the premodern, illiberal, sectarian empire. The analogous movements in Western Europe, in the first half of the nineteenth century, sought to solidify bourgeois liberalism in societies that had become significantly bourgeois and liberal. This is why simple assimilationism was possible. But the Eastern European modernizers of the late nineteenth century fought for socialism in a society that was quite illiberal and certainly not socialist. Nearly the only thing one could secularly assimilate to was the socialist movement.[20] The attitude of Trotsky, discussed in chapter 1, presents a model case. He shed his Judaism without donning, at least intentionally, Christianity or even Russian ethnicity. He was to be nothing more than a Social Democrat. Friedlander's earlier simple assimilationism balked at Christianity but eagerly sought Germanity. The "socialist assimilationists" of Eastern Europe claimed to be fleeing Judaism, not to another particular religious or ethnic identity but to a universalist political culture: socialism. Of course, in spite of their protestations, Trotsky and other socialist assimilationists were in fact adopting Russian (or Polish, or Lithuanian) ethnicity. When Trotsky spoke Social Democrat, he spoke it in Russian. What socialist assimilationism amounted to was a withdrawal from Jewish ethnicity to join the Russian socialist movement *as Russians*. A roll call of prominent revolutionaries of the era would show that this was no small or marginal

---

20. There were interstices for assimilationist liberals in Poland and Russia, but these were not significant. There were also other nonsocialist, anticzarist movements.

grouping. But it was not the path to modernization taken by the mass of Eastern European Jews.[21]

Zionism

As a large popular movement, the origins of Zionism are Eastern European. It was there that many Jews experienced themselves as a people apart who couldn't, wouldn't or shouldn't merge with the surrounding society. They concluded that Jews needed a territory — the establishment of the Jewish people in their ancient home in Palestine. But this common conclusion was reached from various premises, and, as a program, it was animated by various motives. There were socialist Zionists (who themselves came in a variety of forms) who believed that Jews needed their own place in order to develop a normal class structure and so move on to the Revolution or to rid themselves at least of the personality deforming effects of their anomalous class position in the Diaspora. There were pastoral idealists, usually socialists of a kind, who thought getting Jews to work the land would do them a world of good. Cultural Zionists thought a homeland the prerequisite for a renaissance of Jewish culture or perhaps even a necessary condition for its future existence. Finally, there were the Zionists who believed that anti-Semitism was too tenacious in the Diaspora to escape from; Jewish persecution would end only in Jewish territory.

Many Zionists had multiple motives. Some wanted to build socialism *and* create a Jewish cultural center. Others' apotheosis of agricultural work overlapped with their socialism. Belief in the persistence of anti-Semitism played a role in most Zionist views. But besides agreement on a Jewish homeland as the goal, there was one other element that the overwhelming majority of prestate Zionist activists shared; they were secularists. This is unsurprising since Orthodoxy left the end of exile to God, and Reform claimed no longer to be in exile. It is true that Zionists were secularists whose historical attachment to Palestine was transmitted to them through religious tradition. When Theodore Herzl, the founder of political Zionism, considered Uganda as a site for the Jewish homeland, his idea was roundly rejected. But still, a survey

---

21. Immigration to a modern, liberal society was the primary path taken. Once there, Conservative Judaism or simple assimilationism became the dominant modes.

of the leading Zionists, with very rare exceptions, would find none who sought the return to Palestine in obedience to God's will, or who claimed the land as God's gift.[22] This, of course, has changed since the war of 1967. Most leaders and activists of the West Bank settler movement explain and justify their actions religiously. But this is mostly a development of the last few decades.

Zionism is a secularism without assimilation. The traditional faith can be shed, and not only do we not have to become Christian, we do not even have to stop being Jews. The trick is to enter modernity together, as a "normal" nation. The keys to normal nationality are a common language and a home territory—hence, the fundamental Zionist program of building a Hebrew-speaking culture in a Jewish national homeland.

The modern Zionist movement began in the mid–nineteenth century when some Eastern European Jews, influenced by a mixture of traditional Jewish themes, the emergence of ethnic nationalisms, and the dubious prospects of assimilationism, formed small groups to advocate the settlement of Jews in Eretz Yisroel, the Land of Israel. At first these local groupings, called Lovers of Zion, were autonomous and had no unifying organization. In the early 1880s their movement was invigorated by two developments: the pogroms and Leon Pinsker's (1821–91) publication (1882) of *Autoemancipation*.

The pogroms, anti-Jewish riots, although probably government instigated and certainly government allowed, nonetheless demonstrated a widespread and passionate *popular* hatred of the Jews. The vivid manifestation of this hatred caused many Jews, including some socialist assimilationists, to despair of ever being accepted into the majority society. This led Pinsker to first articulate the classic theme of Zionist thought: Hatred of the Jews was an ineradicable historical fact as long as Jews were a minority in a society. Xenophobia was a universal phenomenon, but somehow Jews had become the focus of a particularly persistent form of it. Jews were destined to be despised and oppressed unless they had a land of their own. Although at first Pinsker

---

22. There was a religious faction of Zionists, Mizrachi, formed in 1902. Avraham Kook was its leader. Mizrachi argued that the secular Zionists were instruments of God's will and, therefore, Zionism, though dominated by secularists, was actually a religious enterprise. Since Conservatives also saw God as working through Jewish history, it is not surprising that they were the religious group in the Diaspora most sympathetic to Zionism.

held no special brief for Palestine, the Lovers of Zion, with their religious/historical/romantic attachment to Eretz Yisroel, became his natural allies in the movement to settle Jews in a home of their own. The first significant wave of modern Jewish settlement in Palestine, the First Aliyah, began in 1882.

Thirteen years later, in 1895, Theodore Herzl (1860–1904), a westernized Austrian Jew, who had not read Pinkser, came to the same conclusions: Anti-Semitism was a permanent feature of European culture, as entrenched in Paris as it was in Kiev. Jews could not end their persecution by assimilating as individuals into other nations. They must assimilate as a nation, in a land of their own, into the family of nations. In 1897, in Basle, Herzl organized the First Zionist Congress, where the financial and political foundations for the Zionist movement were created. Herzl himself was committed to neither Hebraicism, Judaism, Socialism, or even Zion (Eretz Yisroel) itself. He was committed to a Jewish state. He embraced the other Zionists, with their varying goals, to pursue that political end.

Ahad Ha'am (1856–1927) was the leading voice of the "cultural Zionists." For him a Jewish homeland in Palestine was to be a national cultural center. In the homeland a modern secular *Hebraic* Jewish culture would be created out of the rapidly dying ancient traditions of the Jewish people. While hardly indifferent to the dangers of anti-Semitism, Ahad Ha'am was more concerned with the threat of the spiritual and cultural death of the Jewish nation than with the physical massacres or civil persecution of Jews. Indeed, Ahad Ha'am expected that the majority of Jews would continue to live in the Diaspora. But only cultural infusions from the vital national center would enable them to sustain themselves as Jewish communities. Ahad Ha'am was less concerned with getting lots of Jews to settle in Palestine than he was with creating the right conditions for the birth of a modern Hebrew Jewish culture. A Jewish homeland was a necessary condition for this cultural renewal (this is why he was a Zionist), but it was far from a sufficient one.

In 1898 Nachman Syrkin (1868–1924) tried to combine socialism and Zionism. Although Syrkin's tenure as a Zionist leader was brief,[23]

---

23. He scandalized the bourgeois leadership and lost popular support by backing the Uganda scheme (Sachar 1979, 69).

his views laid the basis for the emergence of Labor Zionism, which eventually came to dominate the leadership of the Zionist movement. Ber Borochov (1880–1917), in the 1905 essay "Nationalism and the Class Struggle," claimed to derive Zionism from standard Marxist premises. These early socialist Zionists held the general view that persecution of the Jews prevented them from participating in, and/or benefiting from, the class struggle. A Jewish homeland would allow the normal evolution of a Jewish class structure where the Jewish proletariat could make a revolution against a Jewish bourgeoisie.

This orthodox (except for the Zionism) socialist analysis was complemented by the pastoralist and work worshipping ideas of Joseph Brenner and A. D. Gordon. Central to Gordon's and Brenner's "pastoralist" Labor Zionism was a return of the Jewish people to manual labor and to the land. The pastoralists believed the Jewish national character had been distorted and degraded by alienation from labor on the land. The most abnormal aspect of the Jewish class structure in the Diaspora was the absence of a substantial class of manual, and, most especially, agricultural, laborers. Not only did the pastoralist program of "the conquest of labor" fit into the orthodox Labor Zionists hopes for the development of a normal class structure, it was also a bridge to the views of the cultural Zionists, for the pastoralists believed that agricultural work would transform the national character, making possible the revival of national culture.

In theory the orthodox Labor Zionists were socialists who believed the Jewish road to socialism was through Zionism. Actually, from the first, the Labor Zionists manifested a more than instrumental attachment to their Zionism. Not only did the pastoralist wing of the movement see an intrinsic value in settling and working the land; in time virtually the whole movement came under the influence of the cultural Zionists. The men and women who came to constitute the leadership of the Jewish settlement and who founded the State of Israel were largely Labor Zionists of this stripe. They sought the creation of an agrarian socialist society as the home of transformed Jews in a secularized Hebrew culture.

As in most movements, events overtook ideology. The wave of immigrants to Palestine in the Second Aliyah (1904–14) and the Third Aliyah (1919–23) may have been refugees from pogroms, revolutions, and wars, but some form of socialism and Hebraicism still informed their Zionism. The German refugees from Hitler, however, were seeking neither culture nor socialism. They sought a haven. Moreover, the growing importance of bourgeois American Jewry and of the European states, especially Britain, to the success of Zionism, all militated against the Zionist leadership emphasizing the socialist aspect of their Zionism. Increasingly, Zionism as "havenism" became the leitmotiv of Zionist politics. Saving the Jews, not from assimilation or for the class struggle, but in the most primitive sense of saving—from physical annihilation—became the Zionism that *almost* all Jews ultimately came to support. Havenism as the overriding Zionist goal also partially accounts for Zionist attitudes toward the Arabs of Palestine. Although ignorance and European chauvinism certainly played a role, Zionist indifference to Arab sensibilities and interests was largely dictated by the havenist commitment. Even the Zionists most attuned to Arab concerns could not compromise on this point. Binationalist pacifists, like Martin Buber and Judah Magnes, and staunch socialist internationalist movements, like Hashomer Hatzair, would not close off or severely limit the immigration of refugee Jews.

Given the dominant and unifying role of havenism in the Zionist movement, it is remarkable that nonhavenist Zionist ideology shaped so much of Jewish settlement in Palestine. A network of socialist collective farms, kibbutzim, became the backbone of the settlement. The national labor union, the Histadrut, became the most potent actor in the economy. Hebrew was successfully revived and made into a modern language through which Israel has developed a secular Jewish culture. The socialism has eroded in contemporary Israel, but the secular Hebrew culture, although increasingly challenged by religious Israelis, seems permanently entrenched as part of the contemporary Jewish world.

Zionism's most concrete goals have been achieved. There is a Jewish State with a normal class structure. Hebrew is again a living language among Jews. A place exists where Jews will not be persecuted as Jews and are free to create a national Jewish culture. But Zionism as *the* Jewish response to modernity is a failure. Although Israel is widely supported by world Jewry, it has little appeal for world Jewry. Havenism, temporarily revived with the Soviet Jewry movement, is currently of limited use. An insurance policy, however treasured, is hardly an ideology and even less a culture. And until a haven is needed, most

Jews show no inclination to become Israelis. Moreover, only a small portion of Diaspora Jewry is nourished by Israeli culture. Except for eliminating a certain kind of vulnerability (an important exception, I grant), Zionism is a minority adaptation for modern Jews. Israel may have profound psychic effects on Diaspora Jewry, even for Jews critical or appalled at Israeli policy toward the Palestinians, but it does not give a substantial Jewish form to the lives of most Diaspora Jews. Chapter 6 discusses in more detail the potential relationship of secular American Jews with contemporary Israel.

The Yiddishist Movement
Overview

The Yiddishist movement, like Zionism, was a form of national secularism; the Jewish people were to remain Jewish and a people, but without Judaism, the religion of the Jews. As in Zionism, language was to be the key to this national secularization. There were some in the Yiddishist movement who were territorialists,[24] but, unlike Zionists, the main body of the Yiddishist movement was not territorialist. Neither Jewish political sovereignty nor Jewish geographical concentration was part of their program.

Another important ideological difference between Yiddishism and Zionism was the role socialism played in each movement. Although socialism was important to most strands of Zionism, and central to some, it never completely dominated Zionist ideology as it did Yiddishist. During Yiddishism's formative years, there were virtually no Yiddishists who were not socialists. Indeed a large faction of Yiddishists (I will call them *tacticians*) viewed Yiddishism, at least in theory, as little more than a means to bring socialism to the Jews.[25] The only disagreement this group had with socialist assimilationists was over how to do political work among the Jewish people. For the tacticians, Yiddish was a temporary means for bringing about the integration

---

24. These territorialist Yiddishists tended not to be focused on Palestine, although there was a small Yiddishist faction in the Zionist movement.

25. While formally this is identical to what I have called the orthodox Labor Zionist attitude toward the relationship between socialism and Zionism, as I noted above, in practice the Labor Zionists rarely treated their Zionism as a mere tactic. This did happen among Yiddishists.

of the Jews into the international socialist struggle. Ultimately Jews would assimilate into the nonnationalist, secular socialist society.

The more fervent school of Yiddishists (henceforth the *nationalists*) thought that national cultures would be an enduring feature of socialist society. They believed that Jewish culture merited a place in the socialist future. It was not that they loved socialism less but that they loved Yiddishkayt more. In practice these two factions of Yiddishists were often hardly distinguishable. Some tacticians were deeply devoted to Yiddish as a tactic, and all the nationalists were deeply devoted to international socialism as the setting for Jewish culture.[26] Nontheoretically inclined Yiddishists may not have even noticed the distinction, and the less punctilious ideologists also may have conflated the two positions. In practice both schools were dedicated to building a secular Jewish culture that promoted socialist values and socialist action. The more important ideological fissure in the Yiddishist movement occurred with the split in the wider socialist movement over the assessment and attitude toward the October Revolution (Coup?) and the Soviet Union. But that is for later in our story.

Origins

By the nineteenth century, Yiddish had been the language of Eastern European Jews for hundreds of years. A Germanic language with a significant Hebrew vocabulary and written with Hebrew characters, Yiddish also incorporated elements from many other languages. At first, all sects of Jewish modernizing intellectuals scorned Yiddish as a mongrel jargon lacking the resources or dignity of German or Hebrew. But complete disdain, to the point of refusal to employ it, was an impractical attitude. If you wanted to reach Jews — with a message of socialism, Zionism, or any other ideology — you had to do it in Yiddish, the mother tongue of the vast majority of Jews. So modernizers started to use Yiddish before they started to value it.

Valuing Yiddish became easier with the emergence of Yiddish literature in the second half of the nineteenth century. The classic Yiddish

---

26. So, like the Labor Zionists and Zion, the Yiddishist tacticians seldom treated Yiddish as a *mere* tactic. But still, its tactical status for some Yiddishists and not for others did lead to practical disputes among Yiddishists.

writers—Mendele Mokher Sforim (1835–1917), Sholom Aleichem (1859–1916), and I. L. Peretz (1852–1915)—revealed the resources and the potentialities of the language. Their work conferred upon Yiddish the prestige of a great literature. Although all three of the classic Yiddish writers had a popularist and humanist bent, Peretz was of particular importance to the ideological development of Yiddishism. In addition to nurturing a generation of Yiddish writers, Peretz consciously used Yiddish to make traditional Jewish customs meaningful to contemporary secularists.[27] He wove socialist or humanist morals into his pseudofolktales of simple and pious traditional Jews. Yiddishism found its exemplar and inspiration in him.

The historian Shimon Dubnow (1860–1941) is the first systematic idealogue of secular Diaspora Jewish nationalism. Dubnow argued that Jews had reached the highest stage of national existence, where the people's unity no longer depended on racial or political factors. Jews were a "spiritual" nation held together by values, folkways, and, above all, a historical consciousness of a common destiny. Jews, Dubnow believed, should preserve their nationality in the Diaspora by remaining in autonomous communities. They did not need political sovereignty to be a nation; they were beyond that. Culture was the national glue. Although Dubnow first articulated the philosophical bases for a Yiddishist type of secular Jewish nationalism, Dubnow was not a Yiddishist. Though he readily admitted the prominence of Yiddish in the lives of most contemporary Jews, he did not think it the essence of the Jewish nation. The essence, the Jewish spirit, had existed in other languages and might again in the future. Dubnow was a pluralist on the issue of language.[28] It was Zhitlowsky who, using a Dubnovian framework, first prominently argued that Yiddish was the core of the Jewish nation.

Chaim Zhitlowsky (1865–1943) passed through a number of ideological stages in his long career as a theoretician of Jewish life: More or less territorialist, more or less hostile to Zionism, more or less sympathetic to the Soviet Union—through all these changes, the mainstays of his views and influence were always his Yiddishist nationalism and his secularism. Although Zhitlowsky did not believe that all Jews should

27. Howe 1976, 19–20.
28. See Goodman 1976.

necessarily stop being religious, he insisted that religion not be a requirement of Jewishness. An attempt to make religion mandatory for Jews would result in the loss of important and creative elements of the Jewish people, as Spinoza was lost. The Jewish nation consisted of religious and nonreligious groups and individuals. It was one nation by virtue of its common culture. That culture was embodied in the Yiddish language. From his 1897 article, "Why Yiddish?" to his 1939 article, "What is Secular Jewish Culture?" Zhitlowsky held that in Yiddishkayt we find a culture that is the basis for an all-embracing Jewish nationality. The language of the Jewish masses had supported traditional religious life and socialist atheism; it was the vehicle of literature and journalism, family life and business activity, folktales and song lyrics. Zhitlowsky did not completely identify Jewish culture and the Jewish nation with Yiddish. He recognized that there was Jewish culture prior to Yiddish and that there might be Jewish life after Yiddish.[29] But he felt that Yiddish was *the* form of contemporary Jewish culture and *the* basis of the modern Jewish nation. It was Yiddish that had made secular Jewish life possible. Zhitlowsky opposed assimilationists who doubted the possibility or desirability of Jewish nationality (or at least *continued* Jewish nationality),[30] and he opposed Zionist Hebraists who based that nationality on the resurrected ancient tongue. To both he countered with the reality, rootedness, and richness of Yiddish. Jews already had a culture; the task was to maintain and deepen it.

In 1908 Zhitlowsky was chairman at the Czernowitz Conference, which brought together Jewish writers and thinkers to discuss issues related to Yiddish. Although concerned with such matters as standardizing Yiddish grammar and promoting its literature, the main issue of the conference was the status of Yiddish as a Jewish language; was it *the* national language, *a* national language, or just a language that was currently in wide use among Jews. After heated debate the

---

29. In a formal agreement with Dubnow (but, in practice, unlike Dubnow), Zhitlowsky treated Yiddish as the only conceivable vehicle for a Jewish secular culture flowing from conditions then current.

30. Zhitlowsky (1904) argued that Jewish nationalism was desirable because the universal is best realized in the particular, or, as he put it, the more "Yid" a Jew is, the more *mentsch*, — "the more Jewish, the more human." The possibility of Jewish nationality Zhitlowsky thought was an empirical fact, with the actuality of Jewish nationality readily observable. This later point was more plausible in 1904 than it is in 1996.

conference settled on the moderate (and ambiguous) position: Yiddish was a national language.[31] It did not declare itself on whether there were any others.

The Bund

Zhitlowsky's nationalist Yiddishism was preceded by tactical Yiddishism. The earliest Jewish socialists in Eastern Europe were assimilationists who resisted the use of Yiddish as an obstacle to internationalism and a spur to chauvinism. But it became clear to some of them that the circumstances of the Jewish working class had some special features that called for a special approach. Neither the occupational structures nor the cultural lives of the Jews were integrated into the wider social fabric. There was no Jewish peasantry but an abundance of small traders. Jews, living in their own areas, had their own customs and traditions. They were subject to widespread hateful prejudice, even from "class brothers," and they suffered an extra measure of government persecution for being Jews. These factors mandated specifically adapted tactics, most especially the use of Yiddish in propaganda and organizational work. It was primarily this impulse that gave birth, in Vilna (1897), to The General Jewish Workers Union of Lithuania, Poland, and Russia — the Bund. The Bund thought of itself as a part of the international socialist movement, and its delegates were among the principal founders in 1898 of the Russian Social Democratic Labor Party. But from early on, the Bund displayed nationalist tendencies intermixed with its tactician ideology. Increasingly, political equality for Jews seemed to require national equality. Respect for the Jewish masses required respect for their culture and language. The Bund never abandoned its internationalism, but, as time went on, the nationalist aspects of its program grew in importance. Jews needed to be defended against pogroms and anti-Semitic oppression. The cultural life of the Jewish proletariat needed defense and support, too. Eventually Zhitlowskian ideology became almost as prominent in Bundism as was Marxism. Although more consistently Marxist than Zhitlowsky's, like Zhitlowsky's, the Bund's politics fluctuated through the upheavals of

---

31. Liptzin 1972.

twentieth-century Jewish history. But through the changes, until it was decimated by Hitler and Stalin, the Bund remained a major force in Eastern European Jewry's political and cultural life, and it remained steadfast in its commitment to secular, socialist Jewish nationalism. The Bund doctrine of "hereness," of building a Jewish life in a socialist Europe, set it against both Zionism[32] and emigration in general. But disasters to European Jewry — wars, pogroms, and failed (and successful!) revolutions, inevitably drove many Bundists to emigrate. The flowering of socialist politics and Yiddishist culture in America was heavily indebted to these Bundist-formed émigrés.

In America

The massive emigration of Jews from Eastern Europe to America, which began in 1881, was composed largely of traditional Jews. The modernist ideology that most took hold of them was assimilationism, whether simple or socialist. The relative absence of anti-Semitism in America removed the hurdle to assimilation that was so difficult to overcome in Europe. Jews like Meyer London and Morris Hillquit used this political opening to become active in socialist politics. Ex-Bundists, such as David Dubinsky and Sidney Hillman, became leaders in the labor movement. But the liberalism of American society also gave unprecedented scope to the cultural initiatives of Jews. Jewish life in New York, the center of the immigration, blossomed. Ideological assimilationists still had to live their lives in Yiddish or cater to those who did. The politics of London, Hillquit, Dubinsky, and Hillman was directed mostly to Yiddish-speaking workers. There arose a Yiddish press, Yiddish theater, and an American Yiddish literature. Jewish mutual aid societies and social clubs were organized, the most significant of which was the *Arbeterring*, the Workmen's Circle.

At first the Workmen's Circle, founded in 1892, was simply a mutual aid and continuing education society with vaguely socialist inclinations. It had no nationalist component whatsoever; German was the association's official language.[33] Although assimilationists dominated the leadership for over twenty years, from early on the Circle

---

32. The Bund also polemicized against Zionism as petit bourgeois utopianism.
33. Trunk 1976, 358.

was engaged in Yiddish language cultural activities and Yiddish language socialist propaganda. These practices gradually received nationalist interpretation and motivation through the influence of Zhitlowsky and ex-Bundists. By 1927 the secretary general of the Circle would write that much of the Circle's cultural work and its network of schools was "undoubtedly a direct outgrowth of the Bund and its position on general Jewish and cultural issues";[34] in other words, secular, socialist, and nationalist.

Until 1916 the schools the Workmen's Circle ran for children were all English in form and socialist in content. There was no Judaica at all in the curriculum. In 1916 it was decided to establish Circle schools to teach Yiddish to members' children. Within the organization the decision was controversial, and it was not until 1918 that funding was provided for the Yiddish schools. But thereafter the schools grew and settled into a Zhitlowskian-inspired curriculum. And although the assimilationists in the organization fought a rearguard action until 1930, by then the schools' work had been so impressive and become so central to the rest of the activities of its branches that all internal opposition collapsed.[35] Of course, within the larger Jewish community, opposition remained: In 1930 most Jews were still seeking to become "real Americans," and a socialist Yiddishist education did not seem to further that end. As the thirties progressed this changed. The rise of Hitler and the fate of assimilationist socialism in Germany made many progressive Jews more sympathetic to a nationalist alternative.[36]

Besides strengthening the Circle's Yiddishism, the Bundist members deepened its socialist commitment. By the First World War, the vaguely socialist fraternal organization was being pushed by its newer and younger members to become "the vanguard of Jewish radical thought."[37] Although never a disciplined political party or organization, by the early 1920s the Circle was sufficiently immersed in socialist politics to be torn apart by the same issue that split the entire international socialist movement, namely, what to make of the Russian Revo-

---

34. Quoted in ibid., 364.
35. Ibid., 365.
36. Ibid., 371.
37. Ibid., 363.

lution. Buried in this issue were a host of other questions, the answers to which constituted distinct ideologies: socialism and communism.

The socialist movement associated with the Second International began to divide when some sections, national branches, supported their own nations in World War I. The Bund firmly belonged to the camp that condemned participation in the war and, in general, responses to the war did not bitterly divide American Jewish socialists. There was a pacifist consensus. Nor was the Russian Revolution immediately divisive. For a time right after the Revolution, the Bund, which had allied with the Menshevik faction of the Russian socialist party, "critically supported" the Bolshevik-led revolutionary government. In the first few years following the Revolution, some Eastern European sections of the Bund even affiliated or attempted to affiliate with the national communist party. But before long the antidemocratic and antinationalist Bolshevik policies alienated Bundists. And if they did not, Communist persecution of the Bund did. Still, many Jewish socialist assimilationists remained Communists and for a time the Communists allowed space for Yiddishism, at least if it was of a clearly tactician nature. But the more explicitly nationalist elements among Jewish socialists tended to side with the Menshivik/Socialists in the big international split.

The big split was reflected in the Workmen's Circle in 1926, when branches sympathetic to the Soviet regime formed a separate organization, The Independent Workmen's Circle. This breakaway group took with it the bulk of the Circle schools and renamed them the Jewish Workers' Non-Partisan Elementary Schools. The Independent Workmen's Circle evolved into the International Workers' Order, a Jewish socialist fraternal organization squarely communist and tactician Yiddishist in orientation. By 1929 the nonpartisanship of the Non-Partisan Schools was no longer supported by the majority of its members. In 1930, while a minority continued on as a network of Non-Partisan Schools, the majority affiliated with the communist International Workers Order (IWO) to become The Jewish Elementary Schools of the International Workers' Order, the *ordnshuln*.[38] There were other

---

38. Ibid., 381–2.

Yiddish school movements unaffiliated with either the Circle or the IWO. But most students who got a Yiddishist education got it in a school that ladled out class along with Yiddishist consciousness.

Not just the schools but the entire Yiddishist scene was dominated by its Socialist and Communist wings.[39] Housing cooperatives were established. Theaters and choruses were organized. Periodicals proliferated. Youth groups were formed, and a number of children's and adults' recreational summer camps were founded. This "cultural work" was accompanied by intensive political activity and labor organizing. But within the Workmen's Circle and allied Socialist Yiddishist institutions, nationalist concerns were the undisputed primary focus. Indeed as time went on, the nationalism of the Workmen's Circle began to include more and more traditional Jewish heritage and less of those elements of its political and antireligious program that had put it at odds with the majority of American Jews.[40] So, for example, without giving up its secularism, it found ways to acknowledge Rosh Hashanah, and, while remaining adamant in its devotion to Yiddish and Diasporaism, it came to be a strong supporter of Israel. Like other Socialist institutions, the Circle developed an intense anti-Communism that sometimes drove it to the political right. By the 1960s it was not even left enough to support the anti–Vietnam War movement.

The Communist Yiddishists and their allies, like all organizations tied to the Soviet Party line, had an ideological and historical development perverted by the vicissitudes of Kremlin politics. The IWO, later called the JPFO, the Jewish People's Fraternal Order,[41] was at times an ultratactician organization. There were periods in the early thirties when its school curriculum contained almost no nationalist elements;[42] it was straight Communist Party doctrine in Yiddish accents. At other points, when Moscow policy allowed it, nationalist feelings would

---

39. This is not to imply that most Yiddish language activities were socialist dominated. There was a lot of nonideological use of Yiddish as a cultural medium to inform and entertain first-generation immigrants. But activities consciously aimed at the promotion of Yiddish culture, that is, Yiddishism, were largely a Socialist and Communist monopoly.

40. Parker 1981, 504.

41. The JPFO was nominally only a branch of the IWO, but in actuality, it was always the main body of the organization.

42. Trunk 1976, 382. This downplaying of Yiddish in the Shuln may have been abetted by the general assimilationists' urges to become "real Americans," but it was consciously justified on antinationalist, internationalist grounds.

come to the fore. Soviet popular front politics of the late thirties enabled the *ordn-shuln* and the JPFO to give vent to their nationalist sentiments. The schools attracted many students whose parents weren't Communists and other JPFO cultural groups (such as choruses) that could also attract a broader, less political, segment of Jews, were formed.

The 1939 Nazi-Soviet pact was the first in a series of events that not only ended any chance for these Communist Yiddishist institutions to have broad appeal but also began to erode their internal cohesion. It took a lot of rationalization for any Jew to remain active in any organization even remotely connected to a policy of peaceful coexistence with Hitler. The 1941 Nazi invasion of the Soviet Union and the subsequent antifascist Allied alliance brought relief to the tortured consciences of Jewish Communists and permitted a revival of the broadly appealing nationalist politics under a renewed popular front. With the war's end, and after the murder of Europe's Jews, the JPFO could never return to a strictly tactician stance. But its late thirties vitality would never be regained. Externally, the anti-Communist persecutions of the Cold War took a toll. Internally, the increasingly obvious tyrannical nature of the Soviet Union debilitated. General events, like Hungary in 1956 and especially Czechoslovakia in 1968, caused defections. But matters specific to Jews were felt even more keenly. In 1952 word began to leak out about Stalin's murder of the Soviet Union's leading Yiddish writers. From the late forties the Soviet Union took an ever stronger anti-Israeli line, ultimately arming and supporting Arab states in the 1967 and 1973 wars. More troubling, anti-Zionist rhetoric was being used as a thin disguise for officially sanctioned anti-Semitism. Undeviating loyalty to Soviet-true Communism became a hard and lonely row to hoe for a Jewish movement. By 1968 even some of the rocks of the Yiddishist Communist movement quit trying. In that year the *Morgn Freiheit*, revered voice of Yiddishist Communism, broke with the Moscow line.

Whatever harm was done to Yiddishism by sectarianism and obtuseness counts for little in the scale compared to the weight of assimilation. The most clearheaded, principled, and pragmatic politics could probably have done nothing to keep Yiddish alive. The Workmen's Circle and the successor organizations to the JPFO are now shadows of their former selves. In its heyday the Workmen's Circle was the largest

Jewish membership organization in the United States. During the thirties the Circle and the JPFO each had over a hundred schools in their school networks. Both wings of Yiddishist socialism, Socialist and Communist, sponsored organizations and events that created a complete cultural milieu. The American trade union movement drew many of its crucial leaders from the ranks of these Yiddishist socialists. But socialist Yiddishism barely exists today. The memberships of the Workmen's Circle and JPFO successors are much diminished and almost exclusively elderly. The scattered schools educate less than a tenth of the children they once did. The rich cultural life has all but disappeared, an occasional lecture or concert replacing the daily round of activities of previous decades.

It takes no deep insight or subtle analysis to attribute the decline of the Yiddishist movement to the decline of Yiddish speakers. The movement built its nationalism on a vanishing foundation. Yiddish literature and journalism will not be created without writers and readers. There can be no theater without fluent actors and comprehending audiences. A school curriculum cannot be built on a language for which, at best, parents have only a mute nostalgia and children have neither use, affection, nor familiarity. The remnants of Yiddishist socialism have been groping for a revitalizing purpose. Although they have contributed to the transition of Yiddishism from a nationalist ideology to a scholarly discipline and an antiquarian hobby, such activities are insufficient to sustain a national movement. The socialism and communism of the main Yiddishist institutions have passed. The Workmen's Circle has become a liberal, and not always left liberal, organization with trade union sympathies. Most of its schools' explicitly socialist curricula are even less visible than its Yiddish language instruction. Organizational descendants of the JPFO have evolved politically into a mixture New Left–inspired eclectic radicalism and old-style socialist internationalism, but, with its past of rigidly defined secularism and its tactician origins, these Communist Yiddishist spin-offs have had even more difficulty than the old Socialists in finding a Jewish content for their institutions. It is clear to all that Yiddishism can no longer serve as the substance of secular Jewish identity.

Although its old programmatic content no longer suffices, the socialist Yiddishist movement is the direct ancestor of the ideas developed in this book. The belief in the possibility of a nonreligious, historically based Jewish identity — an identity that would reinforce rather than undermine a humane and internationalist sensibility — was a belief championed and explored by thinkers such as Dubnow and Zhitlowsky. It is both the starting point and destination of Secular Judaism. But in the journey from the Jewish secularism of these pioneers to its realization as a usable contemporary Jewish secularism, we must not only revisit some of the old haunts, we must also make some stops that are not on the standard "secular" itinerary. Our first important stop is at the intersection of religion, spirituality, and secularism.

CHAPTER THREE

Secularism, Spirituality, and Religious Rituals

"SECULARIZATION" has come to denote the displacement of God from the center of life in modern societies. In that sense all but the most "fundamentalist" or traditionally religious are secular. Except for sects like the Amish or the Satmar, in America we all, religious and nonreligious alike, spend most of our time in a world that is not dominated or directed by religion.[1] In this sense the typical American is secular, as are the large majority of American Jews. But, if we restrict the definition to those who consciously self-identify as nonreligious, secularism has a much more limited population. It is this self-conscious secularism, built on a principled irreligiosity (although not hostile to religion in others), that is our subject. Why anyone would hold *ir*religiosity as a principle is beyond the scope of this work. I do, however, give a prima facie defense of principled secularism in chapter 7, in the section on secularism. Those who cannot sustain an interest in a discussion of secularism, without first having its value as a creed established, may need to read that section before continuing. In any event, as we have seen in the previous chapter, while there are traditions of such secularism in American Jewry, they are now frail and will not flourish without an infusion of new ideological and organizational blood.

Secular Judaism is an oxymoron to most Americans. On the U.S. census form, *Jew* gets checked off under religion. If an American Jew

---

1. There is a debate as to whether modernization inevitably and permanently leads to secularization, but there is little dispute that secularization has accompanied modernization in the West. See Berger 1995.

wants to declare a national origin, something like *Polish* has to suffice, and under race (itself a questionable category), most American Jews will indicate membership in that great *granfaloon, white*. But if *Jew* is to be part of your American identity, it most naturally identifies your religion.[2] Against this American classification of Jewry, this book tries to motivate, rationalize, and describe an American *Secular* Judaism.[3] By definition we are concerned with nonreligious Jews. But this does not mean that we can ignore the relation of these Jews to the stuff of religion. In part we cannot ignore it because the traditions that any Jewish identity draws upon are thoroughly permeated by religious sensibility. Mordecai Kaplan has called Judaism a religious civilization.[4] An identity that springs from that civilization cannot be completely *religionrein*, cleansed of religion, and still recognizably Jewish. It can be secular in its rejection of the supernatural and its indifference to a possible deity. It can be secular by using only mundane, rational criteria in its choice of practices and customs. But it must still position itself with regard to those practices and customs. In the latter part of this chapter I will describe the relation I think Secular Judaism should have to "religious" observances. But I want first to address another reason why Secular Judaism cannot ignore the stuff of religion. It is in religion that we typically think of one's "spiritual needs" being fulfilled. The claims of the spiritual are strong in contemporary American culture. People want to know the spiritual potential of any identity recom-

---

2. At different times and in different places this has been otherwise. In the Soviet Union *Yivrai* was stamped on one's internal passport to indicate Jewish nationality. The Nazis notoriously thought of Jews as a biological breed. In Israel, whatever *Jewish* may designate, it does not preclude secularity. Indeed one of Israel's great political divides is between secular and religious Jews. There is a large literature on the nature of Jewish identity. I take no position on the issue except insofar as this entire book is premised on the belief that at least one possible Jewish identity is secular.

3. The term *Secular Judaism* is problematic but preferable to the alternatives. The problems arise from the normal use of *Judaism* to refer specifically to the religion of the Jewish people. There is no serviceable word in English to refer to Jewish culture(s) as a whole. The word *Yiddishkayt* is a Yiddish term that best captures our subject. It is most accurately rendered *Jewishness*, but that is too awkward an expression for repeated use. It would also not do to speak of *Jewish Secularism*, since that would imply that our subject was a Jewish variation of some tradition called *Secularism*, when we are actually concerned with a secular variation of Jewishness. So *Secular Judaism* is the term I shall employ to refer to the approach this book is describing. It must constantly be borne in mind that the *Judaism* component encompasses more than the religion, while, at the same time, the *Secular* qualification enables the *Judaism* to not refer to the God-centered part of the tradition.

4. Kaplan 1934.

mended as a cultural fulfillment. To what extent, then, is a nonreligious Judaism a nonspiritual Judaism? It is to this question that we now turn our attention.

Secularism and Spirituality

Secularism began its career as part of religious life. Monks were deemed "secular" if they belonged to orders whose work concerned this world. They were not irreligious; rather, they found their religious fulfillment through worldly work. Secularism retains its this-worldly focus, but now it also connotes an explicit rejection of, or, at the very least, indifference to, other-worldliness. This rejection or indifference has two consequences: The secularist has no belief in God, and the secularist has no belief in the supernatural. God and the supernatural are not of this world, and the essence of secularism is to be of this world. Although not a perfect complement, I will use the term *religious* to contrast with *secular.* In my use of the term *secular,* there can be no secular monks, only monks who do secular things. By definition then, there is no religion in the secularism I am discussing.

To some ears this will sound like a banishing of spirituality from secularism. Indeed the spiritual and the religious have been closely linked and are, to some, synonymous. But they are not synonymous. As we shall see, there is space for the spiritual, *suitably understood,* in the secular world.

A Conception of the Spiritual

The spiritual self has made a comeback. Thirty years ago, at least among secularists, it seemed that mind and body covered it all; a person's parts fit into one of two categories: the psychological and the physical. There may have been some dispute as to whether the psychological was distinct from the physical, but it was assumed that these two categories were adequate for discussing all aspects of the self. This is no longer true. What was recently included in the psychological has been separated into distinct domains. While different "selves" show up on the lists of different taxonomists, the "spiritual self" now appears on most lists. This is not simply due to whatever religious revival may be occurring. Secular professionals in such fields as medicine, nursing, and social work are talking about their clients' "spiritual needs,"[5] and lay people are talking about their spiritual experiences, needs, or inclinations quite apart from any explicitly religious context. Spirituality has become a subject of interest and concern. But what is the spiritual?

Different people refer to different features when they speak of their spiritual selves. For some, their spiritual selves are simply those aspects of themselves, whatever they might be, that are most valued. For others, it is that which accounts for their humanity. For many, it is that part of themselves that is not of, or is unconcerned with, the material world. Some use it to refer to their "higher" functions, their ability to appreciate poetry or to love their neighbors. Spirit has also come to be identified with one's most authentic, true self or that part of the self that experiences awe or experiences God. And so one's spirituality might be one's capacity to relate to God, to be awed, to be oneself, to express intellectual, aesthetic, and moral sensibilities, to be in touch with one's immateriality or essential humanity, or, simply, the capacity to manifest supreme value.

These various notions of spirituality overlap. They support each other and bear the marks of the conceptual origins of the spiritual. The concept of the *spirit* originally referred to that immaterial part of a person that gave life to her body. As the word indicates, it was the breath (re*spir*ation) of life. The concept of spirit evolved to refer to that which would survive the demise of the body. Spirit was the finest part of ourselves in the literal sense of the word: the lightest, thinnest, most ethereal part of the self. But it also began to be thought of as the finest part of ourselves in the more common sense of the term: the highest and most valuable part of the self. Because God came to be conceived of as immaterial, spirit was thought of as that part of ourselves which is most Godlike. It is our spirit that bears the divine image and that accounts for our elevation above the nonhuman animals. We are artists, scholars, and poets because we are in*spir*ed beings. We are morally responsible and free agents because we are spirits. The spirit animates

---

5. In Johnson 1993, an entire section is devoted to the "spiritual aspects of care." "Spirituality, like emotions, is a part of every person. It is what makes human beings unique from the rest of nature" (p. 15).

and creates. It is the best part of us, the enduring, immaterial, Godlike essence of our humanity, which allows us to experience God and divine feelings, and which, ultimately is what we really are.

But what can a secularist make of all this? What of spirituality is to be salvaged if we give up on its divine and immaterial core? Much is to be salvaged. There is a conceptualization of spirituality compatible with a secularist rejection of theism and all forms of supernaturalism. This concept not only captures much of what people now mean by spirituality, it also explains and encompasses much of the older concept. I do not pretend that the concept of spirituality I will propose is what everyone really means when they speak of spirituality, let alone that this is what the term has always really meant. But I do believe that as a conceptualization of spirituality, the following can help us understand the commonalities of spirituality in its historical, religious, and secular guises.

Spirituality is that which preserves us from despair. Despair is the feeling that, because life is meaningless and without purpose, it is not worth living. We can best understand the condition of despair by contrasting it with a meaningful and purposeful life. A life, just like a word or phrase, is meaningful to the extent that it is significantly connected to things beyond itself. We understand a word's meaning when we can connect it to other (depending on one's theory of language) words, concepts, objects, or behaviors. A poem or story is meaningful because it connects to ideas, experiences, or emotions not explicitly stated in the text. So it is with a human life; it has meaning to the extent that it has intelligible connections to things beyond itself.

The denial of intelligible connections is one ground of the existentialist claim of life's "absurdity." Whether it's due to a doctrine of extremist individualism, radical freedom, or an insistence on the contingency of human life, existentialists tend to see people as isolated and estranged, unconnected or only accidentally connected to the world about them. Life is absurd because, although a person is in the world, she does not *fit* in the world. There is no particular place she belongs, no especially appropriate setting, no natural home. Something is absurd when it is radically out of place.

But besides meaninglessness, absurdity is a result of purposelessness. Indeed, purposelessness is just a special case of meaninglessness. To be without a purpose is to be unconnected to a goal or rationale. It is absurd to do something if there is no point to it. And if there is no point to living, no reason or purpose to live, life too becomes absurd. Much existentialist thought can be understood as a response to the sense of life's intrinsic absurdity. Leaps of faith, creation of values, pride in Sisyphean labors, or frank (authentic) acknowledgment of the contingency and emptiness of human existence are attempts to overcome absurdity or to live a dignified life in the face of absurdity.[6] Without an adequate response to life's meaninglessness and purposelessness, we experience dread, nausea, bad faith, estrangement — in a word, despair. There is no point to life, so why go on living? Suicide, said Camus, is the only serious philosophical question.

I take spirituality to be anything that fends off despair. Spirituality is that which gives meaning and purpose to life. Its heart is connectedness. One is spiritual in so far as one is connected to things beyond oneself. Spirituality is a thing that admits of degrees, for one can be more or less connected, more or less at home in the world. No matter how broad and cohesive your purposes are, so long as we can ask about the purpose of your purposes, despair threatens. No matter how well connected you are, unless your connections are connected, there is a perspective from which you do not fit. Ultimately the only guarantee against despair would be a place and purpose in the totality of being. Clearly, most religious schemes do this very well (although some do it better than others). Even if you don't fully understand the divine plan, if you are religious, you usually have a general sense of your role in it. Moreover a connection to God is as connected to all of being as you can get. The religious believer is liable to despair only because she can lose her connection with God. Even if a religious believer thinks human life in general has meaning and purpose, once she is cut off from God, it no longer has meaning or purpose for her. To lose God is to lose your connectedness to the rest of being. It is to deprive your purpose of a final purpose or to ensure that your final purpose will be frustrated. But so long as there is a relation to God, no matter how much suffering and unhappiness one has, one is safe from despair — life retains its meaning and purpose.[7]

---

6. See Kierkegaard 1843, Nietzsche 1886, Camus 1942, and Sartre 1943.

7. The most plausible alternative to a conception of spirituality as significant connectedness is spirituality as transcendence. In this view the spiritual is that which takes you away

Belief in God serves spirituality so well because it is the context for all contexts. Everything finds its ultimate place in the divine plan. There are no loose ends. All purposes serve a purpose, all values are grounded. But God is not the only possible provider of an ultimate context. There are nontheistic philosophical systems that also try to explain it all to you. These philosophies purport to explain why things are the way they are and how you and your life fit into the way things are. Convinced Spinozists or Hegelians can find themselves playing lousy roles in the big picture, but they still have a meaningful part in the script, and the goodness, reasonableness, and, indeed, inevitability of the production literally cannot be doubted. These total world views, with or without God, allow for, or at least aim at, what I shall call *perfect spirituality.* They allow you to be at home in the universe. You are related to all of being. Your purposes can serve the purpose of the universe, and the purpose of the universe is itself not some brute inexplicable fact, but rather some rational necessity that flows from its nature. Nothing is absurd. It all makes sense.[8] While your individual life may be failed and unhappy, while you may lose the true path, there is a path to be found and a worthwhile journey to make. There are no possibilities for genuine despair, only common wretchedness.

Without a total world view, perfect spirituality—a sure defense from despair—is not to be had.[9] But imperfect spirituality, affording

---

from mundane reality. It is related to the notion of the spiritual as the immaterial. The world we normally experience is the material world; the spiritual is the experience of that which is beyond the material world. My characterization of the secular as rejecting the supernatural rules out incorporating this notion of the spiritual into Secular Judaism. But it is not completely unrelated. Insofar as transcendence is movement beyond the immediate, spirituality as connectedness is transcendent. It transcends immediate experiences by linking you to distant times, persons, and events. While the links never go beyond this world, they do go beyond this self. I think that this is the more important sense of transcendence. Although some, such as Kenneth Seeskin (1995) have argued that the essence of religious Judaism is its conception of a transcendent God that is wholly other than this world, it seems to me more significant for Jewish theology that God is concerned with this world, responsive to it, and that we Jews can participate in God's projects, that is, Jews are connected to God. While Jewish Secularism drops the connection to God, it retains connectedness as the core of spirituality.

8. In religious thought the ontological argument is an attempt to show that God is not some unexplained brute fact but rather a rational necessity. This is needed to save religion itself from ultimate absurdity.

9. At least it is not to be had in most cases. One can, I imagine, just have a firm conviction that life is worth living without any rational justification for that belief or attitude. And as

some protection from despair, is available without a comprehensive understanding of all being. There are halfway houses between God's plan and my immediate desire for a chocolate chip cookie. There are localized connections that add meaning to life, although they still leave you without significant relations to much of reality. Without God or the Absolute you may be lost at sea, but it makes a big difference whether you are alone in a rowboat or on a large, well-furnished ocean liner filled with sympathetic fellow passengers. Meaning and purpose come with context, and context comes in various sizes. There is a sense in which your spirituality is constituted by the ties you have to the largest context that you feel significantly tied to. If the largest context to which you feel significantly tied is very small, your spirituality may be so paltry that it hardly seems to deserve the name. Below I will discuss what makes a context large.

For many religious believers anything less than perfect spirituality is too paltry to merit the appellation. But I think we can better describe human experience if we acknowledge that there are degrees of spirituality and if we set the threshold for naming spirituality and reflecting on it some place short of perfection.

Two Imperfect Spiritualities

The two most common arenas for spirituality short of the totality are nature and history. The spirituality of nature or history is no sure defense against despair. It is possible to view the endless chemical or social reactions as futile movements without meaning and purpose. But if such spiritualities do not completely fill the void, they still furnish vast areas that otherwise might be empty.

There are people who feel themselves part of nature in a way that gives their lives meaning and value. It is when they are communing with, or absorbed in, nature that they feel most spiritual. Life is meaningful and worth living because it is a part of, as the theme song of the *Lion King* puts it, the circle of life. That Disney never tells us what

---

long as it is an unshakeable belief, one would be safe from despair, and, as I have defined it, such a conviction would constitute perfect spirituality. On the other hand, even with a total world view, the possibility for despair exists, since one can lose faith in that total world view.

good the whole damn circle is does not completely vitiate the message. There can be spirituality without foundations. Or rather, if the foundations are big and rich enough, it matters less if they are ungrounded. Nature is one big, rich, albeit ungrounded, foundation of spirituality. This form of spirituality is reflected, not only by the sustenance Wordsworth gets from the landscape of Tintern Abbey and the awe Kant feels at the starry heavens above, but also by the truly religious activity Einstein believes "earnest research" to be, as he seeks in science to understand the "thoughts of God." Nature can spiritually situate us and does so for many.

History is another large, albeit metaphysically ungrounded, source of spirituality. Smaller than nature but more germane to the peculiarly human, history can show us our place in the human story. By identifying with historical movements, our personal purposes can merge with past and future purposes. Our ends do not die with our end. While it is still intelligible, the question "why is the civil rights movement worthwhile," is far less compelling than the question "why are my personal goals worthwhile?" Social movements do not float quite as freely as personal projects; history is not as ephemeral as biography.

In some ways history can better serve spirituality than can nature. Although history may be as purposeless as nature appears to be,[10] unlike nature it is filled with the purposes of its subjects. Insofar as our self-understanding takes the form of a story, we best give that story weight by making it part of a larger narrative.[11] The events and goals of my life become the results of other events and goals, or emblematic of them, or contributions to them. They are not unconnected, isolated, and out of place. You do not have to feel part of the "march of history" (if you "ain't a-marchin' anymore") to have historically based spirituality. Even if you reject the view that sees history as a progressive movement with a clearly marked measure of progress, life is richer if viewed as part of the flow of history, which, for all its eddies, currents, and unpredictable courses, is a stream containing the travails, strug-

---

10. This ought to be qualified in two ways. First, nature, insofar as it contains humans (and perhaps some other animals) contains purposes. Second, nature does not appear to be without purpose in some religious and philosophical views. Still, to most secularists, most natural processes contain far less purposes than most historical processes. And, of course, correctly understood, Darwinism attributes no purposes to evolution.

11. Cf. MacIntyre 1984.

gles, triumphs, and dreams of humanity. Hence I think that this "historicist spirituality" has an advantage over naturalist spirituality.[12] My preference for history-based spirituality over nature-based spirituality may just reflect a "Western" mind set. Even *religious* spirituality in the West has preferred a historical mode. The circle-of-life nature-based spirituality seems more the secular counterpart of Eastern religious sensibility.[13] Of course, large-souled individuals can combine both.

My account of spirituality may be charged with taking no account of its qualitative aspects. Is there no more to spirituality than extensive meaningful connections? Doesn't the degree of spirituality depend on the intensity of the connections as well as their extent? Might not a single intense connection be more spiritual than a lot of mild, although still meaningful, ones? And, apart from intensity, doesn't the connection have to be of a certain type to be spiritual, a type not sufficiently specified by the vague term *significant?* Might not even intense connections not be spiritual in nature?

Although it is obviously true that one intense connection may be more spiritual than a dozen qualitatively similar mild ones, it is not obvious what to make of intensity. If we assume that love between two people is a spiritual connection, it seems fair to judge that the intenser the love the greater the spirituality. But what makes one instance of love, which is of the same type as another instance of love, more intense? We are inclined to say that the bonds are stronger. But where strength is best understood, it turns out to be, on closer inspection, a quantitative matter.[14] Hence, I suspect that there is literally more to a greater love than a lesser one. And, just as a strong rope has more strands than a weak one, an intense spiritual connection is one composed of many small connections. Spirituality is measured by density as well as size of context. It is not merely a question of how big a

12. Divorcing history and nature is not justified at the deepest levels. Nature has a history and humans emerge from, and remain a part of, nature. Although contemporary ecologists, and in different ways Darwin and Marx before them, have taught us the importance of viewing humanity in its natural context, still I think there exists these distinctive modes of spirituality I have called historicist and natural.

13. I certainly do not mean to imply that the "West" has shown little sensitivity to nature. Only that, when thinking of its place in the world, the historical setting has played a greater role and the natural setting a lesser one than in some other cultures.

14. I do not think this is just Pythagorean. I think that contemporary science as a whole does not feel fully satisfied with an explanation until it is cast in mathematical form.

picture you fit into, but also of how snugly you fit. And snugness itself is just a matter of number of points of contact.

The overall intensity of spirituality may be a quantitative affair, but two qualitative requirements are necessary for a connection to qualify as spiritual in the first place. One is that the connection be significant and not just an external relation to which you can be entirely indifferent.[15] The other is that the connection connect you to something you judge to be "good." This is an important issue elaborated below. But any significant connection to a perceived good is spiritual, for such connections all provide some meaning, and meaning fends off despair, which is simply awareness of an absence of meaning. Of course if you define despair differently or think of spirituality as a conqueror of other human travails, you will only admit certain kinds of significant connections as spiritual. If spirituality is the antidote to mortality, only eternal connections will count. If spirituality combats pain, only comforting connections will count. If spirituality defeats evil, only connections to a fully redeeming justice will be spiritual. These indeed have been hallmark characteristics of spiritual connection, but this is only because God has been the most common and best provider of meaning, and divine connections come with a package of extra benefits. The spirituality available to secularists not only gives less meaning than God, it also must forgo some of the qualitative extras. Still, because nongodly connections can offer meaning, I think that they make for spirituality.

Secular Jewish Historicist Spirituality

Ethnic identification is a poor, but unfortunately common, substitute for historicist spirituality. Although ethnic identification can be a part of historicist spirituality — and an understanding of one's ethnic origins must be a part of it — as a replacement for historicist spirituality, its inferiority is twofold. First, it is a smaller domain. The connections one can forge are fewer and more limited in scope. An ethnic group simply contains less than human history. Second, an ethnic identification not situated in a wider historical identification is almost always rooted in

---

15. This caveat requiring significance is meant to rule out relations such as, "I am x miles distant from the moon." (Although for some, I guess, this might be a significant connection.)

falsehoods. It rarely recognizes its diverse sources, its multiple and conflicting tendencies, its blurred boundaries. Therefore Secular Judaism, like any other ethnic tradition, should not be the sum of one's spiritual life but merely an important and central component of it.

But as a central component of historicist spirituality, Secular Judaism functions particularly well. In part this is because the religious tradition from which it emerges is itself so historically conscious that both the values and folkways that have seeped into secularism from Judaism are already historically framed and ready for use in a historicist spirituality. In addition the history of the Jewish people, more obviously than most people's, is integrated into world history. There are few nations on earth whose history is completely irrelevant to Jewish history, and there is a long list of nations that play leading roles in the Jewish story. Feeling seriously connected to your Jewish past requires serious connections to the pasts of Egypt, Iran, Greece, Italy, Iraq, Spain, Poland, Russia, Germany, and the United States, to name just a few of Jewish history's most prominent players. England and France have some star turns and there are delicious cameos for Brazil and China. A complete cast listing would leave out no European, North African, Middle Eastern, or Central Asian nation. But sub-Saharan Africa, South Asia, East Asia, and the Americas would also be well represented. A person tied to Jewish history is tied to world history. Jewishly based historicist spirituality can be intensive and extensive, for it is composed of many and long connections.

There is a well-recognized danger in historical consciousness. John Sayles has a character say at the end of his film *Lone Star,* "forget the Alamo." There is an obvious appeal in this advice. But history can be studied and "felt" without an eye to reliving, revising, or avenging the past. There is a difference between understanding one's emergence from the past and a romantic, anachronistic wallowing in it. Romantic and narrowly ethnic historical consciousness will be constricting, but not all historical consciousness need be so.

The political lineage of Secular Judaism makes it qualitatively well suited to serve as a natural route to a broad historicist spirituality. The socialist movement within which classic Jewish secularism was formed, emphasized the meaning and purposes of history. In chapter 4 I discuss the importance of maintaining progressive politics as a key element in Secular Judaism. Here I only want to point out that by connecting it to a world of historical values and goals, progressive politics enhances the spirituality of Secular Judaism. I have spoken of spirituality as that which keeps despair at bay by providing a person and her purposes with meaningful connections to contexts beyond her individual life. We must now recall the proviso that these larger contexts and purposes, if they are to ground spirituality, must be perceived as good. This proviso has been implicit in much that has already been said. We have defined despair as the feeling that life is not worth living. Well, it might not be worth living because it has no purpose, but equally it might not be worth living because it has no *good* purpose. Spirituality is the yearning to be connected to something good. Meaninglessness may loom large in modern nihilism, but valuelessness is the traditional soul of nihilism. Religion comforts because, in the face of all the evidence to the contrary, it assures us that not only are we part of it all, but that all of it is good. Any spirituality will have to assure us, or at least allow for the possibility, that we are part of something good. That is another advantage historicist spirituality may have over nature-based spirituality. It is easier to see moral intentions in the stories of human actions than to find them in the workings, however beautiful, of an unconscious, godless nature. A godless nature is beyond, or below, good and evil; but godless history is mired in the moral.

Because of the required moral component of spirituality, the spirituality of Secular Judaism needs progressive politics as part of its tradition: It makes Secular Judaism part of something that is good. There are two senses in which religion and progressive politics might make an individual "part of something good." The first is that she contributes to a good cause or plays a role in the existence of a good thing. This is a sense that is shared by progressive politics and most Western religions. In the religions, God's world and God's plans are good. You inhabit that good world and are part of that good plan. In progressive politics you are part of a movement that is good, insofar as it tries to create a good world. But religion also offers the comfort that you personally can experience the goodness: You can be saved, redeemed, blessed—you, not just the world as a whole, are going to be all right. Justice will prevail in general, as well as in your personal case. Progressive politics, except in its nutso Laws-of-History/Scientific-Socialism-Inevitable-Triumph (e.g., "vulgar Marxism") guise, cannot guarantee even the realization of the good it seeks, let alone that any particular individual will experience that good. This is an important limitation on any secular spirituality — the only personal goods it ensures are the satisfactions and benefits that come with participation in a good cause. These are necessary and substantial aspects of the spiritual life. But we must acknowledge that secular spirituality lacks the comfort of guaranteed personal salvation that is so important in more standard spiritualities. But then again, the value dimension of progressive politics is similar to that of religion in that this promised good seems to be belied by the evidence. More of this and the relation between progressivism and Secular Judaism in chapter 4. Here we only note that spirituality requires connecting to a larger good, and that, while not as large or as good as God, a secular Jewish identity interwoven with the progressive political tradition is not without grandeur in its scope or goals.[16]

Why call this *spirituality* rather than *ethical life,* a term that describes how one lives within a conception of the good, without being laden with the supernatural and theistic baggage carried by *spirituality?* Since most people are reluctant or unable to shake the religious connotations of *spirituality,* why burden our discussions with it?

Although ethical life is an essential part of spirituality, and although I am at pains not to include in my conception of historicist spirituality God or magic, two of the typical constituents of the spiritual, I cannot substitute *ethical life* or any of its synonyms for my purposes, for there are crucial aspects of what are commonly considered spiritual experiences, which are not merely ethical but are also not related to transcendent mysteries. That which fends off despair has an emotional component. It is the emotional experience that results from consciousness of connections to, and participation in, a historically worthy movement that fends off despair that I am calling *spiritual. Spirituality* captures this emotional dimension and the emphasis on connectedness. This is not to deny that one's ethical life can be saturated with emotions and

---

16. Because Michael Lerner (1996, 34) equates Jewish secularism with "an ethnic identity whose primary rallying point is a set of ill-defined holidays observed as historical memory but without any contemporary spiritual meaning," he is scornful of it, which would be reasonable were his characterization definitive. Although his description captures much of the contemporary secularized Jewish community, it does not apply to a Secular Judaism that, while indeed based on a historical sense of peoplehood, adds a spiritual dimension by linking those people to the *secular historical* quest for a world of justice and moral equality.

connections. But they are not defining elements of the ethical life, merely possible concomitants. But because emotional engagement and a sense of connectedness are essential attributes of Secular Judaism, I stand on the word *spiritual*. And although it runs counter to theists' and mystics' possessiveness about the term, this nonreligious employment of *spirituality* is in line with much current usage.[17]

Secularism and Religious Rituals

The spiritual potential of a secular Jewish identity flows from its world historical and progressive sources. But that potential is realized through the various specifically Jewish ties connecting us to the sources. So one question we must ask is, "What elements of the Jewish story and Jewish tradition connect us to a broader human perspective and to progressive values?" for there are spiritual reasons to appropriate those elements.[18]

How is it with religious Jewish customs and traditions? Severed from their theistic, perfect spirituality and their supernatural rationales, is there any role for them to play in Secular Judaism? Should traditional Jewish rituals form a part of historicist spirituality? Do they advance other purposes of Secular Judaism?

Although these questions require a ritual-by-ritual, custom-by-custom answer, in general I think that many traditional religious Jewish practices, suitably modified, should be a part of contemporary Secular Judaism. Historicist spirituality is strengthened by their incorporation, as is the capacity to realize other goals of Secular Judaism.

Anything that forges meaningful connections to the human past deepens historicist spirituality. Knowledge of the past is one connection to it. But continuity of practice is another. Practice is a form of knowledge. Knowing that Jews observed the Sabbath is not knowing as much as knowing how they observed the Sabbath. And in some

---

17. See, for instance, Thomas Moore's bestseller which tries to demystify "soul" in a similar manner (Moore 1992). Also, the answers Sidney Schwartz (1994) gets from his adult students to his question concerning the nature of spirituality.

18. There may be elements of judaica that should be appropriated by Secular Judaism even if they don't contribute to historicist spirituality. As I discussed in chapter I, there are many reasons to be a Secular Jew and some practices might serve some reasons but not others.

ways actually observing the Sabbath adds a still deeper layer of knowledge. But it does more than that. It places one of your activities in the context of a long-standing practice. Not all of the traditional meanings of the practice can fit into a secular context. But some of them can, and the sheer similarity of behavior with past generations is itself a strong tie: "I am doing as my ancestors have done." There is something counteralienating in this, even if you cannot share any of your ancestors' rationales and have not devised new ones of your own. Moreover, the noncognitive dimension of spirituality, the "feeling of oneness" that may flow from certain beliefs but is not identical with them, is also cultivated by continuity of practice.

But very often there are secular reasons for practicing traditional religious rituals, beyond the spiritual bond created by tradition for tradition's sake. Sabbath observance is a good example. Although the religious rationale is primarily to fulfill God's command to commemorate the first divine vacation, it is easy to extract secular rationales for some kinds of Sabbath observance.[19] Sabbath celebrates labor, requires a day off for all workers, encourages contemplation, fosters respect for nature, and encourages family togetherness. Most Jewish holidays can be adapted to secular purposes. Secularists have long recognized the value of Hanukkah, Purim, and Passover as ways of celebrating courage, freedom, and solidarity. But secularists can also use Yom Kippur, the most religion-soaked of Jewish holidays, as an opportunity for moral self-reflection and regeneration. Tu b'Shevat is an ideal environmental festival, Sukkot a time to appreciate food and shelter. (See appendix B for a sample of a secular Rosh Hashanah service.)

Jewish milestone rituals can also find a place in secularism. In chapter 1 I spoke of the thinness of American culture. There is, for example, no specifically American (non-Christian) way to mark the birth of a child. Handing out cigars does not cut it. A *bris* is a rich and detailed way of cutting it. Even if one has moral or medical reasons for objecting to the central act of the ceremony,[20] male infant circumcision, the form of a ritual is available. The actual circumcision can be replaced

---

19. Lots of people have worked on this, for instance, Larry Bush 1986.

20. In our current state of knowledge, I think these objections are ill founded. See my article in defense of *brit milah* in Silver 1993.

75

with some other symbolic act. The obvious and deep inadequacy of the *bris,* its inapplicability to girls, is also remediable. Much work has been done to create rituals to welcome the birth of girls.[21] These *simchot bat* use selected aspects of a *bris* but add to it and change it in accordance with egalitarian values. This ritual can be secularized just as well.

There may be rituals that are so thoroughly religious or so morally objectionable to a secularist that they are incorrigible (for instance, the custom of "ransoming" the first-born son back from God, or the daily prayer thanking God He has not made one a woman).[22] These should be abandoned. Others, although innocuous, may not be reformable into relevancy. They, too, should be put aside. But secularists ignore an invaluable cultural source if they refuse to truck with any Jewish ritual whose origins or original meanings are religious. The secularist can use Jewish ritual to mark most human events — such as birth, death, marriage, or acknowledgment of adulthood — and to teach most human values. Jewish rituals help the secularist do that for which American culture provides little help and for which a secularism that rigorously avoids all rituals would be of no help. Moreover a secular Judaism so scrupulous in maintaining the purity of its secularism, and taking this to require that there be no dealings with anything "tainted" by religious origins or potential interpretations, might be impossible and certainly would not last. Jewish civilization, as noted above, was a religious civilization. Everything that this civilization has bequeathed to contemporary Jews has a religious past. If there is to be anything Jewish about a secularism, it inevitably involves traditions that *were* religious. Even the classic secularists celebrated Hanukkah, Purim, and Passover, which for all there secularist meanings, have undeniably religious origins. The great figures of classical secularist literature, Sholom Aleichem and I. L. Peretz, write about religious people in a religious world. The classical Jewish secularist attempt to build a culture with minimal use of a religious tradition seemed plausible only because of the existence of Yiddish as a popular Jewish language.[23] With the de-

---

21. See Diamant 1988.

22. Some traditional practices may be morally objectionable to the religious as well.

23. But even here Yiddishist intellectuals were aware of the danger of throwing out the baby with the bathwater. In 1904 Zhitlowsky told a lower East Side audience that "if we are dissatisfied with the joyous bonfires that our skeptics lit in honor of free thought, it is not because we have gone back to believe in [supernatural beliefs or the contents of the Shulkan

mise of Yiddish, it is clear that any viable Jewish secularism will have to draw upon the full range of Jewish traditions. Not all traditional rituals will be used. What will be used will be adapted. Different secularists and different secularist communities will make different choices and adaptations. But to reach its goals, and even simply to exist, a vibrant secularism will have to call upon Jewish religious traditions.

Secularists, in addition to using ritual practices, can appropriate values and attitudes forged in a religious setting. The writer Tony Kahn associates his father's refusal to name names during the McCarthy era with the traditional Jewish religious refusal to become apostates. He connects this secular act of loyalty to friends and principles, this willingness to personally suffer for a cause, to the historical stiff-neckedness of Jews. Traditional Jewish stiff-neckedness was religiously rooted, but by connecting it to his father's steadfastness, Kahn finds a context that enriches and deepens his father's stand.[24] Many Jewish religious values and attitudes will not find a secular analogue, and important Secular Jewish values and attitudes will not fit into any traditional religious context. But a sustainable Secular Judaism must be willing to recycle many resources from religious Jewish traditions.

The standard secular objections to religion do not apply to traditionally religious rituals and values appropriated to a secular setting. The rituals invoke no supernaturalism and therefore promote no obscurantism. There are no promises of a heavenly afterlife, no pie in the sky or divinely engineered messianic future to blunt the need to work for justice here and now. Attitudes and practices are purged of their reactionary origins and effects, or they are abandoned. The rituals that remain are not opiates to dull and pacify; they are stimulants to connect and reflect. The values retained do not celebrate the "God-made World to Come" but the human-made world that we may make come.

Will these rituals and values, deprived of their numinous setting, become pallid, empty charades? Without the terror, sublimity, authority, and mystery God brings to the table, will our Secular Jewish feasts

---

Aruch] but it is because [the skeptics] have tossed onto their bonfires so many things that should not have been burned under any circumstances" (Zhitlowsky 1904, 24).

24. Tony Kahn made remarks to this effect from the audience at a lecture on Hollywood and the Jewish Left.

consist of unseasoned, stale, rewarmed dishes? I think not. Although some religious traditions are highly liable to become hollow without God, Jewish religion is already so historically and ethnically conscious, so attuned to the moral judgments of human reason, that most of the emotional and intellectual reverberations of the practices will carry over into a secular context. It is the Maccabee's courage, rather than the miracle of the oil, that moves even most religious celebrants. It is the historical experience of exile and oppression, not the belief in divine salvation, that gives depth to the Passover Seder. The power infused in a *bris milah* by its possible primeval origins in the sacrifice of the firstborn, and its status as the fulfillment of a divine commandment, has long been supplemented, if not replaced, by the consciousness of it as an irrevocable physical marking tying the child to the fate of the Jewish people. Even a fast day for moral self-assessment requires no divine judge for it to achieve solemnity. This is not to say that God is a superficial or superfluous appendage to the Judaism of the religious; it is to say that there is enough genuine historicist spirituality in traditional Judaism to make a secular variant an authentic, potent, and living extension of the tradition. Dubnow dubs Jews "the veterans of history." Isaiah Berlin claims that "all Jews that are at all conscious of their identity as Jews are steeped in history."[25] Some may be steeped in God, but all are steeped in history. And on this rock we can build *our* synagogue.

---

25. Berlin 1965, 252; Dubnow 1903, 180.

CHAPTER FOUR

Secular Judaism and Progressive Politics

It is not necessary to complete the work, but neither can you
refrain from advancing it.

RABBI TARFON, *Babylonian Talmud*

THE PROGRESSIVE political tradition is a crucial element in *Secular* Judaism. I am tempted to claim it is an essential element, for although it is logically possible to have an apolitical or politically conservative Secular Judaism, I think that this possibility, for reasons I discuss in this chapter, cannot be successfully realized. A vigorous Secular Judaism will be progressive. In addition I argue that a Jewish identity will add vigor to one's progressivism. But before these arguments can be made, we must prepare the way with some definitional work.

What Is Progressivism?
Political Labels

Dislike for being labeled is often caused by a dislike of the available labels. Pigeonholes would be more happily inhabited if they were custom made. This general desire for personalized descriptions is especially powerful, at least in contemporary America, when it comes to political categorization. Americans, more than most peoples, bridle at party identifications and ideological classifications. None of the available political labels can be worn comfortably. This is nowhere more true than on the left of the ideological continuum. *Liberal, radical, socialist,* and *progressive,* suggest much, but *precisely* specify nothing, about a person's politics. Even *relative* ideological placement is tricky.

It is not easy to say what is a further left position on any given political question. In part this might be because left/right is no longer a relevant political dimension or because other political dimensions have taken on greater importance. But I think the problem mostly stems from confusing the essence of a political philosophy with the actual positions that happen to flow from it at a given time. I believe there is an underlying belief that is the philosophical essence of leftism.

Before trotting out this essence and putting it through its paces, a few methodological caveats are in order. First, I do not really believe in essences. I do not think there is a single belief or even set of beliefs that all leftists have held and that accounts for their leftism. And I certainly do not believe that there is some abstract form that a political position must match to be a truly leftist position. The left represents a historically changing family of doctrines, attitudes, movements, organizations, platforms, parties, beliefs, and individuals.[1] There are different types of resemblances and relationships in this family of the left. Some members are almost completely unlike others. Indeed family membership is frequently at issue. I do not think we can discover the family essence, for there is none. But we can make sense out of the family by imposing an organizing principle on its members. We can invent an essence that helps explain what the family is all about. This kind of procedure is sometimes called a *rational reconstruction*. It makes no claim about how things actually came to be the way they are; instead it shows how they might reasonably have come to be that way. The following, then, is a rational reconstruction of leftist political philosophy. But first, a caveat to this caveat. Although proposed only as a rational reconstruction, this essence of the left that I will speak of has, I believe, played a real and significant role in the history of leftist thought. It may not be a real *essence,* but it is a real and important phenomenon.

The essential leftist belief is that human beings can intentionally change things for the better. The amount and speed of the change called for determines how far left a position is. Notice that, in and of itself, this is a morally neutral characterization. Mahatma Gandhi and Martin Luther King, as well as Robespierre and Stalin, all seem to

---

1. The general "family resemblance" analysis of universals is due to Wittgenstein (1953).

merit the left label (although it is unclear that Stalin cared or believed that any changes he sought were *for the better* in any nonself-serving sense). This definition makes sense out of much intuitive political labeling. Sakharov was to the left of Brezhnev, Aristide to the left of Duvalier, Roosevelt to the left of Hoover but to the right of Norman Thomas. The further left position is held by the person seeking more or deeper social change. The definition explains why a position that was once left may no longer be so. A desire to censor *Playboy* in the 1950s was almost exclusively a rightist position; in the 1990s it may well be on the left. Forty years ago the uncensored distribution of photos of naked women was advanced as a change for the better. Today the prohibition of such distribution is advanced as a change for the better. Our intuitions want to put the young Hugh Hefner and the contemporary Catharine MacKinnon on the left, and the proposed definition does just that. But it also explains why political labeling is so baffling. The *Playboy* example illustrates why. Not only would MacKinnon like to censor *Playboy*, but so would Jerry Falwell, yet we do not feel he has a left position on this issue. The problem is that change is a relative thing. Do those who want to *reverse* a course of change deserve to be called leftists because this reversal would itself be change? No. Those calling for change to some original status are not leftist. MacKinnon wants censorship to protect women in a way she believes they have never been protected. Falwell wants the same censorship but in order to return to a previous moral atmosphere. Whether MacKinnon's position would make things better in a new way is another question. Her rationale is leftist. Falwell's is not. Similarly, Sakharov was to the left of Brezhnev, but Solzhenitsyn is not. Even if a return to a czarist, holy mother Russia were a radical improvement over the Soviet state, it would have been a change back to a lost good. A liberal democratic Russia was advocated as an advance to a new good. Hence, although Hitler demanded apparently radical change, he was not of the left. Too much of Nazi ideology expressed a desire *to return* to some racially pure, warlike German society for Nazi radicalism to be classified as leftist. That Hitler wanted to return to a society that never actually existed makes his views no less reactionary.[2]

---

2. Isaiah Berlin (1996) states that "Hitler had a professed aim of undoing the results of the French Revolution."

There is nothing very new about this definition of the left. Most basic political labels reflect it. We have "progressives" on the left: "we can make the world better"; "conservatives" in the middle: "we had best leave well enough alone"; reactionaries on the right: "we must undo past changes."[3] "Radicals" can be of the left or right depending on whether they want a sharp and fast reversion from the status quo or sharp and fast progress from it. When describing political positions in terms of their basic location on the left/right spectrum, these are the most useful labels. A liberal or a monarchist, a free marketer or a socialist are left or right only in specific contexts. But a progressive is always on the left and a reactionary always on the right.[4]

Full-Blown Progressivism

Stripped to her philosophical political essence, a progressive simply believes in human-made human progress. Yet in earlier chapters I have used the term *progressive* to stand for particular political values and, in some cases, particular political positions. This is because some values and positions, through long association with the conceptual essence of progressivism, have attached themselves to its very meaning. Therefore the term should be understood as referring to its essential skeleton *and* the flesh that is tightly attached to it. Although not of the essence, this flesh is not an inexplicable, arbitrary growth; it is the historically evolved incarnation of the progressive idea. The progressive believes in and wants a better world. Certain visions of that better world and certain ways of realizing these visions have tended to dominate progressive thought. Progressives have fairly consistently believed that human equality makes for a better world. For great stretches of history, an expansion of individual human liberty was viewed as progressive, as

---

3. Here and in what follows I discuss the progressive, conservative, and reactionary as pure archetypes. Obviously any sane progressive has some skepticism concerning how much can be done to improve the human condition, just as a sane conservative must believe some improvements are possible and a sane reactionary realize that some past conditions are unrestorable.

4. Eric Hobsbawm describes the great ideological divide leading to World War II as pitting the descendants of the Enlightenment — liberals, socialists, and communists alike — against the foes of the Enlightenment. He notes that the original terms used to describe these opponents were the forces of "progress" and the forces of "reaction" (Hobsbawm 1994, 144).

was the support for cooperative activities. The ultimate eradication of violence and poverty has also long been at the core of most progressive visions. These goals and means have become so closely linked with progressivism that some think of them as its essence. But a conservative might well value equality, freedom, peace, and prosperity. She just does not believe that there is much we can do to achieve them. Worse, she believes that attempts to achieve them will only make things worse. Therefore, conservative social activism is aimed at stifling progressive social activism. But not necessarily because a conservative has different ultimate values. The conservative's heaven is usually as free, peaceful, and bountiful to all as is any leftist utopia. But because she disbelieves in efforts to make heaven on earth, as a practical matter, she does not champion policies aimed at the realization of these values. Since it is up to progressives to fight for these values, quite naturally they become a part of progressivism in a way that they are not part of conservatism. Since the values do not constitute practical political goals for the conservative, it seems to the progressive that conservatives do not genuinely share these values. And, of course, there is a sense in which they don't. Conservatives will not work for equality or solidarity, and they try to thwart those who do. But, still, it is not the ultimate values that define the left/right spectrum but the ultimate beliefs. Leftists should not look upon conservatives as evil, only as unduly pessimistic. Conservatives should not view progressives as evil, only as unduly optimistic.

Of course, progressives and conservatives may suspect each other's respective optimism and pessimism is merely a cover, an excuse to pursue callously selfish, amoral goals. And since progressives and conservatives are human beings, they are to a large extent correct. Selfish, amoral goals can be, and have been, callously pursued using leftist and rightist rhetoric. Indeed, most progressive and conservative politics are a mixture of sincere principle and disingenuous selfishness. And, as in most areas of life, it is hard to disentangle human motivations (including our own) in any given instance. It seems to me that conservatism better lends itself to selfish insincerity or selfish self-delusion, at least on the part of those living well under the status quo. It is convenient to think that things cannot be changed for the better if you are content to leave things as they are. But I may be only indulging a progressive bias; and, in any case, there is no shortage of historical examples of insincerity and self-delusion on the left.

The progressive believes in the possibility of making things better. The deepest progressive traditions hold that a world of equality and liberty, free from poverty and war, is that better world. Other progressive traditions hold that certain means, such as free speech or labor unions, are especially effective in building that better world (or constitute it in a more fine-grained way than is described by the broader values such as equality and liberty). When I refer to progressivism, I speak of this entire progressive tradition, its optimistic essence *and* the historically associated ideals. It is this broad tradition that, I think, can be supported by a Secular Jewish identity. It in turn gives a needed substance to, Secular Judaism.

Jewish Identity and Tradition as a Prop for Progressivism

I know Jews who claim that they maintain their Jewish identity solely through their progressive politics and who think that it is un-Jewish to be right wing. This goes too far. Being a Jew and being a progressive are distinct things. But I do think there is an affinity between Jewish history, traditions, and progressive politics. The long list of prominent Jews on the left, and the consistent sympathy for progressive politics of a high percentage of Jews, is neither random nor caused by a minor contingency of modern Jewish history. There are no necessary connections present, but there is a deep, tenacious bond. Let's begin with the sustenance received by the progressive from being a Jew.

History

We start with Jewish history. Jews have been afflicted with most of the burdens progressives seek to eradicate. Denied land or access to certain crafts, Jews have been condemned to poverty. Disenfranchised, they have known political powerlessness. Religious outcasts, they have experienced social ostracism. Repeatedly uprooted and expelled, Jews are the archetypal refugees. Relentlessly pressured to abandon their faith, Jews suffered for centuries on account of their convictions. Jews have been history's premier scapegoats — blamed for plagues, criminality, debauched morals, degenerate art, degrading science, capitalist

84

exploitation, communist oppression, war, and the murder of God. Jews have been the perennial target of violence and victims of war. And Jews have suffered from the most acute episode of racial persecution in history. Teach someone what it has been like to be a Jew for the past two thousand years and you give her vivid lessons on the evils of inequality and persecution. This passion of the Jews is not the whole story, but it is a true story. Jewish history provides Jews with strong reasons for progressive partisanship. Insofar as contemporary Jews are taught to see Jewish history as their own, progressive politics comes to coincide with the politics of self-interest, for Jews have good reason to believe that the tolerance of inequality, authoritarianism, and oppression will work to their disadvantage. But even if a Jew believes that her situation is now so secure that she has nothing personally to fear from conservative politics, Jewish history should help her to empathize with those who will be harmed by a conservative regime, a regime willing to abide social injustice. Having felt the horrors of racism and having labored under the burdens of inequality and oppression, Jews should understand and share the impatience of the downtrodden for change.[5]

Jews were the historical counterculture in Christian Europe. They were seen by the ruling majority and by themselves as the Other. This outside, marginal social position gave them the motive and perspective to question the dominant ideology. Official talmudic doctrine eschewed any disobedience to the state and enjoined a "lets keep our heads down" quietism. But no amount of "the law of the land is the law" talmudic pronouncements could fully counter the effects of the Jews' existential situation. A millennium of experience as cultural opposition forms a habitual skepticism about the goodness of the status quo and the wisdom of conventional thought.

In addition to having a history that groups them with the alienated and the wretched of the earth, central traditional Jewish values also make Jews natural allies of progressives. The importance of the individual's life and dignity, communal solidarity, equality before the law, and the emphasis on education are all core values in Jewish tradition

---

5. While making this identification with the downtrodden via an identification with oppressed Jews of the past, we need to be careful to avoid the "claim to historical grandeur and historical tragedy which [is] unearned and emotionally self indulgent," [that Eva Hoffman, quite rightly, disdains (Bershtel and Graubard 1992, 72).

85

and are, or should be, mainstays of the progressive vision, for they remain the most hopeful path to a better world.

Education

Even a passing familiarity with Jewish tradition demonstrates its devotion to learning and education. Study is the dominant form of serving and worshiping God. In traditional Jewish societies, scholars have the highest status. Universal male literacy was an ideal closely approached in many Jewish societies, well before it was a norm in most other cultures. Education for the poor was a community obligation.

Progressives, too, value education. On the one hand, improvement of the world would seem to require knowledge of it. We must learn how things work so we might work them better. As one prominent leftist scion of a rabbinical family has noted, "philosophers have only interpreted the world, but the point is to change it."[6] But it is not simply the accumulation of new knowledge that is valuable; widespread distribution of the knowledge we already have also improves the world. Ignorance contributes to poverty, violence, and inequality. Better education, more widely distributed, has long been high on the progressive agenda.

This pragmatic attitude toward knowledge is also found in Jewish thought. The primary purpose of the voluminous Torah commentaries is for learning how to apply the law. Scholars are judges and their scholarship helps them render wise judgment. Jews have sought new understanding and deeper insight so as to make a better world. In addition, Jews have believed that the democratic dissemination of knowledge throughout the community is crucial to creating that better world.

One particular aspect of education associated with the progressive outlook is the development of critical acumen. Social change requires the ability to question and challenge accepted doctrines. Indeed much of the theoretical underpinnings of various progressive traditions are built on the negation, deconstruction, or critique, of dominant institutions or ideologies. Progressive schools are "dialectical," or "criti-

---

6. Marx 1845.

cal." Progressive education does not simply consist of learning what is "known," it involves questioning it. And here, Jewish educational tradition is inspiring. The higher reaches of traditional Jewish study consist mostly of inquiries into competing interpretations of texts, the clash of authoritative citations, the quest for an original and synthesizing insight, and, above all, the logical construction and *undermining* of support for some judgment. *Pilpul,* the heart of the yeshiva curriculum, is Yiddish for "dialectics."

In the Jewish tradition the questioning of authority runs deep. Abraham argues with God over the justice of destroying Sodom. There are *aggadot* (anecdotes, parables, tales) whose moral is that God should not attempt to override human understanding and application of Torah.[7] No authority, no matter how exalted, should impose its will without the rational consent of the community. God commands and Jews must obey. But Jews retain the duty to question the commands, and God is duty bound to reveal his rationales. And of course, under all circumstances, the right to kvetch is inalienable.

Laws, Individuals, and Community

Another progressive feature of Jewish traditions is the prominence of the law in human affairs. Of course, the content of a legal system can be conservative, and most legal systems have been just that. Jewish law, too, is rife with conservative elements. But the idea of law is progressive,[8] and its existence indicates a belief that humans should not be ruled by superior strength or arbitrary authority whimsically applied. The logic of law also tends toward equality, for laws are general rules that are meant to govern all community members. Of course the law can recognize kings and castes. It can enshrine inequality. But I think the notion of equality before the law is not simply an external ideal that happens to be attached to some legal systems. Rather it is an ideal embedded in the idea of the law that will be expressed with the law's development. Jewish law expresses this ideal. There are 613 com-

---

7. The story is told of a rabbi's attempt to invoke God's direct authority to counter a decision of a majority of sages. God weighs in but is told by the majority to mind his/her own business.

8. Cf. Habermas 1992.

mandments and they apply to every male Jew. A rabbinical court's judgment is not to be based on the (nongendered) status of the parties to the dispute. Everyone has access to the law; all can seek legal redress. And since the law rules so many facets of traditional Jewish life, this equality of rights and duties permeates much of traditional Jewish existence.

Although a legalistic *form* of life is progressive, this could be easily outweighed by a primarily conservative content. Jewish law is not devoid of conservative content. Far from it. But before looking at some of its conservative content, I will point out two major progressive features of Jewish law.

First is the overriding importance placed on the saving of human life. All Jewish laws, save three, give way to the commandment to preserve human life. The principle of preserving human life as first priority is known as *pakuach nefesh*. The three exceptions to it are the commandments against idolatry, murder, and adultery/incest. More about them in a moment. For now I want to focus on the great value traditional Jewish law has placed on the individual life. A famous talmudic precept is that to save a life is equivalent to saving the whole world.[9] The same passage stresses that each human life is unique. It is not simply the loss of an individual, but the loss of *this* individual, that is tragic. All things must defer to saving *this* individual. Apart from the exceptions, traditional Judaism enshrines preservation of the individual as its supreme law. One of the "exceptions" is really not an exception at all. The prohibition against murder forbids the sacrifice of one individual to save another. This does not weaken individualism, it merely combines it with egalitarianism. Each life is supremely valuable, none should be purchased at the cost of another.

There is a characteristic of traditional Jewish individualism that deserves special mention. It is not simply the individual biological life that is so precious; equally valuable is the dignity of the person whose life it is. Humiliating a person is in some ways tantamount to killing her. Traditional law is full of rules aimed at maintaining the individual's dignity. For example, the highest form of charity is double-blind anonymous giving, in which case neither benefactor nor benefited

---

9. Mishna Sanhedrin 4:5.

know each other, thereby protecting the recipient from any humiliation attached to being the object of charity and protecting the donor from vanity. This brings us to the second and third exceptions to the priority of preserving life: idolatry and unchastity. A life should be preserved, except at the cost of the fundamental dignity of the individual whose life it is. What is sacred is not the mere biological process, but the unique divine image that that physical entity bears. Given the talmudists' theological and sexual beliefs, choosing death over idolatry or unchastity is plausibly understood as a defense of the individual's dignity. The idea that the achievement of an individual's highest good may at times be incompatible with her continued life, may, in this instance, be based on beliefs we do not share. But they are not a retreat from individualism. If anything, they represent a rich concept of the individual that includes her dignity. And this is very much in line with progressive thought.[10]

Much of progressive tradition can be understood as a quest to realize universal human dignity. The "dignity of man" has been emblazoned on the banners of progressives since the French Revolution. Political rights, decent working conditions, education, health care — practically every progressive initiative in history — have been advocated in the name of human dignity. Even the basic material well-being of humans was not viewed merely as an end in itself but also as a means to recognizing the dignity of each individual.

Although leftist thought of the last century has tended to value the collective and rail against "bourgeois individualism," from the larger historical perspective, the emergence of the value of each individual is

---

10. One must be careful here about seeing all possible goods as somehow accruing to individuals and thereby making any set of values a reflection of individualism. But the above argument for the individualistic value of Jewish tradition does not rest on such broad but empty foundations. Substantive individualism requires that the individual's good be highly valued and the individual's choices be greatly respected. Related to these requirements, although not necessarily derived from them, are the principles that certain goods of an individual should never be sacrificed for the sake of other goods (even for the same goods of other individuals) and that, as I state above, the community's good consists of the well being of its individual members. I think the idolatry and chastity imperatives are not primarily aimed at the good of anyone other than the individual they enjoin. Nor do I think they were experienced as thwarting the pursuit of one's own good, that is, I do not believe individuals felt that their individuality was constrained by the laws against idol worship and fornication. Therefore, they are not major evidence of a retreat from the individualism enshrined in *pakuah nefesh*.

highly progressive. That part of the leftist condemnation of "individualism" that is progressive condemned the hypocrisy that made some individual rights (and some individuals) inviolable while ignoring other
individual rights (and other individuals). There was also the justifiable
condemnation of an individualism that falsely conceived of the individual as a thing apart from society. But leftist anti-individualism that
actually denigrated the individual and valued only the collective is
more plausibly viewed as reactionary than progressive. Stalinist or
Maoist collectivism may have been dressed in progressive rhetoric, but
it was not a transformation to a higher plane of individualistic society;
it was an attempt to avoid or reverse the valuing of every individual.
These collectivisms were a throwback to those despotic societies in
which most individuals are dispensable. The individualism expressed
by the Jewish tradition of *pakuach nefesh* flows with the mainstream
progressive tradition, running from the Enlightenment through classical liberalism, social democracy, anarchism, and left libertarianism, all
of which have sought a society that highly values all individuals.

Progressive individualism conceives of the individual as part of a
community. It understands the individual as finding her fulfillment in
that community and in solidarity with it. The individualistic right and
collectivist left agree that either a society can primarily value individuals and their rights or it can value the community and its rights. The
individualistic right opts for individuals, the collectivist left for community. Centrists recognize the conflict and seek compromise — sometimes favoring individual rights, sometimes community needs. But
right, left, and center agree that the individual and the community have
opposing interests. Progressive individualists deny the conflict.[11] They

---

11. As Joel Greifinger has pointed out to me there are those who would consider themselves "progressive individualists" (or whom others might so consider) who would not only
not deny the conflict between individual and community interests, but indeed believe its
denial is the high road to totalitarianism. The denial of an ultimate, essential conflict between
individual and communal goods looks like a conflation of them and opens the way to
claiming that the former is *really* served whenever the latter is. Moreover, it justifies the
public administration of the individual's good since the communal good is bound up with it.
This point is brought home when we consider the collectivist right, which makes the individual's good compatible with the communal good by obliterating the individual through complete absorption into the community (*volk*, state). These are deep and complex matters that I
will not develop here. I will simply state my position that: 1) Potential for reconciliation is
not tantamount to identification between the things reconciled. 2) Reconciliation is the goal
worked toward, not always the immediately achievable condition (and so, sometimes, cen-

hold that neither individuals nor communities can flourish without each other. Progressives believe that this is not just a contingent fact about the relations between individuals and communities. It goes to the very heart of what an individual and what a community are. An individual person is a biologically based social creation whose humanity is constituted and sustained by continued interaction with others. Outside a community we have no truly *human* being and certainly no human good.[12]

Individuals cannot be truly valued without the valuing of their communities. But the dependency is mutual. A community is constituted by

---

trist compromise is best). 3) The totalitarian upshot attributed to the reconciliationism I am endorsing is the result of either outright fraudulent collectivist lip service to individualism or a more subtle bad faith, wherein the reconciliation is only judged from the communal perspective. 4) Reconciliation of individual and communal interests does not obliterate the distinction between the public and private spheres. It is a communal, as well as an individual, interest that some matters be under the complete, unfettered control of the individual.

Of course an individual's *particular* interest, even an important one, can be ultimately irreconcilable with the community's interest. As a guilty murderer, it may be in my interest to have a corrupt jury that would be open to bribes. But individualism is not advanced by corrupt juries. But the right to a fair trial and to the presumption of innocence does serve individuals as individuals. In my view, these sorts of "generic-individual" interests are completely compatible with the community's interests. It is on the level of social policy that I believe there does not have to be a choice between community and individual; the right policy will give each its full due. But, of course, John Doe may have a particular interest that conflicts with his community's interests. And while I believe it is a community interest to give weight to the category of particular interests (as we each have our own particular interests and the community ought to protect idiosyncratic tastes and situations), certain particular interests may not be reconcilable with generic-individual and communal ones. While I remain hopeful about the ultimate reconcilability of generic-individual interests and communal interests, I recognize that the vagueness of the distinction between generic and particular interests, combined with our always imperfect social knowledge, will forever require compromises—so much so that my claim of an ultimate reconcilability might be thought to be reduced to an otiose theoretical possibility. Theoretical as a fully realized society it may always be, but not otiose. It remains useful as a spur for finding reconciliation in particular matters. Reasonable members of a sane society will always need to be prepared to settle for less than they want or feel they deserve, but the settling should not end the continuing quest to find a solution that makes everyone happy.

I should also state that my belief in the possibility of reconciling individual and community interests is not a denial of the value of pluralism. I take no position here on whether there are a multiplicity of things that are intrinsically good. There may be many good things in the world without there being an ultimately irreconcilable conflict between individual and community interests.

12. Although hermits may realize some human good outside of a community, it is arguable that even that good is parasitic on the existence of social life. The hermit had to learn the values and techniques of a reclusive ideal somewhere, not to mention the basic knowledge needed even for reclusive survival. In any event, neither traditional Jewish nor progressive thought values the recluse focused exclusively on her own spiritual well-being, uninvolved with the world. There is no Jewish or progressive good life outside of social life.

individuals and has no existence separate from them. A community's well-being is the well-being of its individual members. Not only can a community not exist apart from its individual constituents, but it also has no interests that it does not share with them. There are no community interests that are not reducible to the interests of individuals — past, present, or future. This is not to deny that a community is an "organic whole" with its own features and properties. But it is to deny that one of those features is a good of its own, a good that does not accrue to individuals in the community. While there are things that are true of a community that are not true of its members (for instance, a community can be five hundred years old), it cannot be true that a community is doing well and that all its members are doing lousy.

The upshot of all this is that, as the progressive enlightenment ideal teaches, a community should serve individuals, and, as the progressive socialist ideal teaches, individual well-being requires communal bonds. In this century progressives have stressed the communal aspects of progressivism, largely because, at least formally, individualism became the consensus ideology in the Western world. Ideologically speaking the individualistic program of progressives had triumphed. Individual voting, legal, religious, and contract rights were becoming the norm. Further progress seemed to require movement on the communal end of things. Reactionary collectivists in progressive cloaks used this perception to repress the individualistic aspect of the progressive ideal. But it is increasingly clear that a progressive philosophy will value individuals and community, not as separate ideals, but as individuals in community.

This may sound like the contemporary political philosophy called *communitarianism,* and in some ways it is; communitarians have developed the insight that individuals essentially exist, and find their good, in communities. But many communitarians conclude that this insight suggests a need to reign in individualism. Communitarians are thereby tacitly buying into the collective/individual dichotomy. By calling for a tilting toward community needs, even at the expense of individual rights, some communitarians are not very different from the "centrists," who propose a compromise between the competing needs of the individual and the community. I believe that the progressive and traditional Jewish position would correctly deny the conflict. Which is not to say that individual or community "rights" falsely conceived (that is, the right of an individual to own a factory or the right of a community to hear only the majority language spoken) might not come into conflict with each other or with genuine human interests. As I have said above, I also disagree with communitarians who believe that a community has interests that transcend the interests of all and each of its members.

We have already seen how Jewish tradition values individuals. If we now turn to its attitude toward the community, we shall find an equal respect. *Klal Yisroel,* the Jewish people taken as a whole, is a moral priority throughout the tradition. We are taught that each Jew is responsible for all Jews. Charity, support of the community poor, is morally obligatory, it is a mitzvah, a commandment. Jews have forever collected money to ransom other Jews. No matter how poor a community is, it is duty bound to rescue kidnapped Jews. The troubles of each Jew are the troubles of the Jewish people, and the troubles of the Jewish people are the troubles of each Jew. Community solidarity has been a corollary of the value placed on each individual. No virtue has been more esteemed than a love of the Jewish people. This community-mindedness, this strong sense of social responsibility, is an important resource for progressives seeking to foster human solidarity. It is all the more valuable for being integrated with a deep concern for each individual.

As has oft been noted, the ultimate manifestation of Judaism's community-mindedness is its concept of salvation. The central Jewish drama is not about whether this individual is saved or that individual becomes enlightened, it is about the redemption of the entire Jewish community. There is no hint of "every man for himself" in this theology, no worrying about the fate of your own soul as opposed to that of the communal soul.

Jewish Materialism

Alas, the phrase "Jewish materialism" conjures up the anti-Semitic canard, to some extent internalized by Jews themselves, that Jews are a greedy, acquisitive breed, obsessed with their possessions and indifferent to the finer, more spiritual aspects of human life. Whether it is as the Shylock moneylender, the Fagin swindler, or the Bloomingdales habitué, we see that this materialistic image persists throughout Western culture. The anti-Semitic employment of this degrading insult should not blind us to the genuinely progressive materialistic insight of Jewish tradition: "If there is no flour, there is no Torah." Judaism realizes that human spirit requires a material base. The same idea forms part of the moral foundation of Marx's work. True human history, the realm of human freedom, commences when abundant productivity frees humanity from the drudgery of alienating work and spirit-killing poverty. Although occasionally romanticized in Jewish tradition, for the most part, poverty is seen as a curse to be overcome. We cannot expect a mensch to act as a mensch when she is preoccupied with her animal needs. No flour, no Torah.

Of course compared to classic socialist thought, the traditional Jewish philosophy of history is out-and-out idealism. God's struggle with the Jews, not the class struggle, is the key to history. But even if the fulfillment of God's Torah — rather than the eradication of poverty, the abolition of private property, or the democratic control of production — has been the main item on the Jewish historical agenda, it is an idealistic agenda with a prominent materialistic moment. For, unlike the main variants of most religious traditions, the spiritual task of Judaism — the fulfillment of Torah — is a very "this worldly" enterprise. Social, *material* justice is a part of Torah. This is not (to the credit of Jewish thought) the crude materialism of simplistic socialist traditions. Nor does it approach sophisticated "materialistic analyses" that, although probably still quite inadequate for their aspirations, have garnered an important place in progressives' understanding of the world. Traditional Jewish materialism is encased in a religious idealism. But it is not an idealism that, in order to advance the human cause, would have us focus exclusively on things of the spirit while the suffering flesh of our common humanity is despised as a petty distraction. Jewish respect for the flesh should be entered as a progressive credit in our ledger.

Nonprogressive Parts of the Tradition

Some readers will feel that I have provided a one-sided interpretation of Jewish tradition. Are there no conservative or even reactionary elements in the tradition? Indeed, isn't even the progressivism cited open to question? Think of the gloss a progressive, cynical about Jewish tradition, might offer: education: "theocratic elitism"; solidarity: "tribal chauvinism"; the value of the individual and her dignity: "sham rhetoric covering an oppressive patriarchy." Are not these, the cynic might ask, the real core of Jewish tradition?

I think not. But in a way, it doesn't matter. The issue is not whether Jewish traditions are *really* progressive. It is enough, for our purposes, that they can plausibly and effectively be used as a foundation for a progressive philosophy and as a framework for a progressive education. There certainly are clearly conservative, even reactionary, elements in Jewish traditions. But they do not undermine the possibility of an overall progressive interpretation. Moreover the nonprogressive features can be used as object lessons in what needs to be overcome. Progressivism works for progress and does not expect to find things already good. The reactionary chaff in the tradition is grist for the secular educator's mill. Traditional Jewish patriarchy, for instance, should be highlighted by progressive Jews as the central *conservative* element in the Jewish tradition. No progressive spin can be put on it. But progressive purposes can be served by its study: It can be shown how patriarchy conflicts with other ideals; the connections between sexism and racism (and therefore anti-Semitism) can be explored. In general, Jewish patriarchal tradition can serve as a vivid example of the nature of, the contradictions in, and the injustices of sexism and the need to struggle against it. It also shows the possibility of changing it. Most Jews, but especially secular Jews, do not approach Jewish traditions as a take it or leave it package deal. That Jewish identity can be meaningfully embraced through evolving traditions, while Jewish patriarchy is emphatically rejected, is an important progressive lesson. Many contemporary Jewish feminists, from the secular to the religiously orthodox, are learning and teaching this lesson.[13]

Acknowledging and studying the injustices in Jewish tradition has the further progressive use of countering the chauvinist tendencies among Jews. As I said, I think that the ideal of *klal Yisroel*, Jewish love of the Jewish people, is progressive. I believe that it is a model for community responsibility that can be expanded to a broader human solidarity. Nonetheless there are chauvinist aspects of Jewish tradition and

---

13. For example, Plaskow 1990, Pogrebin 1991, Falk 1989, and Heschel 1983.

folk attitudes. Philip Roth has depicted these mind-sets in much of his work. In one memorable passage in *Portnoy's Complaint*, Alexander Portnoy sets forth a ranting exegesis on the kosher laws, in which they are interpreted as the expression of Jewish moral control contrasted with barbarian "goyishe" self indulgence: "[A] diet of abominable creatures well befits a breed of mankind so hopelessly shallow and empty headed as to drink, to divorce, and to fight with their fists. All they know, these imbecilic eaters of the execrable, is to swagger to insult, to sneer and sooner or later to hit." Portnoy concludes that the implicit message of his Jewish upbringing is the superiority, intellectually, but especially morally, of Jews. The "stupid goyim . . . will eat anything" and "they will do anything."

Roth's parody captures a significant current in twentieth-century Jewish psychology. This current may have sources deep in the tradition, perhaps going back to the idea of a chosen people. It certainly has swelled as a result of Jewish experience in the first half of this century. (It is hard not to feel morally superior to a world that is largely indifferent to the torture and murder of your children.) A progressive Jewish education should begin its study of Jewish chauvinism by explaining how persecution can lead to a reactionary xenophobia and racism.[14] It might then point out that no tradition or culture is immune from doing injustice or beyond the need for moral criticism. Studying and criticizing Jewish chauvinism has multiple progressive effects. First, it can directly lessen chauvinism and concomitant xenophobia and racism. Put under a clear light, the stupidity and pernicious effects of chauvinism are more readily seen. It cannot remain in the shadows as a subconscious belief, influential but not subject to analysis. Studying chauvinism directly undermines it.

Second, by owning up to any Jewish evil, we indirectly combat the particular evil of ethnic chauvinism among Jews. Harsh judgments of others and feelings of superiority are shaken when one sees the mote in one's own eye. Belief in one's moral superiority is undercut somewhat by any motes you find there, but a particularly striking mote is noted when the very belief in moral superiority is understood to be evidence against moral superiority.

---

14. Although it is clearly a complex phenomenon, this is surely *part* of the explanation of contemporary anti-Semitism among some African Americans.

Third, study of Jewish chauvinism affords an opportunity to distinguish between pride in a tradition and contempt for other traditions. This is of special importance. In chapter 1 I argue that there is no necessary tension between devotion to a particular ethnicity or culture and devotion to the enlightenment ideals of universal equality, solidarity, and mutual respect. But a tension can easily arise when (in addition to the other, more material factors, such as economic equality and general prosperity, mentioned in chapter 1) patriotism is confused with jingoism or an intelligent appreciation of one's own heritage is replaced by an ignorant contempt for others.

Fourth, the scrutiny of Jewish chauvinism spurs the exploration of conflicting tendencies within the Jewish tradition. Along with the idea of being a chosen and holy nation, Jews have a tradition of considering themselves displeasing to God, in dire need of reform and redemption. Reactionary Jewish chauvinism is coupled with progressive Jewish self-criticism. Alexander Portnoy's imagined parental jeremiad against the "goyim" brings us to Jeremiah's cries against our own wickedness. The final progressive lesson to be drawn, then, from looking at nonprogressive features of the Jewish tradition is the realization that all traditions are a mixed moral bag, all in need of preservation *and* change.

One of the changes that a tradition might need is reinterpretation. In chapter 2, regarding religious ritual, I spoke of reinterpreting religious practices so that they can have secular meaning. But doctrines and practices may need new interpretations to appease moral and political, as well as metaphysical, scruples. Some parts of the tradition are morally hopeless. They should be abandoned. This is the case with much of the sexism of traditional Jewish life. But other apparently nonprogressive parts of the tradition may be susceptible to progressive refashioning. A number of efforts have been made to give the idea of "choseness" a universalist meaning.[15] This sort of effort is worthwhile. A

---

15. There is a long history of contrasting Jewish interpretations of the "chosen people" doctrine. Judah Halevi, the medieval Jewish poet, emphasized the uniqueness of the Jews in the doctrine. Some kabbalists give the idea a racist slant, with Jews having superior souls to gentiles. A more standard rabbinical approach makes the choseness primarily the function of the extra duties Jews took on in accepting the Torah. The modern Reform movement stresses the universalist interpretation — there is nothing special about Jews beyond their willingness to bear God's message — a willingness any person can participate in. Reconstructionists, in their 1945 *Sabbath Prayer Book,* seem to have despaired of giving a universalist twist to the doctrine and decided to abandon it.

tradition is constituted by continuity, and reinterpretation maintains as much continuity as is compatible with a progressive vision. A successful progressive reinterpretation shows, while not needlessly weakening the tradition, that even in humanity's darker corners there flickers a potential spark of enlightenment. Of course, sophistry will only feed cynicism, but if honestly and insightfully done, reinterpretation can nourish the optimistic heart of progressivism.

What Progressivism Does for Secular Jewish Identity

I have been discussing how Secular Judaism can support progressive values. I now turn to the support progressivism gives to Secular Judaism, for Secular Judaism is more dependent on progressivism than progressivism is on it. Most of the world's progressives are not Jews. Their progressivism is embedded in either another tradition or a fairly self-standing ideology. One clearly need not be any sort of Jew to be a robust progressive. But it is not at all clear that one can have a robust *secular* Jewish life that is unallied to progressive values. For a religious person, doing God's will serves as a unifying theme that gives life coherence and moral value. The secular Jew needs a functional analogue. Although lacking the certitude or completeness of the divine vision, a progressive vision can tie Jewish life to a coherent set of moral values. Humans can have satisfying lives and fulfilling identities without serving God, but not without serving something. What ultimately makes life worthwhile is that you are doing something worthwhile with it. Although a Secular Judaism with no moral compass is logically possible (for one can follow certain traditions without giving them any moral significance), it is not sustainable. It cannot be successfully taught or passed through the generations. It cannot be successfully taught because no persuasive motive to learn it can be given. It cannot be passed through the generations because its amoral stance generates no loyalty. It is not sustainable because it does not sustain us.

Granted, progressive values are not the only values possible for Secular Judaism. Jewish tradition can be made logically consistent (insofar as it is internally consistent) with a wide range of politics and morals. Some textual or historical support can be found for almost any position. Jewish history is long, its texts massive and the work of many hands. If the devil can quote scripture, it is no surprise that Republicans can cite Talmud. A group calling itself *Toward Tradition* has claimed that "Judaism and its eternal values have little in common with modern American Liberalism," and that "Judaism is a conservative and traditional religion."[16] The group's advertisement implies that Jewish law endorses deregulation, support for the U.S. military, lower taxes, capital punishment, and capitalism. So it is not only logically possible to place Jewish tradition in a conservative moral framework, it has actually been done. But the strain is clear. Toward Tradition acknowledges that "many Jews with a multi-generational loyalty to the Democratic Party were troubled" by the conservative tide in the 1994 congressional elections. (Indeed 78 percent of Jews voted Democratic.) To make the case for an essentially conservative Jewish tradition, the group must claim that "many people nowadays seem to misunderstand the true nature of Judaism." Quite so; most Jews do think their traditions are most at home on the left, although whether this is a "misunderstanding" is another thing. Unlike Toward Tradition, my argument need not make any claims about the politically "true nature" of Judaism. I only claim that progressivism is a comfortable moral setting for Jewish traditions and that Secular Judaism needs a moral setting.[17]

Certainly there are many individual conservative elements in Jewish traditions. Toward Tradition types can point to them. The richness of Jewish traditions, along with the ingenuity of commentators, allows for many moral interpretations of the tradition as a whole. But a *secular* Jew, needing to motivate Jewish practice without recourse to God, will find a progressive interpretation most sustaining. Earlier I spoke of

---

16. Advertisement in *The New York Times,* 16 December 1994. This conservative interpretation of Jewish traditions was challenged in a liberal counter-ad on 3 January 1995. Bershtel and Graubard (1992, 251–4) give some historical depth to the Toward Tradition position by noting that most enlightenment liberals thought of Judaism and its traditions as anything but progressive, and the majority of late nineteenth-century radicals still considered Jewish traditions reactionary. Bershtel and Graubard claim that the "myth" of an ancient progressive Jewish tradition was created when the Bund sought to exploit the traditional religious sentiments of Jews to win them to the cause of socialism. No doubt the Bund did do what it could to give progressive slants to Jewish traditions. But that does not imply that its interpretations are unfounded. The image of Jewish traditions as progressive may indeed be of relatively recent origin, but this is irrelevant to the actual political nature of these traditions. In any event, I am not claiming that the traditions have an actual political nature, but only that they have a rich progressive vein to mine.

17. It is interesting to note that Toward Tradition excludes secularists from the Jewish traditions it believes are conservative. There seems to be an implicit acknowledgment that Secular Jews, at least, are naturally progressive.

progressive spins on Jewish ritual as examples of Jewish contributions to progressivism. This sort of spin makes tradition relevant to progressivism. But we now see the symbiotic nature of the relationship. The progressive spin also makes Secular Judaism relevant to life. This does not operate only at the level of particular practices. It can encompass an entire moral vision. Perfect faith that the Messiah will come, though she may tarry, reflects the progressive's optimism in a world of justice, though it too tarries. The Jewish responsibility to *work toward* the Messianic age is given secular application in progressive social activism. Progressive ideology rationalizes, organizes, and helps interpret Jewish traditions. It not only gives a secular meaning to Jewish history, it gives a secular meaning to Jewish theology. Without such meanings, Secular Judaism is doomed to temporary adjunct status in the life of a few generations of American Jews. Allied to a progressive vision, Secular Judaism might become a vibrant force in American Jewish life.[18]

An Apology for Progressivism

I have been arguing that being a Jew enriches a progressive life and that being a progressive is crucial to a *secular* Jewish life. But these arguments will count for little if progressivism is judged a misguided politi-

---

18. Bershtel and Graubard (1992, 258–59) assert that "the historical moment has passed . . . [when] . . . radicalism could provide a powerful basis for Jewish organization, identification, and community allegiance." But the only reasons they offer to support this assertion—that Traditional Judaism has been historically apolitical, that there are non-Jewish venues where Jews can be radical, that people's leftism can be sustained through non-Jewish sources, and that the image of Jewish radicalism has dimmed—are inadequate. At best they only show that you do not need to be (or to remain) Jewish to be a progressive or be progressive to be Jewish. All of which is true. But they do not show that there are not possible ways of being Jewish rooted in progressivism or that communities of Jews can form around those ways. And they certainly do not show that secular Jewish identity does not benefit from, if not require, a strong progressive component. Contra Bershtel and Graubard, Leonard Fein (1994) argues that only a Judaism of progressive social activism can possibly reintegrate what he terms *non-Jewish Jews* securely into the fold of identifying Jews. Fein goes even further, claiming that progressive social activism is ultimately the recipe for a flourishing Judaism of all varieties. Here I think Fein goes too far. While I agree with Fein that, as I have argued above, any Judaism must serve some "good," I disagree that that good must be identified with a progressive social agenda or any political agenda at all. The good, for religious Jews, might well be sufficiently realized by doing God's will, and there is no requirement that God's will be understood in liberal or progressive terms. But Bershtel and Graubard say nothing to diminish the essential centrality of progressive politics for the Judaism of what I have been calling *Wicked Children* and Fein's roughly equivalent non-Jewish Jews.

cal philosophy. Although it is beyond my present ambition to argue for the superiority of progressive politics, I do want to defend it against the charge that, as I have defined it, progressivism is foolish, for I have claimed that the essence of progressivism is a belief in humanity's ability to improve the world, and some think this belief is obviously false.

Most conservatives would claim that the world is as good as it is going to get. Or at least as good as we can make it. They would argue that the human world is not conducive to human-initiated general improvement. We humans are too wicked and weak to be the agents or embodiment of a better world. It is not simply a case of enormous complexity outstripping our limited powers of understanding (although there is that); there are also natural forces that can never be overcome. Disease, selfishness, limited resources, innate aggression, sexual competitiveness, and other deadly sins pervert our intentions and accomplishments for social improvement.[19]

But the conservative feels that, more than any theory, it is the historical evidence that decisively refutes the progressive's "optimism." The world has not grown better, and our efforts toward that end, especially our political efforts, have only made things worse. How can anyone at the end of the twentieth century be optimistic about the human prospect? Can any sane person be sanguine about the results of human wisdom and intentions? Better leave well enough, even if it isn't quite well, alone.

I do not find the history of social progress as unequivocally disheartening as the conservative, but I concede that it is not a record that justifies bright expectations. But the "optimism" animating progressiv-

---

19. As I pointed out in note 1 of this chapter, this political classification scheme does not pretend to capture neatly all who would most commonly be labeled progressive or conservative. Karl Popper–type conservatives, who believe in the possibility of social progress but believe only incremental, modest attempts are wise (Popper 1962), I would reclassify as fundamentally progressive (unless incrementalism becomes a ploy for quietism). My taxonomy would also reclassify Nozickian "conservatives" who also have no beef with the possibility of social progress but simply insist that it should not be achieved by violating individual rights (Nozick 1974). So stated there is nothing a progressive should disagree with. Most progressives, however, do not share the Nozickian account of individual rights and believe that this account of them stands in the way (perhaps, on the part of some who hold these views, intentionally, and certainly self-servingly) of making progress. In my scheme such ill-conceived individualism makes one a de facto, but not a philosophical, conservative. I should again stress that the traditional leftist critique of Nozickian individualism is often as misconceived and ill motivated as the object of their criticism is accused of being.

ism is barely touched by the dismal historical record, for it is primarily a moral rather than an epistemological stance. The progressivism I am commending is not a belief that predicts a good outcome, it is an attitude that aims at one. It is an outlook that not only acknowledges all of the obstacles to making a better world, it also acknowledges that it may be unlikely that we will achieve a better world.[20] It is compatible with an intellectual pessimism rooted in the horrors of history and the amoral callousness of nature. In purely intellectual terms, it can be as pessimistic as most conservatisms; it only demurs at a pessimism that believes progress an absolute impossibility. It is a practical, not a theoretical, stand. It tell us what to do, not what to believe.

The progressive is typically accused of naiveté or dishonesty. She is either innocent of the facts of life or misrepresents them to herself and others. But a nondogmatic progressivism need not ignore or hide anything: neither the difficulties of making or recognizing progress, nor the bleak prospects of achieving it. All this can be accepted to whatever degree a clear-eyed, honest assessment leads. And as long as this assessment does not judge progress impossible, progressivism remains a rational attitude.

If used as a guide to action, conservative pessimism will make our probable bleak future a certainty. Whatever small chance there is for progress would be snuffed out by a despairing, inert humanity. Although the platitudes of sports coaches seldom persuade, it is true that you are not going to win if you do not try to win. In addition to counseling self-defeating passivity, pessimism robs the present of meaningful hope. There is a kind of hope that believes in the possibility of a future good that it is powerless to help realize. Conservatives can have such hope. But it is empty compared to hope that informs action. It is this living, fertile hope that conservatism destroys. Surely it is not certain that things cannot get better; what justifies an attitude that would have us act as if they cannot?

---

20. This optimism is even more pessimistic than the type of pessimism Gramsci was endorsing with the slogan he popularized, "Pessimism of the intellect, optimism of the will." Gramsci wanted us to squarely face all the obstacles to progress and realize that the struggle will not be easy; we would have to work through much adversity. But Gramsci did not go further and claim that even our best, most correct efforts might prove (let alone probably would prove) ultimately futile. See Gramsci 1975. A fortiori, the optimism I commend is different from traditional American optimism. The "can do" attitude includes "will try" and "will succeed." All I am calling for is a "should try" attitude.

The conservative's reply can take different forms. First she may contend that false hope is less comforting than reconciliation to a bleak world. But the progressive responds that the hope she offers is not false; it is neither a guarantee of historical triumph nor a denial of the pitfalls to progress. Indeed, it is many a conservative style "reconciliation" to this vale of tears that is premised on the false (to most secularists) hope of pie in the sky justice and joy in the hereafter. Without *that* false hope, what is there to recommend reconciliation? Where is the comfort in resignation, without heavenly recompense. It is hard to reconcile yourself to hell. It is the rare sensibility that finds more solace in acceptance of utter hopelessness than in even a glimmer of hope and the scope to act on it. Conservatives who tell us to abandon "false" hope for this world, but don't provide hope for another, offer nothing. Conservatives who tell us to abandon "false" hope for this world and provide otherworldly hopes, offer nothing a secularist can believe in.

The conservative can deny that she is a hopeless pessimist. She may believe that things might or even will get better; she just doesn't think that we can do anything to make the advances. We are more likely to make things worse. Maybe much worse. The conservative need only be pessimistic about our abilities, not our prospects. To counter, the progressive can plausibly point to some successes, some areas where it appears that human efforts have improved human welfare. But I do not believe progressives can disprove the conservatives' claim that in general we cannot make things better. We can, however, note that this claim draws a picture of humankind as without effective practical reason. It sees us as unable to shape means to ends. Maybe we are so unable. But our self-image as rational practical agents runs deep. All prudence and at least a substantial part of morality assumes it.

Now perhaps the conservative only wants to claim that collective action or action aimed at the common good is doomed to failure; practical reason has a place in individual life but not in social life.[21] But this seems an arbitrary thesis. First, how do we separate individual

---

21. One can even further narrow the conservative's claim to "it is only 'government's' ability to do good that is denied; individual's and nongovernmental collectivities are allowed moral efficacy." What is distinctive about government? It can only be that it has coercive powers. So this narrow "conservative" claim reduces to the assertion that coercion cannot further the good. Hardly conservative in its historical associations and quite compatible with the essential progressive vision.

from social life? Can I improve my life, but not my family's? My neighborhood's? My workplace's? My civic group's? And are the coordinated efforts of effectively rational individuals condemned to ineffective irrationality? Do not some teams, corporations, and unions reach their goals because of what *they* do? And is not the group sometimes better off as a result? We certainly act as if we think we can make a positive difference in our lives. Does the conservative really want to say that, even is we do act this way, we should not because we cannot? I doubt that the conservative would recommend this to individuals and see no reason to embrace the advice for groups. Furthermore, most conservatives would be reluctant to deny that humans can intentionally aim at *evil* ends with great success. Why then deny that we can aim at good ends with a reasonable chance of success? Obviously one can have a theory of human nature or social psychology that explains why the Gestapo can succeed where Amnesty International cannot. But it seems to me that there is as little support for a theory of thoroughgoing original sin as there is for one of thoroughgoing natural nobility.[22]

Finally, there is the conservative fear that the quest for progress risks disaster. The progressive can share that fear and should have as deep an awareness of the catastrophes brought about by some genuinely progressive intentions, not to mention the horrors done by pseudo-progressive ones. But the rational response to these dangers is not an abandonment of the progressive project. Rather we should yoke progressivism to the humility and carefulness appropriate in light of the dangers. Most important, progressive social activism should be allied to a morality that constrains what can be done in pursuit of progress. Many of the past disasters came about because it was felt that anything was justified in the name of progress. Eggs have to be broken to make an omelet, and therefore bodies had to be broken to make a revolution. The conservative can call history to testify against a morally uninhibited progressivism. But there are no reasons that progressivism must be morally uninhibited. An epistemological modesty and historical sen-

---

22. Nelson Lande points out (personal communication) that the conservative can argue that destruction is simply easier than construction and requires less skill. Granted. But is it plausible that we inhabit a social world in which, not only is destruction easier than construction, but it is the only possible form of effective action? Moreover some evil involves construction, and some progress may require destruction.

sitivity allow and promote a morally restrained progressivism.[23] The strict morality and enormous decency of many progressives establishes the possibility. Stalin only proves that pseudoprogressive rhetoric can serve a lust for power and vindictiveness. Lenin and Robespierre only prove that a *perhaps* genuine desire for progress can accompany an abandonment of moral restraint and engender great evil. But there are reactionary and conservative moral monsters, too. The existence of Hitler and Czar Nicholas I does not taint every reactionary and conservative. And the lives of Dorothy Day and Mohandas Gandhi, Martin Luther King and Judah Magnes, Pete Seeger and Riguberto Michu are all real models of progressivism within the bounds of morality.

Hopeful in spite of the evidence, engaged but heedful of obstacles, rightly done, Jewish tradition and progressive politics both embody an illusionless utopianism. While a plausible argument can be made that Jews have been ill served by their utopian visions — religious and secular — and have suffered greatly from attempts to realize them, one wonders how long the Jewish people would have endured and what sort of people we would have been without our utopian hopes.

So far we have been concerned with the philosophical basis for a Secular Jewish identity in America. In what follows we turn to issues regarding the realization of this identity in the education of Secular Jewish children. A defense of historical optimism requires that we first turn to the role of the Holocaust in progressive Jewish education, for historical optimism is most dramatically challenged by the slaughter of European Jewry. If progressive, that is, optimistic, politics at the heart

---

23. The issue is more complex than I indicate above. What I am calling *morally uninhibited progressivism,* its advocates would argue, is only uninhibited by phony, shallow, or limited morality. There is nothing immoral, they would argue, in either sacrificing a few for the sake of many or ignoring the strictures of a "morality" whose real purpose is the maintenance of social domination. With regard to the second point, I agree that some "moral" rules really do only serve domination, but I do not count among the phony rules prohibitions against killing the innocent or torturing anyone. As to the first point, although my theoretical-consequentialist bent puts me in sympathy with the need to suffer lesser evils to avoid greater ones, as a practical matter, I think evil is best minimized if we give great weight to prima facie prohibitions against certain acts. For instance, I believe that progressives, like everyone else, should have such a strong bias against violence that they would find it almost impossible to ever justify armed struggle and actually impossible to ever justify terrorism. Although these things may be justifiable, experience teaches that a readiness to justify them usually leads to moral hazards and avoidable tragedies.

of Secular Judaism, then our understanding and teaching of the Holocaust poses a central challenge to Secular Jewish ideology. The second
half of this book, which attempts to lay out the philosophical ground of
a Secular Jewish curriculum, therefore begins with a discussion of the
role of the Holocaust in the educational program of Secular Judaism.

CHAPTER FIVE

The Holocaust
in Secular
Jewish Education

THE TORTURE and murder of European Jewry resists decent commentary. Trivialization, exploitation, distortion, and superficiality accompany most classroom Holocaust discussions. At the very least, discussions of the Holocaust feel terribly inadequate. Mindful of these difficulties, some believe no discussion is appropriate — "what we cannot speak about, we must pass over in silence."[1] But silence itself is clearly a form of distortion and trivialization. The dilemma is unavoidable: Our speech will fail to do justice to the Holocaust, yet it must be spoken of.[2]

My task in this chapter is slightly removed from this dilemma. For, rather than speaking directly about the Holocaust, I will discuss *why and how* it should be discussed — more specifically, why and how it should be taught to children. Nevertheless, the dangers native to all Holocaust discussions will not be far off. We cannot explore the rea-

---

1. While not referring to the Holocaust, Wittgenstein's comment perfectly expresses some thinkers' attitudes toward it. Edward Feld reports that some rabbinic leaders would observe the Holocaust Commemoration Day with silence, apparently in the belief that words cannot express what happened. Feld argues against this attitude (Feld 1995, 39). Lawrence Langer's work (see Langer 1995) strikes me as the culmination of this tradition of Holocaust thought, although his own essays and collections of testimonies clearly show that he does not advocate a total ban on Holocaust talk. Starting with Theodor Adorno's famous, but cryptic remark, "to write poetry after Auschwitz is barbaric" (Adorno 1967, 34), through George Steiner's claim that the Holocaust is "extraterrestrial to analytic debate" (1995, 121), there is a clear tradition of thought that fears that all Holocaust discussion will inevitably be banal, vulgar, or absurd. I have more to say about this in the text at the end of the chapter.

2. I use the term *Holocaust* although it has been subject to criticism as a vogue term with inappropriate connotations of religious sacrifice. While I prefer the Yiddish *Churbn*, *Holocaust* is now too embedded in English to be discarded.

sons and ways to teach the Holocaust without talking about the Holocaust itself.

Why Teach the Holocaust?
Honoring Victims, and Frustrating Evil Designs

That the Holocaust should be taught, especially to Jewish children, is fairly uncontroversial. There may be technical disagreements about the appropriate age of introduction, but its place in the curriculum is not disputed. The rationales for its inclusion vary. A prominent one, and to my mind one of the most persuasive, is the strong desire of many Holocaust victims to have their story told. Witnessing and testifying are repeatedly cited as primary motives for outlasting the Nazi slaughterhouses. Insofar as simply telling what happened accedes to the wishes of the victims of the Holocaust, it is worth the doing. Undeserved suffering merits whatever meager recompense we can provide. And that the Nazis did not want the story told also makes it worth telling. Evil designs should be frustrated to whatever extent possible.

Emil Fackenheim built a philosophy from the imperative to frustrate the Nazis. "Thou shalt give Hitler no posthumous victories," has become, Fackenheim says, an eleventh commandment. He understands this mostly as a duty to work for the survival of Jews and Judaism.[3] Others have seen it as a demand that Jews cherish and nourish the values and sentiments despised by the Nazis.[4] I discuss both these points elsewhere.[5] But here I note only that, by itself, failure to tell of the Nazi crimes violates Fackenheim's commandment. The murderers kept secret and tried to destroy the evidence of their massacres. Himmler told the SS that their work could never be publicly acknowledged. Euphemisms in Nazi documents indicate that they tried to hide the truth of what they were doing, even from themselves. Contemporary self-styled Nazis deny that the Holocaust ever happened. If there are to be no posthumous victories for the Nazis, at a minimum, we must describe the crimes they would deny.

---

3. See, for example, Fackenheim (1970), 84.
4. See Steiner 1995, 121.
5. See the discussions in chapters 1 and 4.

Historically Significant Truth

Testifying for the victims is one good reason to study the Holocaust, but a more fundamental imperative perhaps justifies Holocaust education, namely the imperative to teach historical truth. The Holocaust did happen, so we ought to teach it.

But this is too simple. We do not, cannot teach everything that happened. The teacher, like the historian and the artist, selects. While there are many plausible pedagogical principles of selection, the most general is that we teach those truths that are important. But importance is a relative term. Important to whom and for what? Should we teach historical events that most impressed or shaped the lives of past peoples? Or the events that seem to have most shaped our lives? Or the items that will be most useful to know for shaping our future? Or the ones most likely to enrich our present? Clearly the dominant principle in most educational plans is to teach those things that the pupils will find most useful to know in their lives (or what the powers that be decide is most useful to have students know).

How does the Holocaust measure by these standards of importance? As a shaper of the past and present, especially the Jewish past and present, the importance of the Holocaust is unquestionable. The thousand-year-old homeland of Jewish civilization was destroyed. Yiddish culture was smashed beyond recovery. Over a third of all the world's Jews were murdered. All Jews became, to varying extents, traumatized survivors. The State of Israel, which eventually *may* have come into being without the Holocaust, was soon established. Its politics and the politics of world Jewry have been significantly informed by the Holocaust. Europe lost whatever shreds of moral self-confidence that had remained after World War I. The human potential for unlimited cruelty, callousness, and degradation received demonstrable proof. No moral taboo remained unenacted.

Today the Holocaust plays a central role in Jewish consciousness and communal life. The most successful Jewish fundraising is devoted to its memorialization and study, to organizations devoted to preventing its recurrence, and to the pursuit of its aging at-large criminals. No other Jewish institution, neither Torah nor Israel, unites contemporary Jewry as does Holocaust commemoration. Liberals and conservatives, Zionists and non-Zionists, doves of Yesh Gvul and hawks of Gush

Emunim, secularists and orthodox—all agree on the importance of Holocaust commemoration. Jews who agree on nothing else are respectful in common of Yom HaShoa. From Buenos Aires to New York to Moscow to Tel Aviv, Jews with almost nothing else in common understand the Holocaust to be their great commonality. To be sure, there are voices that protest the emergence of the Holocaust as the dominant, in some cases sole, substance of Jewish identity. But these protests are not meant to denigrate the importance of the Holocaust as much as to bemoan the loss of other content in Jewish identity. They don't object to "Never Again!"; they just don't think it should replace the Shema. They dissent to the relative place of the Holocaust in Jewish life; they do not deny its absolute importance.

Making Lessons of the "Lessons"

The historical importance of the Holocaust as an element in our Jewish past and present is, then, easily established. It is therefore ironic that its pedagogical justification is so often sought in its usefulness for the future, for here we are on much more problematic ground. Take, for example, the old saw that we are condemned to repeat unstudied history. Santayana's epigram notwithstanding, we will not repeat history in any case; nor does the deepest historical knowledge seem to prevent moral and practical blunders very like those of the past. For if the devil (and "Toward Tradition" conservatives) can always quote scripture, policy-makers can always cite history. The Balkan wars of the 1990s are called new Vietnams and Somalias as often as they are called new Munichs and Auschwitzes. It is difficult to believe that more or better Holocaust education would have prevented the genocidal massacres in Indonesia, Cambodia, Rwanda, and Guatemala (to name a few) of recent decades. Or that, if the Nuremberg trials were better known, we might have avoided the near ubiquitous reemergence of torture. Holocaust education will not inoculate the world against atrocity.

The "future use" justifications of Holocaust education can be sorted into two broad categories: useful in teaching good general political and moral attitudes and useful as specific guidance for political and moral action. I have considerable sympathy for the former (attitudinal) justifications, very little for the latter (pragmatic) ones. But in either case there is an awkwardness in making lessons of "The Lessons" of the Holocaust. There is something repulsive about using the Holocaust as a device for furthering any particular political/moral agenda. When we look at some of the "lessons" that are extracted from the Holocaust, they do indeed seem to epitomize its vulnerability to vulgar exploitation: "the triumph of the human spirit," "the inevitable defeat of evil," "the ineradicability of anti-Semitism," "the justification of Israel," "the possibility of heroism," "the cruelty and callousness of human nature," "the horrors of racism, fascism, and homophobia," "the absence of God." I do not say that the Holocaust is irrelevant to these issues or sheds no light on them. But whatever light it sheds is of a highly complex coloration; any washing out of the hues, in order to highlight a feature that illustrates one's pet lesson, distorts reality and shows disrespect for the victims. Worse, the attempt to analogize the Holocaust to contemporary social and political problems and then draw practical conclusions from the analogy, cannot help but ignore disanalogies, often leading to intellectual, moral, and political foolishness. Let us go over "The Lessons" one by one, starting with the practical ones.

"Never Again!"

"Never Again!" This, the ballyhooed arch lesson of the Holocaust, has proven painfully vague. Someone should not allow something. But just who should not allow just what? Clearly Jews and Jewish organizations should not allow the Nazi party to come to power in Germany and to start persecuting and exterminating Jews. But we need no impassioned sloganeering, let alone a developed curriculum, to tell us that. Does "Never Again!" also dedicate us to vehemently opposing all state-sponsored massacre? All ethnic persecution? All torture? All turning away of refugees? All war atrocities? All indifference to unjust human suffering? This would seem the most humane and enlightened interpretation of "Never Again!" — but it is of little practical value, as is evidenced by the blatant disregard of the slogan by many of its most prominent declaimers. It would be tiresome and depressing to rehearse the violations of the "Never Again" oath. And, alas, the violations are so obvious and numerous that the rehearsal is unnecessary. Besides, are these principles so morally subtle that they would go unremarked without study of the Holocaust? Surely the moral framework that would inform most curricula would affirm these principles even in the absence of a Holocaust unit.

What of the more specific lesson that anti-Semitism must be quickly and strongly confronted lest it lead to genocide? Here the Holocaust is at least as likely to mislead as to enlighten. Nazi anti-Semitism, although constructed from the elements of classic anti-Semitism, had a unique program. The Nazis were determined to murder all Jews. Their enmity was not political or economic. They were not primarily interested in the land, wealth, power, or status possessed by Jews. Ultimately they showed that they would not be satisfied by simply plundering or enslaving Jews or by separating themselves completely from Jews. Only the death of each and every Jew, the annihilation of the Jewish people, would do. This was not a minor item in the Nazi program. It was a matter of high principle, arguably the Nazis' most fundamental ideological commitment. Resources desperately needed to defend Germany in the closing months of the war went instead to murdering Jews. Jew hatred had Hitler's dying words.

The proper response to such a program in which a major state power is profoundly devoted to the literal death of all Jews would be ill fashioned as a response to more mundane anti-Semitisms. Although some sort of response will usually be in order, there may be some manifestations of anti-Semitism that are best ignored. Some call for friendly education. Still others for aggressive propaganda campaigns, community organizing, electoral politics, or economic boycotts. There may be cases, short of a return of the Nazis, requiring self-defense and even preemptive military action. But if the Holocaust is taken as the model of anti-Semitic activity, our response *always* will be an all fronts, no holds barred, uncompromising mortal battle, because that is what should have been done in the face of the Nazis. It was not done, in large part, because Jews could not conceive of such hateful and irrational enemies. The Holocaust now allows us to conceive it. But it should not lead us to perceive everywhere what was inconceivable only a few generations ago. Neither Louis Farrakhan nor Hafiz al-Assad is a Nazi — Nor are teenagers painting swastikas on suburban synagogues or suicidal terrorist bombers in Tel Aviv. These characters are certainly not benign; their activities merit vigilance and counteractions. Their motives no doubt include heavy dollops of Jew hatred, and their actions can be murderous. But whatever potential evil they represent, it is not Auschwitz. We cannot usefully teach a wise response to them through the study of the Holocaust. Holocaust lessons cannot be justified on the grounds that they teach us how to deal with anti-Semites.

If anything, our Holocaust consciousness has blinded us to morally and prudentially intelligent reactions to a number of conflicts with non-Jews. The conflict between Jews and Arabs is illustrative. At bottom this is a political dispute over land. Secondary features involve questions of political, economic, and cultural domination. In the course of the conflict, many Arabs have been more or less infected by anti-Semitism (as, for that matter, Jews have been by anti-Arab racism). But for many Jews "Never Again!" is meant to provide practical guidance on Middle East politics. Now, if the Arabs were as depraved, immoral, and irrational as the Nazis, it would be obviously foolish to negotiate, compromise, or reason with them. There can be no peace with Nazis. Give them an inch and they take Poland. Tolerate their economic boycotts and they make Babi Yar. Likewise, (reasons the learner of Holocaust "lessons") give the Arabs Nablus and they will take Tel Aviv. Share Jerusalem and they will get a piece of Haifa. Just talk to them and they will murder you.

I am not, here, arguing Middle East politics. There is room for reasonable people of good will to disagree about the demands of justice or even the dictates of (Jewish) prudence in the Middle East. But too frequently the emotional power of "Never Again!", with its inapt invocation of Holocaust imagery, overwhelms all attempts to reason about the Middle East. This has been a great misfortune for the Palestinians and Israelis, and it has done considerable harm to all Jews.

The Need to Repress Bigotry and Hatred

Another practical "lesson" often squeezed from Holocaust study is the necessity for squelching ethnic hatred and all bigotry at its earliest manifestation. "If the result of racism is Auschwitz, then its first buds must be ruthlessly nipped." The problem here is one of counterproductive overkill. Racism is pernicious enough to merit a serious response even if it is not, and it usually is not, heading toward genocide. But if we urge people to fight racism because racism leads to extermination camps, we risk them concluding that racism is not so bad in the more usual cases where it only results in oppression, poverty, indignity, and injustice.

Moreover the Holocaust, in most instances, suggests inappropriate means for fighting racial persecution. In retrospect, armed resistance — even in the face of insurmountable odds — was a sane response (maybe the only sane response) to the Nazis, for the fact that almost everyone will certainly be killed is not an argument against fighting. And, as we now know, almost every Jew in Hitler's clutches was killed, even if she did not fight. Even under the horrendous racial oppression of antebellum American slavery, a slave may have reasonably concluded that an attempted armed rebellion (as opposed to escape or some other form of resistance) may not have been the wisest strategy. And armed resistance to the deep and damaging racism that still permeates America would be downright foolhardy. The very purity and extremity of Nazi racism makes the Holocaust a poor model for suggesting practical strategies for combating racism in general.

Moral Lessons

But not all lessons are "how to" instructions. Some try to inculcate beliefs and attitudes. And one kind of rationale for Holocaust education is that through the study of the Nazis' persecutions and murders we can shape beneficently the minds and characters of the young. Ultimately I am going to agree with this kind of justification and indeed use it as a guide for the type of Holocaust education I recommend. But first I want to examine its drawbacks and abuses.

Some beliefs that can be taught are specific propositions about the past: "This is what happened: So and so many Jews were killed here; these were the methods used; this is how it was organized; this is what was said; here are the forms resistance took." This sort of straightforward account is justified, as I said before, because of the historical importance of the Holocaust to Jews. Of course such an account involves value-laden interpretations. Moreover, by calling it straightforward, I do not mean it is simple or uncontroversial. But the controversies and interpretations are concerned with what actually happened.

In contrast we have interpretations that not only give versions of the story; they provide the moral of the story as well. The story is said to illustrate a precept or to instantiate a generalization. I turn to the precept use shortly. But using the Holocaust as evidence for generalizations is almost always spurious. By its very nature, the specificity of a historical event makes it a poor basis for generalizing; and of all historical events, the Holocaust is least suitable for generalization. So, for instance, while the Holocaust certainly demonstrates that assimilation does not guarantee an end to virulent anti-Semitism, it does not demonstrate that assimilation has *no* tendency to reduce anti-Semitism. Yet one crude Zionist argument points to the fate of German Jewry as a warning to American Jewry.[6] The Holocaust tells us what is possible; it does not tell us what is common.

But a story with a moral does not have to claim that things are usually as they are in the story, only that they might be as they are in the story. It asks us to consider possibilities. We can grant that the wolf is unlikely to turn up and still think it worthwhile to tell about the boy who cried wolf. For crying wolf does erode credibility, and even the unlikely possibility of a wolf's appearance helps one appreciate the value of a reputation for credibility. A story illustrates a possible set of connections, and even a unique story does that. All the more so when the story is historical. For in a fictional tale, we can always wonder whether the apparent possibility depicted is an illusion.[7] Perhaps some subtle impossibility is buried in the account. It is the undeniability of the possibility of an actual event that makes true stories the best candidates for morality tales.

Morals the Holocaust Doesn't Tell

I do not think that the Holocaust as a whole illustrates any general truth, other than the disheartening one that any imaginable cruelty is part of the human repertoire. It cannot honestly support other morals that have been foisted upon it. The Holocaust does poorly as a picture of the human spirit triumphant. The overwhelming majority of "bystanders," non-Nazi Germans, occupied Poles or French, allied gov-

---

6. Shlomo Riskin (1996) says "the most aware [Jews] will not wait to be rejected by their host countries. . . . [They] will always opt for Israel as the only ultimate haven."

7. Different kinds of fictions try to establish different kinds of possibilities. Science fiction, by definition, does not claim its stories are now possible. But, if it is good science fiction, the story must be possible given the laws of nature, and even the wildest fantasy tales ought to portray logical possibilities.

ernments, Catholic clergy, and so on, were either callous, indifferent, obtuse, cowed, or fearfully paralyzed. Most victims were bewildered and terrified, and, if not quickly murdered, ultimately degraded. As a whole the Holocaust cannot make you feel good about humanity.

The Holocaust is not a good example of a great evil defeated for, although the Nazis fell short of their thousand-year reign, their greatest evil intention was largely successful: The Jewish presence in Europe was decimated, and the heartland of traditional Jewish creativity and vitality was destroyed. The Nazi movement did come to a bad end but not before it achieved many of its bad ends. And too many individual Nazis eluded punishment for the Holocaust to be a lesson in justice victorious.

Nor is the Holocaust a good vehicle for depicting the evils of racism, homophobia, or anti-Semitism. As I discussed above, these things are evil even if they do not lead to Auschwitz, which is neither their inevitable or even likely result. It is simply false to say, "this is *the* upshot of racism," and while it is true that this was, in part, *an* upshot of racism, its atypicality makes for a bad paradigm of how bigotry results in evil.

Although often invoked for the purpose, the Holocaust either does not demonstrate the absence of God or is not needed to demonstrate the absence of God. Conceptually, the existence of *any* logically unnecessary evil is incompatible with the existence of an omnipotent and perfectly benevolent God. On this basis — long before Hitler — Leibniz, firmly committed to God's existence, concluded that ours must be the best of all possible worlds, and Hume, firmly committed to the admission that real evil exists, concluded that an omnipotent benevolent God could not possibly exist.[8] You can conclude what you will from the presence of apparently unfathomable evil — no God or no *real* evil (i.e., the apparent "evil" is a logically necessary ingredient of the highest good) — but you do not need the Holocaust to establish the premise that the world is *apparently* full of profound and inexplicable evil. An unwanted pimple gets the argument going, and human history before 1933 and after 1945 makes the argument as vivid as anyone could want.[9] The Holocaust is philosophically otiose.

---

8. At least this is the view of one of Hume's characters in *The Dialogues Concerning Natural Religion* (1779).

9. It is hard to imagine needing a more vivid portrayal of gratuitous evil than Dostoyevsky provides in the chapter "Rebellion" in *The Brothers Karamazov* (Dostoyevsky 1880).

Psychologically the Holocaust has an ambiguous effect on faith. The faith of some believers, among both survivors and observers, was destroyed. In other cases, atheists became believers. Most carried on in their pre-Holocaust belief or disbelief.[10] So not only does the Holocaust fail to advance the philosophical argument against the existence of God,[11] it is also psychologically indeterminate. Of course the Holocaust has the psychological power to shake faith. But it just as readily serves to strengthen faith. Therefore any manipulation of the Holocaust story to deny (or, as is less often done, establish) God is abusive. This is not to say that it is inappropriate to make theological reflections in light of the Holocaust. But this is very different from teaching children a lesson or drawing a moral about the existence of God from the murder of Europe's Jews. As a lesson in religion, then, the Holocaust is as unreliable psychologically as it is superfluous logically.

There is no denying the overall rhetorical power of Holocaust imagery, however. All the general morals and principles I have just claimed the Holocaust does not or should not teach can be brilliantly burnished with Holocaust rhetoric. We can stir the heart with chants of *Am Yisroel Chai* (the people of Israel live), slake our thirst for justice with Nuremberg Trial quotes, make racism repellent with photos of Birkenau, and deride belief in God by citing the death of two million Jewish children. The Holocaust makes effective rhetoric. But rhetoric divorced from historical, philosophical, and psychological truth has no place in a morally sound curriculum, and none of these general lessons can be taught from a truthful study of the Holocaust. Even the one general lesson of the Holocaust that I do admit, the establishment of the human *potential* for unlimited depravity, is usually distorted by making the Holocaust a proof of actual universal human depravity.

Morals the Holocaust Might Tell

Bereft of general truths to impart, Holocaust study might still properly play a role in moral education. Its proper role in moral education must be ancillary to its role as part of historical education. The primary justification for studying the Holocaust is that it happened and that it

---

10. See Berkovits 1973 and Brenner 1980.
11. I do not mean that the philosophical argument is not sound — only that if it is sound, it is so without the Holocaust.

was important; it has shaped modern consciousness, and it is climactic in Jewish history. The morality tales we include in our Holocaust curriculum must be compatible with a fastidious historical integrity. There are morality tales that allow for that. Although I have argued that no moral lessons can be extracted from the Holocaust as a whole, stories with moral content, derived from aspects of the Holocaust, can honestly be told. And since all history teaching is selective, why not select those elements that we believe will aid moral development? There are many ways to teach the Holocaust. None give the whole, completely objective truth. Some are a denial or gross distortion of the Holocaust. Others involve subtle, but significant distortions. But among the many relatively, and one might even say equally, nondistorting potential Holocaust curricula, some can be formed with an eye to having preferred moral effects. This is the type of curriculum I propose.

The moral lessons of the Holocaust should be taught by using some of its elements as exemplars. The Holocaust, after all, does show us a horrific specimen of racism. We need not claim that all racisms are like this, to engender a horror of racism in general. The general horror of racism can be induced even as we point out the distinctive features of Nazi racism.[12] The indifference of most of the world to the slaughter of European Jewry is revolting. Without ignoring the particular circumstances surrounding that indifference we can, by exploring it, show students how inaction can be morally repulsive. Students may thereby be encouraged to question their own or others' inaction in the face of injustice. There were moments of surpassing courage and humanity during the Holocaust. We can note how rare they were and still expect them to inspire our students.

To be sure, this is a rhetorical use of the Holocaust, but it is rhetoric rooted in honest history. We hope for certain psychological effects, but we neither distort history nor manipulate the students in order to achieve these effects. Unaccompanied by any moralizing, a judicious selection of anecdotes will tend toward certain moral effects. We point out real events and allow for natural responses. If we pick the events to further our understanding of good and evil, of noble and ignoble be-

---

12. Blum seems to say this and *Facing History* seems to do this, although I think *Facing History* sometimes run afoul of my prohibition on empirically generalizing from the Holocaust (as opposed to morally generalizing, which, in some forms, I endorse (Blum 1995).

havior, we merely do intentionally and knowingly that which will happen willy-nilly. And what we don't do is make any claims beyond the claim that this specific thing happened. We explicitly assert no moral principles, let alone offer the incident as evidence for a historical generalization.

The Holocaust stories selected for moral education should not be offered as typical in any way. As discussed above, the extremity of Holocaust events makes them particularly ill suited as historical analogues. One need not subscribe to claims of unusual historical uniqueness to recognize that events drawn from the Holocaust are even more difficult to generalize than are most historical events. In addition, many of the incidents selected will be atypical even among Holocaust events. When we teach of the Gentile Lithuanian librarian who risked her life repeatedly to smuggle books and resistance communications into the Vilna Ghetto, we are not highlighting the most representative Lithuanian. Many more Lithuanians were vicious, anti-Semitic collaborators. Most just kept their heads down and tried to be left alone. These facts must be clearly and explicitly told to the students. But if there were a hundred Lithuanian persecutors and a thousand bystanders for every active Lithuanian rescuer, are we thereby bound, if we are to tell specific Holocaust stories, to tell mostly stories of bystanders? Must we concentrate on, in statistically proportionate fashion, persecutor tales over rescuer narratives? I think not. It is incumbent on us to tell what happened, to provide as accurate an understanding as we can. But we can do that while concentrating on events that vividly portray our moral fears and hopes. History tightly constrains the intellectual understanding we must teach. But it is our moral vision that frames the values and attitudes we should build. Specific events included in a Holocaust curriculum should not be chosen, or not exclusively chosen, because they reflect the most common Holocaust occurrences. Moral importance is a permissible criterion of selection. And what is morally important does not simply tell us what we are, it also shows us what (for better or worse) we might be. Besides telling generally what happened and why it happened, the study of the Holocaust, through specific indelible examples, provokes moral reflection. Moral reflection, in turn, shapes character. At least that is the hope.

In so far as this is Holocaust study as moral education, it is Aristotelian moral education. Rather than rigid adherence to set principles,

Aristotle believed that morality required sound judgment in particular cases. Sound judgment emerges from sound character, which in turn is formed by exposure to moral exemplars.[13] Aristotelian moral education requires no moralizing; good and evil are depicted, not defined.

Exploiting the Holocaust

But even without explicit moralizing, this is still a use of the Holocaust to further a moral/political agenda, and that is troubling. It is troubling because it suggests that the Holocaust is redeemable. To put the Holocaust to a respectable purpose might make it metaphysically respectable; it might provide the Nazi murders with a raison d'être, even if it is not the one the Nazis had for creating it. Analogously, some find it morally obnoxious to use data from immoral, sadistic Nazi medical experiments, even if the data can be put to good use — for good usage can seem to imply ex post facto justification of the experiments.[14] Even without moralizing about it, isn't the conscious employment of the Holocaust to shape morality similarly obnoxious? Isn't there something wrong with turning the suffering of Holocaust victims into the instruments of *our* ends?

Something in this line of thought is not completely unsound, but other considerations outweigh the misgivings. The Holocaust should be taught because it is important history and because its victims have wanted their stories told. These are sufficient reasons for teaching it that would justify its place in a curriculum even were it to have no moral benefits for the future. But if it is taught, it will have moral effects. Different ways of teaching it will have different moral effects. In making our pedagogic choices, choices that are unavoidable in any event, how does allowing random moral effects respect the victims more than aiming at good effects? It does not. And, if we have reason to believe that the good effects aimed at would be ends endorsed by the victims, we partially shed the burden of using their suffering for our ends. If we dwell on the stories of righteous Gentiles (without, as I must

---

13. I believe there is a theoretical circularity here that prevents me from endorsing this as a full account of morality. Still, as a practical pedagogy, I think it works.

14. It turns out that there are scientific as well as moral problems in using the "medical" data. The two sorts of problems may be connected for indifference or blindness to moral norms may indicate a mind-set insensitive to rational and scientific norms.

repeat, implying that they were anything other than exceptional) in the hope that their example will inspire our students with a sense of human solidarity, if we highlight the militant Jewish resistance to murderous persecution (again, being clear that this was not the rule) in order to strengthen our students' fighting spirit against oppression, then we do indeed tell victims' stories for our own purposes — but not *only* for our own purposes. Human solidarity and the stand against oppression was the cause of the victims, too. Even if it was not the cause of all or most Holocaust victims, it clearly was the cause of the particular victims and rescuers whose stories we tell. We have not reduced them to means; we have joined forces with their memory for mutual ends.

Lawrence Langer has argued most prominently against trying to see anything good or make anything good out of the Holocaust. He takes this "good-making" as a form of Holocaust denial, as an inability to confront the full dimension of the horrors and failures of the Holocaust.[15] While right to resist the vulgarity and moral superficiality in the proliferating attempts to make Holocaust memorialization into occasions for feel-good events, Langer's approach flirts with a vulgarization of another kind: The Holocaust becomes, in Roger Gottlieb's words, "encapsulated . . . in a sterile shroud of mystery . . . a permanently inexplicable and horrible enigma."[16] Langer, unlike some others,[17] does not emphasize the unintelligibility of the Holocaust. His concern is its unredeemability. But they go together. "There is nothing to understand," and "there is nothing to be done" represent linked attitudes toward our knowledge and memory of the Holocaust. They are attitudes that implicitly reject Holocaust education or restrict that education to a recital of an absurd, inhuman episode to which the only permissible responses are anguish, shame, and guilt.

This position seems founded on a demand for intellectual and moral integrity, but I believe it is primarily based on aesthetic considerations. Let me repeat why the approach I am recommending is not a violation of intellectual or moral integrity. A truthful account of the Holocaust,

---

15. See Langer 1995b, 16.

16. Gottlieb 1990, 4. Langer himself is a subtler and more complex thinker than the position I call Langerism, and he could justly complain that I have caricatured his position. As I define it, Langer might disclaim Langerism. Still I have baptized the trend in his name because he is its most prominent representative.

17. See, for example, Steiner 1995, 121, or Rubinoff 1993, 148–9.

or at least as truthful as any, can accommodate Aristotelian moral education. No shade of dishonesty need accompany our telling of the Holocaust in a way calculated to make our students hate injustice and love righteousness. Intellectual integrity does not require a Langerian approach. Nor must we ignore the suffering of the victims in order to teach morals from the Holocaust. On the contrary, we must attend carefully and in detail to their suffering (without any pretense that we can feel or fully understand what they felt), if we are to make moral impressions on our students. In addition we are not pursuing moral ends that would be alien to Holocaust victims. Hence, moral integrity does not require Langerism either. But the aesthetic pull of Langer's stance is not so easily dismissed.

The aesthetic essence of Langer's attitude was most famously expressed by Theodor Adorno: "[To] write poetry after Auschwitz is barbaric."[18] Whatever Adorno may have meant by this remark, it does seem to capture the deeply felt sense that some things are no longer appropriate after the Holocaust. Perhaps it is the creation or appreciation of beauty, or the attempt to distill meaning out of experience, or the claim to portray a consoling or significant truth, or the pretension to transcendence through art that is no longer appropriate. But whatever it is, it is an aesthetic inappropriateness. While there is certainly such a thing as moral barbarism, Adorno seems to suggest that writing poetry in the shadow of Auschwitz involves aesthetic barbarism. It is not *wicked* to write poetry now—it is in bad taste. A civilized sensibility recoils at post-Holocaust poem-making.

This is a justifiable aesthetic but not the only one. An alternative is rooted in the progressive faith I discussed in chapter 4; it is reflected in the spirit of *"Ani miamin*—despite the evidence pointing to an unsalvageable human condition, and without ignoring that evidence, I continue to believe that, although he may tarry, still the Messiah will come." This traditional Jewish belief, reportedly clung to by many in the camps and ghettos, is not best understood as an epistemic expression, a prediction about the future. It is much more an aesthetic choice about how to face the world. The refusal to go on after the Holocaust is an appropriate, civilized response. It conscientiously acknowledges the

---

18. Adorno 1967, 34.

magnitude of the evil that has occurred. Langerism does not call for universal suicide; it is, rather, an aesthetic refusal to go on. But given that, biologically, we intend to go on, the attempt to hew meaning out of the most recalcitrant matter ever presented to humankind is as valid as — and perhaps a deeper, aesthetic response than — the refusal to seek meaning. Surely all meanings yielded, all insights gained, all purposes pursued, must be incomplete and tentative.[19] Langerism is far better than the hucksterism that finds a thousand easy uses for the Holocaust. But widespread vulgar exploitation does not preclude the possibility of serious, thoughtful employment. The Holocaust cannot be the centerpiece of Secular Jewish identity or education. But it is ineluctably part of who we are and what we must teach.

The State of Israel is another contentious, and unavoidable, subject for the Secular Jewish curriculum. While many American Judaisms have made Israel the core of their identity and educational program, and almost all give it a highly privileged place, the Yiddishist secular Jewish tradition has minimized and largely ignored Israel as a component of Jewish identity and education. What should the attitude of Secular Judaism be toward Israel? In particular what role should it play in the curriculum?

---

19. Gottlieb (1990, 4) makes a similar point.

CHAPTER SIX

Secular Judaism
and Israel

SOME SECULAR progressive Jews
may not like it, but Israel is now central to contemporary Jewish identity. Religious Jews cannot ignore the religious implications of Israel's existence, and no Jew can ignore Israel's historical and cultural
implications.

This was not always so. During the nearly two thousand years of
Jewish history when there was no Jewish state — however much the
ideas of exile and an eventual return to Zion loomed in Jewish consciousness and self-identity — there was no corresponding social or political reality influencing Jewish life.[1] Even in the early years of the
Zionist movement, both the movement and the Yishuv (the Jewish
community in Palestine) could be, and were, peripheral or irrelevant to
the lives and identities of most Jews. Orthodox Jews considered Zionism a usurpation of God's role, Reform Jews considered it a retribaliza-
tion of a universal ethical creed (see chapter 2). Many Diaspora Jews,
especially those of Western Europe and America, believed Zionism
called into question their nationality as Germans, Americans, British
or French. Although Zionism had a substantial following in Eastern
Europe, even there the religious traditionalists, along with the socialist
assimilationists and socialist Yiddishists, constituted a non-Zionist
majority. All these Jews lived without reference to Zionism, except,

---

1. This is so despite the fact that, throughout most of Jewish history, there has been some
Jewish presence in Palestine and that often Diaspora Jewry had significant relations with
Jewish Palestine, going there to die or on pilgrimage. At times there were influential Jewish
communities there — Safad, for instance, in the sixteenth century. But Palestine never became
a social or political factor in the life of postexilic Diaspora Jewry. Nor remotely was its role
analogous to that of contemporary Israel's role in the Diaspora today.

perhaps, as a topic of discussion and controversy. Insofar as they considered themselves Jews, political and cultural Zionism played no large part in their Jewish self-understanding.

Progressives and Israel

The distancing from Zionism had some particularly strong motives on the left. Although Zionists were mostly men and women of the left, the mainstream left had varied and principled (but not always consistent) criticisms of Zionism: Zionism was a nationalism, and nationalism was generally classified as reactionary; Zionism sought to coalesce a nation out of a religious grouping, and, for leftists, the sooner religious groupings disappeared, the better; Zionism was building its nation on an elitist/religious cultural basis—Hebrew and the Promised Land—rather than on the culture and territory of the Jewish masses—Yiddish and Europe. Although not a prominent leftist criticism at first, Zionism came to be viewed as a variant of European expropriation of other people's lands and hence imperialist. In the twenty-five years following the 1967 Arab-Israeli War, the view of Israel as a militarized, racist, apartheid-like agent of American imperialism became standard in many leftist circles.

These left criticisms of Zionism, are complemented by other secular discomfitures with Israel. The stereotypical Israeli ideal type contrasts with both traditional and more modern Diaspora Jewish ideals. There is a current of thought that holds that Jewish morals, creativity, and uniqueness has been attributable to our dispersed, "homeless" state. A number of characters in Philip Roth's *Operation Shylock* are eloquent spokespeople for "Diasporism," a reverse Zionism that promotes the resettlement of Israeli Jews in Europe:

> The roots of American Jewry are not in the Middle East but in Europe—their Jewish style, their Jewish words, their strong nostalgia, their actual weighable history, all this issues from their European origins. Grandpa did not hail from Haifa—Grandpa came from Minsk. Grandpa wasn't a Jewish nationalist, he was a Jewish humanist, a spiritual, believing Jew, who complained not in an antique tongue called Hebrew, but in colorful, rich, vernacular Yiddish. . . .
>
> There is more Jewish spirit and Jewish laughter and Jewish intelligence on the Upper West Side of Manhattan than in [all of Israel]—and as for

Jewish *conscience,* as for a Jewish sense of *justice,* as for Jewish *heart* . . . there's more Jewish heart at the knish counter at Zabar's than in the whole of the Knesset. . . .

[Diaspora Jews] [are real Jews . . . truly superior people, whom I admired, whom I loved. . . . the vitality in them, the irony in them, the human sympathy, the human *tolerance,* the goodness of heart that was simply *instinctive* in them, people with the Jewish sense of survival that was all human, adaptable, elastic, humorous, creative, and all this they have replaced [in Israel] with a stick! . . .

[T]he only Jews who are Jews are the Jews of the Diaspora.[2]

However convincing you may find this paean to Diaspora Jews (I confess it has considerable appeal to me) and the concomitant disdain of Israelis as macho, arrogant brutes, "Diasporism" is now, inescapably, parody. Regret over historical developments does not reverse them, and chagrin at the importance of certain realities does not lessen their importance. Israel is a state that is officially Jewish. It has an 80 percent Jewish majority and the only Jewish-dominated government, military, economy, and civil society. Israel contains over a third of the world's Jewish population and is the focus of much of Diaspora Jewry's philanthropy, politics, tourism, and education. While Israeli history and Jewish history are not now synonymous, the latter, for the time being, does not have an existence separate from the former. Secular Jews, whose identity is so dependent on identification with the Jewish people and Jewish history, cannot ignore the contemporary central fact of Jewish history and peoplehood: the existence of Israel. There are many viable attitudes one can have toward Israel, but for a Jew serious about her identity, indifference is not one of them.

An engaged, active hostility toward the entire Zionist enterprise and Israel itself *is* a possible attitude for a serious Jew (whatever one may think of ultraorthodox traditionalists, such as Neuteri Karta, there is no denying that they are serious Jews), but, I will argue, it is not a *justifiable* attitude for secular progressive Jews. Zionist ideology and history, along with Israeli politics, confront the progressive with grave concerns. But even apart from the hopes engendered by the recent "peace process," a closer view of Israeli history and politics than the ones encouraged by either the American-Israel Public Affairs Commit-

---

2. Roth 1993, 47, 122, 126, 171.

tee or the Popular Front for the Liberation of Palestine reveals moral and political complexities demanding a complex response from Jewish progressives.

While many morally significant details of Zionist and Israeli history are still hotly disputed, the broad outlines and major events are clear enough. The anti-Israeli left construes this history as a stock case of a European settler imperialism combined with a stock case of a regional puppet regime: First, "white" Europeans, with the backing and approval of the dominant imperialist power, Great Britain, started settler colonies in Arab-inhabited Palestine. A mixture of methods, not excluding outright military force and terror, were used by the settlers to take the land. The settler state that was established reduced the remaining Arabs to, at best, an exploited second-class citizenry and at worst, a rightless, oppressed, occupied minority. Israel became a racist *volksstaat* with a master group defined by ethnicity. The Arab population under occupation has been subject to widespread imprisonment without trial, collective punishment, torture, and massacre. Moreover, Israel has been pumped up militarily by the United States in order to serve U.S. imperial interests. It has armed and trained tyrannical dictatorships in Central America, and it stands ready to use its military strength to enforce U.S. interests in the Middle East. The end of the Cold War and the collapse of Arab resistance have allowed Israel to soften the form of its racist and imperialist-client nature, but it has not changed its essence. No progressive can have anything supportive to do with such a state.

The equally familiar Zionist counterstory is of the return to their never-forgotten ancient homeland of a people horribly and persistently persecuted. They came to live as peaceful neighbors with the Arabs who had, in small numbers, been living there during the Jews' long absence. Murderously attacked by the Arabs, with absolutely no alternative refuge from the world's genocidal intentions, Jews defended themselves. Assigned half the land by the world's most representative institution, the United Nations, the Jewish community was prepared to live in a cooperative peace with all its Arab neighbors. Arabs rejected any Jewish presence in Palestine and waged perpetual war against Israel. Palestinians, who never had any political independence, have not been accepted and integrated into the Arab lands they live in, but, rather, have been scorned, harassed, manipulated, and used as a weapon against Israel by undemocratic Arab regimes. Israel defends itself vigorously against completely unscrupulous enemies whose hostility toward Jews is unbounded. Given the existential threat, Israeli self-defense measures have been remarkably restrained and humane.

The Progressive Apology

There are no outright falsehoods in either of these accounts. But neither provides an adequate basis for making moral or political judgments about Israel. Nor does an adequate account emerge from a simple fusion of these one-sided, broad-grained tales. Presently I am more concerned with analyzing the leftist critique, because its misleading unsubtleties are the ones that might stand in the way of, or distort, a progressive Jew's relationship to Israel. Of course, *for the world Jewish community at large, the pro-Israel tale has been more beguiling and is more in need of correction.* But readers of this book need a truthful, progressively inspired apology for Israel more than an elaboration of the moral and political failings of the Jewish state. Progressive are already painfully aware of these failings and must wonder how and why they can relate to Israel in spite of them.

European Colonialism

Let us start off with the conception of "white" European settlers. For the most part, *whiteness* is a concept — with very little, if any, morally defensible function — devised and employed to make invidious comparisons between peoples. Some Europeans designated themselves as white to justify excluding, conquering, enslaving, disappropriating, or slaughtering others deemed nonwhite. A superiority was attributed to whites to explain an entitlement to despoil nonwhites. Who was white and who nonwhite depended very much on who was in a position to do the despoiling and whom they wanted to despoil. Indeed, all whites were ethnically part of some European people (although, in certain times and places, non-Europeans got the bureaucracies to classify them as *whites*), but often all sorts of Europeans were not counted as whites. It took awhile in the United States for Irish immigrants to become white, and southern Mediterreans did not make it until decades after that. According to Nazi schematics, of course, there were degrees of whiteness (using *Aryan* to give a pseudohistorical basis and profundity to the essentially same concept): The French had less than the Swedes, and the Russians had none at all. In spite of the wholly arbitrary nature of whiteness, except as a reflection of the desire and power to dominate, its ideological trappings often commanded sincere beliefs. Many people have thought that their whiteness amounted to more than inclusion in a dominant caste. But it never did.

Polish Jews, who made up the bulk of the early Zionist movement and settlers, were among the Europeans furthest from whiteness. They were considered "racially" different and were subject to all sorts of social and political disabilities. They certainly did not belong to those classes of Europeans that conceived and implemented the European colonization of the world. Nor did they themselves identify with the white colonizers. In the film *The Education of Duddy Kravitz,* a second-generation Jewish immigrant to Canada can, with perfect coherence, refer to the alien Gentile Canadian establishment as "the white man." Of course European Jews incorporated the general European condescension toward all non-Europeans, so most early Zionists brought some of this mind-set to their relations with the Arabs in Palestine. But the socialist orientation of most early Zionists greatly mitigated the European chauvinism they carried to Palestine.

More important than attitude were the actions and circumstances that shaped the early Zionists. It matters little that the Zionists were not thought of, and did not think of themselves, as conventional colonialists, if they acted as conventional colonialists. But their actions and circumstances were hardly a paradigm of colonialism. Although pre-state Zionists got some crucial, if ambivalent and occasional, support from Britain, they never were the agents of, or had the consistent backing of an imperial power. From the 1939 White Paper prohibiting Jewish immigration to Palestine, until the establishment of the state, Jews in Palestine considered Britain an adversary, and some wings of the movement took up arms against the British. No imperial power looked upon the Jews in Palestine as British nationals. Jews were certainly nothing like the British in India or the French in Southeast Asia.

The similarities to "settler states" are stronger, but still not strong. Most European peoples of settler states sought land and economic opportunity. This was seldom the primary motive for Zionists. Each significant wave of Jewish immigration to Palestine can reasonably be described as consisting of refugees fleeing active persecution.[3] While this is true of symbolically important segments of European settlers in America or southern Africa, it does not characterize the mass of immigrants to these countries. While the motives of the settlers may make little difference to the people whose homeland is being settled, it does make a difference to an objective assessment of the morality of a settler movement.

Imperialist Conquest

Settler states have tended to initiate their realm through outright aggressive wars of conquest, the upshot of which has been the massacre or reduction to servitude of the indigenous people. Europeans fought wars to push the North American Indians off desired lands. South American Indians were enslaved or slaughtered, aboriginal Australians nearly exterminated, southern Africans reduced to forced labor or poverty of various kinds. In most cases some combination of all these occurred. Although Israel acquired much of its present territory through war, these were not wars initiated by Israel as wars of conquest. Prior to 1948 — although Zionist land acquisition techniques merit moral scrutiny — Israel, unlike other settler states, did not engage in outright, massive, and aggressive military conquest. Surely Israel seized the opportunity occasioned by the war in 1948 to expand. Some Zionists hoped for the war and welcomed it for this reason. (The current, fall 1997 Israeli government coalition leadership is the ideological heir to that wing of the Zionist movement.)

But the record seems fairly clear that an Arab acceptance of partition would have prevented the war and subsequent Israeli conquests. Nor is there much doubt that, whatever other motives the Israelis had in 1948, for them, this was primarily a defensive war of physical survival. And though the motives for the 1956 Sinai war are questionable, it was not fought for, and did not result in, any territorial gains. The origins of the 1967 war are murkier, with some evidence that Israel

---

3. The first three Polish-Russian-dominated aliyot are connected to the pogroms of 1882, 1905, and 1917. German Jews emigrated with the rise of Hitler; Arab and Persian Jews emigrated after the anti-Zionist backlash against Jews in those lands, coupled with the generally xenophobic attitude these postcolonial states directed toward minorities. The Soviet emigration was also largely motivated by fear of persecution.

was spoiling for a fight in order to acquire territory. But again the record seems clear enough that the provocation by the Arab States (Egyptian removal of buffer peacekeepers, an Egyptian naval blockade, Syrian mobilization, and a Jordanian first strike), the Arab refusal to make peace, and the Arabs' consistent use of bellicose rhetoric justified a defensive Israeli war or at least took this war out of the category of simply an aggressive war initiated for territorial conquest. The 1982 war in Lebanon was aggressive and unjust, but its aim was not new land for settlers, and there is little doubt that Israel will relinquish control for guarantees of a peaceful northern border.

The point of my sketch is not to depict Israel as blameless in these wars or to deny the substantial use of force, fraud, and terror in pursuit of the territorial ambitions of Zionism. But the history of Zionist expansion in Palestine is not readily classified and judged under the general headings of *colonialism* or *settler state*. Perhaps serious attention to the details of any history would disallow summary classification under any general heading. In any case, the territorial expansion of Zionism cannot be understood as colonialism or imperialism without wholesale and gross historical distortions.

A Racist Society

The charge of standard "white European racism" has limited, albeit real, application to Israel and Zionism. The treatment and status of non-European *Jews* testifies to both the reality of "white" racism (in this case, assumption of European superiority) and its *relative* mildness. Yemeni, Moroccan, and even Ethiopian Jews were sought out and welcomed. Official ideology proclaimed their full and equal citizenship. The discrimination they have suffered is a grave moral blemish on Israeli society. But it is a blemish common to most human societies and by itself gives insufficient reason to dissociate oneself more from Israel than from most other nations and states. Israeli racism toward non-European Jews was and is nothing like South African apartheid or American Jim Crow.

But Israel and Zionism may be more deeply implicated in another form of "racism," for Israel is the "Jewish State," a state that legally excludes and discriminates against non-Jews. All non-Jews are at best second-class citizens in Israel; Arab non-Jews are a class below that.

That we must speak of "Arab non-Jews" is telling. It is insufficiently acknowledged that almost half of Israel's Jewish population are best described as Arab Jews. The immigrants from Morocco, Yemen, Iraq, Egypt, and Syria were at least as culturally and phenotypically Arab as European Jews were European. The more troubling part of Israeli racism is not directed against these Arab Jews. It is directed against non-Jewish Arabs. The logical conclusion is that we are confronted with a "racism" based on creed. But Zionism began as an overwhelmingly secular movement, and much of its social and political elite remain irreligious. Nor do Israel's religious Jews really care about the theological beliefs and practices of Muslims per se. The source of the special discrimination suffered by Arabs in Israel, that is, the discrimination suffered beyond that directed at all non-Jews, is political. In the absence of the Israeli-Arab conflict it would have no moorings. We could expect that with peace, in time, Arabs would be treated in the same way as all non-Jews. But that is problem enough.

Israel is not unusual in being a *nation*-state, a state that recognizes it has a special relationship to a particular nationality. All such states are at moral risk; they discriminate among citizens and noncitizens on the basis of nationality. The discrimination may take the hardly avoidable (but important) form of having an official language (France) or the gratuitous form of a requirement of national ancestry for fast-track citizenship (Germany). One can reasonably debate whether any nation-state, or even any multination-state with legally recognized nationalities, can be morally sound. Misgivings about that possibility have led some to proclaim that the United States is (or ought to be) a "universal-state," united solely in loyalty to a constitutional democratic order.[4] That controversy is beyond our concern here. It is enough to note that, although there is something prima facie morally problematic about the nation-state, these moral problems are ubiquitous and no cause for *special* condemnation of Israel. What might give rise to special condemnation are the consequences of having a nation-state made up of such an odd nationality, Jews. Figuring out how best to conceive of the Jewish people has always been tricky, especially post-emancipation. But the trick becomes morally perilous when *Jew* be-

---

4. This analysis of, or vision for, the United States is rejected by Michael Lind (1995). Among others, he attributes it to Lincoln, Melville, Robert Penn Warren, and George Will.

comes a political designation. In the past, this moral peril was borne by Gentiles (Jews bore the social and physical dangers). In Israel, Jewish state power reverses this, putting Jews in moral peril and others in social danger.

Is the legal status accorded "Jews" in Israel so morally objectionable that no progressive should identify with the country? Yes, if it entails either of the following: first, that the State of Israel is structurally incapable of evolving to a polity of equal citizenship rights for all its citizens; second, that the current legal regime makes it impossible for non-Jews to lead a decent life in Israel. The first of these criteria turn on the question of whether the privileged status of Jews in Israel is reformable. Since Israel's whole being is rooted in its being the Jewish homeland, it may appear that it is not open to the needed changes. But this is not so. Israel can remain Jewish without giving any unusual privileges to Jews or denying equal citizenship to non-Jews. It can become Norway: established "church," official language, state holidays associated with a particular cultural tradition, and a common cultural background to a majority of its population. There may be disadvantages and inconveniences to being a cultural non-Norwegian living in Norway, but there are no political disabilities.

Israel can and should become a state of this kind. It would be a state mostly of Jews, but it would be by and for all Israelis. Its history and demographics would give it deep and natural ties to Jewish history and the Jewish Diaspora. It could serve as a potential haven for Jews, without a special "Law of Return," for it could be expected that such a state would be quick to offer asylum to Jewish refugees. The possibility of this evolution means Israel as a Jewish country is not irremediably a caste society.

A possible road to equality would be of little solace if the current regime mandated inegalitarian horrors. And there are many incidents of such horrors in Israel. But they are not the norm. All state-imposed political inequality is objectionable, but most non-Jewish *Israelis* can, and many do, lead decent lives. Neither property, nor due process, nor educational opportunities are fully denied them. Most occupations are legally open to them, and non-Jews have almost full democratic rights. This contrasts with the old South African apartheid regime, which not only discriminated against, but thoroughly repressed, its nonwhite population, making it impossible for them to lead good lives.

The contrast with other settler states is largely the result of Zionism's labor ideology. Zionists dreamt of a society of self-reliant Jewish laborers, especially agricultural laborers. Not only did Jews come to Palestine without plans of exploiting Arab labor, the use of Arab labor was considered politically incorrect. There would be no haciendas with Arabs in the fields and Jews in the big house, no sweat shops owned by Jews and filled with Arabs. This nonexploitation of Arab labor changed substantially after the 1967 war, but in its crucial formative years, Israel did not partake of this vital component of colonialism. In sum, the history and core structures of Israel are as troubling, but not especially more troubling, than those of other nations. Eventually Israel may have to choose between being an essentially democratic state that is contingently a Jewish country (although that can be a contingency supported by certain government policies), and being a Jewish state that indulges in democratic norms only while they are convenient. That choice has not yet, and may never be, forced. But if it ever is, and Israel chooses wrongly, Israel will have crossed a great moral divide.[5]

The Possibility of Reform

Israel's particularly nettlesome moral issues are mostly a result of the conquest, occupation, and settlement that followed the 1967 war. Following this war we see the beginnings of widespread exploitation of Arab labor and the attempt to control a population that has been denied all political rights. Imprisonment without trial, collective punishment, summary expulsion, political assassination, and torture have become routine. *Nothing in Israel's history or circumstances, however much these circumstances may explain the actions, can justify these human rights abuses.* When it comes to state-endorsed torture, the existence of worst state tortures among Israel's enemies is no defense. Israel's terrorizing of Palestinians is not made less despicable by some Palestinian's use of terror against Israelis. Moral superiority to Hafiz al-Assad, Saddam Hussein, or Abu Nidal confers no justification. In the last thirty years, Israel has systematically engaged in activities that

---

5. Ruth Gavison (1996) has helped me think about the matter in terms of democracy versus Jewish statehood.

deserve unqualified condemnation. But, although at times they have threatened to become so, none of these activities are (yet) intrinsic to Israel as a society or a state. If they were, the only morally permissible relationship one could have with Israel would be that of a revolutionary. Apartheid South Africa required the abolition of the regime and the dismantling of the social system. Israel requires a policy change.

Policies can be so enduring and central to a country that they become part of the national structure. Policies shape structures and can merge into them. The occupation of the West Bank has already transformed Israel's economy, "security" services, and military in unprogressive ways. Much of Israel's (and Diaspora Jewry's) Zionism has become dangerously reactionary as a result of occupation politics. The occupation of the West Bank and Gaza was verging on embedding itself into the very marrow of Israeli society. It is unclear whether the current Netanyahu government will resume policies leading to the entrenchment of the occupation, thereby turning Israel into a full-fledged apartheid society. As I write, Israel still *seems* to be hesitating before this moral abyss. Be that as it may, as long as the occupation, and the evils that flow from it, are reformable policies, "constructive engagement" (a term discredited by Reagan's cynical employment of it) describes a progressive approach to Israel. Support for, and involvement with, the peace and human rights movements in Israel are particularly apt ways for progressive Jews to relate to Israel. Simultaneously they can participate and take an interest in broader aspects of Israeli life, without moral or political stain. There is, of course, no guarantee that Israel will remain above the moral and political threshold of decency. The "national/religious camp," in power as of this writing, daily injects racism, militarism, and undemocratic values deeper into the Israeli body politic. One cannot help but be alarmed at the rapid moral degeneration of Israeli politics. Some day frighteningly soon, progressives may be obliged to put themselves in total opposition to an apartheid Israeli state. But that is not yet, and if progressive Israelis and Diaspora Jews do not despair, it may never be.

All this merely clears the way for involvement with Israel by removing the pariah status. But the progressive American Jew still needs reasons to tread the path that has been cleared. Israel may not be a moral leper, but does this give us reason to embrace it?

The Role of Israel in Secular Judaism

This chapter began with one of the reasons secular American Jews should care about Israel: its sheer weight in Jewish history and contemporary Jewish affairs. That is the crucial fact compelling all Jewish interest in Israel. But there are others.

Havenism

Sara Bershtel and Alan Graubard claim that American Jews pretend to fear anti-Semitism as a way of showing respect for the suffering of past generations of Jews.[6] This is a perceptive comment. American Jews do behave as at home and comfortable as any group of Americans. They are well represented in all sectors of America's elite, and they feel welcomed by all but the most marginal groups of Americans. American Jews entertain no live expectation of persecution. Much of their refusal to appear complacent about the possibility of dangerous American anti-Semitism is a public acknowledgment of the historical horrors and tenacity of Jew hatred.

Much, but not all. True, the acknowledgment functions as an expression of respect for the experience of past Jewish victims. But it is also just what it seems to be: *an acknowledgment of the historical horrors and tenacity of Jew hatred.* Implicit in this recognition is an intellectual acceptance of the potential vulnerability of American Jewry, however invulnerable we may actually feel. The refusal to be complacent both honors the past and admits the fallibility of our firm belief in a secure future. In light of the position of American Jews in American society, it may strike some that Jews are overcautious about anti-Semitism. But Jewish experience has led many Jews to feel that you cannot be too cautious. It is okay to be secure here, so long as we never act with a smug unconcern.[7]

---

6. Bershtel and Graubard 1992, 86.

7. Whether there is any *realistic* potential for an outbreak of anti-Semitism serious enough to harm American Jewry is, I think, an open question. Undoubtedly America has historical and structural features that distinguish it in relevant ways from the European homelands of anti-Semitism. It is also true that the degree of American Jewish power, influence, integration, and acceptance is unprecedented in the Diaspora. Moreover, insofar as these things can be accurately measured, anti-Semitic feelings among non-Jews seems to be of low incidence and usually mild. Finally, the Holocaust is often thought of as having

Justified or not, the existence of Israel goes a long way toward making American Jews feel secure, and support for Israel is a primary means of demonstrating an awareness of our potential vulnerability. Even Jews who would never consider immigrating to Israel, who have no desire to visit Israel, who dislike Israelis and hate the Israeli governments' policies, Jews who would seek asylum in France or England if it ever came to it (and who staunchly believe it will never come to it), even such Jews take a strong measure of comfort in the existence of Israel. From a political or historical perspective, it can be argued that this measure of comfort is unjustified; Israel's existence may endanger Jews by stoking anti-Semitism and making Jews the object of anti-Zionist attacks. Israel may be of no avail against state-sponsored or state-sanctioned American anti-Semitism. But the existence of an asylum of last resort, when such an asylum has been glaringly absent throughout Jewish history, is of powerful psychological comfort. You may plan on joining the multicultural resistance to the White Christian Reich of the U.S.A., but if you do survive the destruction of the "Brooklyn Ghetto," it is helpful to know that you only have to make your way to Tel Aviv and that you do not have to wrangle a visa to Shanghai.

Given this psychological attachment to havenism, which non-Zionist, progressive, secular Jews share with most other Jews, honesty demands that Israel play a special role in Secular Judaism. A tacit reliance on Israel should be complemented by a knowledge of the country and by an involvement with it. It is foolish to be totally ignorant and indifferent to a homeland of last resort.[8]

"inoculated" the West against anti-Semitism, perhaps through guilt, perhaps through a sense of the harms that could recoil to non-Jews from anti-Semitic politics. Still, there is no question that all the traditional anti-Semitic beliefs still have a foothold in America in their most virulent forms. Given the staying power of Jew hatred in the Christian West, where vicious anti-Semitism has been a cultural staple from the beginning, it is implausible to say, just fifty years after the Holocaust, that the danger in any Christian nation is safely over.

8. It may be thought that, if this psychological reliance on Israel is irrational, we should wean ourselves from it rather than indulge it or accept its entailments. Israel, it is said, would not avail American Jews were the United States anti-Semitic enough to threaten the well-being of American Jews. But one does not have to ignore the limitations of Israel as an insurance policy — realizing that it may not provide coverage in many circumstances — to still get some comfort from having it. Surely, even with an anti-Semitic United States, there would be many conceivable circumstances in which Israel would be a haven for American Jews. There could be an expulsionist rather than an exterminationist United States, or one that simply imposed too much Christianity in public life for the comfort or prosperity of

Havenism also raises our already high moral stake in Israel. Israel is a place with lots of Jews, and it is controlled by Jews. Anyone who feels a part of the Jewish people is going to feel pride or shame in relation to Israel's actions. But when we add that we count on Israel, however remotely, as an asylum from murderous anti-Semitism, our moral stake increases. Escape to a land that is an indecent society is an un-reassuring and scandalous plan. If we are to take comfort in Israel's existence as a haven, it should be a place that we can go to in good conscience. Of course, if persecution were driving American Jews into exile, we would not have the luxury of worrying about the moral status of our asylum. But now, prior to any persecutions it behooves us with our tacit havenism to work for a just haven.

A Secular Culture

Zionism has been the dominant secular movement of modern Jewry, and in Israel a secular Jewish culture has been created, but it is not a secular Jewish culture that can well serve the needs of American secular Jews. There are American Jews who use Zionism and transplanted Israelism as the whole substance of their Jewish identity. As a prelude to immigration to Israel this approach can succeed, but as a permanent American form of Judaism (secular or religious), it must fail. Americans are not going to create and sustain a foreign national culture in America. Even Israelis who settle in the United States see their children become Americans. If Israelis cannot perpetuate Israeli culture here, how much less can Americans. The Secular Judaism that might flourish in America must be compatible with American nationality — a supple-ment to it, not a substitute for it. So Israel's secular Jewish culture cannot be the Judaism of secular American Jews. But it should also not be ignored as a resource for American Secular Judaism. Israel offers much Jewish cultural content without religion. It is not adequate as the entire content of Secular Judaism,[9] but it can provide vital elements. Foremost among these is modern Hebrew.

Jews. In a bleak scenario, Israel can even serve as a locus for organized resistance to mur-derous anti-Semitism.

9. It may not even be adequate as the entire content of Israeli secular Judaism, but that is another issue.

Over the past hundred and fifty years Hebrew and Yiddish have been pitted against each other in a struggle for the cultural soul of the Jewish people. American assimilation, Nazi murders, and the rebirth of Hebrew as the language of Israel have decided that struggle. In the final chapter I argue that Yiddish should still have an important role in Secular Judaism — equal to, if not greater than, Hebrew's. But Jewish secularism can no longer dismiss Hebrew as simply a liturgical language without interest to the nonreligious. Such a dismissal has been unwarranted since the Haskalah, when *maskilim* (learned, enlightened people) employed Hebrew for poetry, journalism, history, and philosophy. Indeed, the dismissal was never really well conceived. Hebrew has been the major source and vehicle of Jewish culture from the beginning. And though the Jewish culture that Hebrew has embodied has been religious, much nonreligious cultural content was also created. It is a truism today that the Hebrew scriptures are history, ethical codes, mythology, fiction, and poetry as much as they are theology. The religiously inspired poetry of medieval poet Judah Halevi can be of as much interest to secularists as the poetry of John Donne, the philosophy of Hasdai Crescas as absorbing as the views of Aquinas. So, apart from its secular life in Israel, Hebrew is important to secularists as a key to the historical culture of the Jewish people.

In addition, Hebrew *does* have a secular life in Israel. Jewish (not just Israeli) politics are debated in Hebrew, Jewish theater is performed in Hebrew, Jewish novels are written and Jewish songs sung — all in Hebrew. These are not Jewish because they are concerned with Jewish religious themes, and they are not Jewish simply because they are in Hebrew. They are Jewish because they are by Jews, about Jews, and forged from the Jewish experience. There is too much contemporary secular Jewish cultural action taking place in Hebrew for a wise Secular Judaism to discard.

Moreover, Hebrew is the language of the world Jewish community. Although more Jews speak English than Hebrew, and even an Argentinean Jew is more likely to have English than Hebrew as a second language, as *Jews,* Hebrew is the lingua franca. Orthodox religion is dominated by Hebrew, and Hebrew plays an ongoing (and increasing) role in more liberal religious Judaisms. This is as true in São Paulo and Bombay as it is in Borough Park and San Francisco. The common language heard at religious services in Mea Shearim, Cincinnati, Cochin, and Kiev is Hebrew. The only "Jewish" nation, with a third of the world's Jews, is Hebrew speaking. Any international Jewish conference that does not take place in English will be in Hebrew, and many will be bilingual. Hebrew, then, is not only an opening to Jewish history and culture, it is an opening to Jews. There is no good reason for progressive American secular Jews to exclude themselves from the Hebraic culture of world Jewry. But although desirable, it may be unrealistic to expect Hebrew competency from most Secular American Jews. But songs, poems, words, and phrases should be part of Secular Jewish education and customs. One can hope that this will inspire some American Secular Jews to become Hebrew speakers. But if not, it will at least create an open, accepting attitude toward Hebrew.

In addition to Hebrew, Israeli music and dance can make a contribution to Secular Judaism. Israel has developed a particularly rich body of folk dances. These dances are not only enticing community events that appeal to a wide range of ages, they also can be prominent and joyous features of family and community celebrations. The dances should be systematically taught as part of a Secular Jewish education.

Israeli music is, in part, the inheritor of folk music from the entire Diaspora, and it can serve as an introduction to that inheritance. But Israeli music is also very much a part of international contemporary popular music. Exposure to Israeli pop music can engage Secular Jews with its Jewish variation on their broader musical interests and tastes.

A Source of Themes

Finally, as a chapter in Jewish history and a locus of Jewish current events, Israel furnishes a progressive Secular Judaism with rich veins to mine. There are heroes for progressives to study and honor, such as Judah Magnes, a founder of Hebrew University and a principled fighter for nonviolence and recognition of Arab rights; Henrietta Szold, a Magnes ally and the founder of Hadassah; and Simcha Flapin, social critic, crusading journalist, and peace activist. There are inspiring social movements, such as the Israeli peace movement (Shalom Achshav, Yesh G'vul, Women in Black), the Palestinian occupation resistance, and the Israeli and Palestinian human rights movement (B'Tzs'elem). The Zionist socialist past and institutions that flowed from it are worthy of study. Kibbutzim are of special note as attempts at radical socialist and democratic life. And, of course, as we have seen, Israeli history also provides ample scope for political criticism and moral self-reflection.

Study of Israel also offers an entrée into issues and controversies in current Jewish life. Who is a Jew? What is a proper understanding of Jewish pluralism? What are the prospects for, and value of, the preservation of Jewish identity in the Diaspora? What should be the main philanthropic concerns of Diaspora Jewry? the main political ones? Such questions arise naturally and are given shape when Israel is discussed by Diaspora Jews.

Israel also serves as a fruitful object in a progressive Jewish curriculum because it is a society of recent and continued immigration. The difficulties and possibilities of social integration and cultural blending are dramatically illustrated in Israel. We can see how subtle, unintentional, stubborn, and destructive attitudes of superiority can be. We also witness the creation of strong new cultural forms from the disparate material of Jewish Diaspora communities. These "melting pot" issues that Israel exemplifies are, and will remain, in the forefront of interest for American progressives.

Summary

Israel is too central to contemporary Jewish history and communal life to be left out of any defensible Jewish curriculum. But a secular, progressive curriculum has particular reasons for including Israel, and particular ways of doing it. Because of the emphasis of Secular Judaism on Jewish ethnicity and on Jewish peoplehood, it has to include the significant portion that is Israeli. The fact that this branch of the Jewish people has created a secular Jewish culture is of special interest to American Secular Jews. Israel's cultural creations can support and augment our own.

For Jewish progressives Israel is an unavoidable arena of engagement. As Jews we have declared our solidarity with other Jews. Progressives understand that this means, not only concern for what is done to Jews, but also responsibility for what Jews do. Israel is a key front of Jewish moral action as well as cultural action. Just as progressive Americans could not absent themselves from the civil rights or anti–Vietnam War movements, progressive Jews must be on the barricades in the fight for justice in Israel. That we are Jews and that we identify with Israel and Israeli culture gives us some standing in this fight. But ultimately, for American Secular Judaism, Israel is a cousin, not a father or mother, son or daughter. A close, interesting, creative cousin who may take us in some day and whom we may have to take in. A cousin we can help, teach, learn from, and argue with, about all things Jewish. A cousin in whom we can take pride or feel shame, for she reflects on the family. But it is a cousin from whom we are neither a direct descendant or to whom we are a direct ancestor. Our cousin's story isn't our story, however much it overlaps. The potential community of progressive, secular American Jews should embrace Israel, but it cannot live off of or through Israel.

These last two chapters have dealt with two outstanding issues in Secular Jewish education. The final chapter outlines the complete vision of Secular Judaism and the educational program that would animate it.

CHAPTER SEVEN

From Wickedness
to Wisdom

THIS BOOK began by describing the Wicked Child, the Jew who was estranged from Judaism but not yet prepared to abandon the Jews. She may not have wanted to sit politely at the seder table as if she understood or endorsed the proceedings, but she still wanted to be there. Although she could not articulate the reasons for the hold that being Jewish had on her, she wanted them to hold her children as well. In chapter 1 I argued that the Wicked Child's desire to maintain and pass on a Jewish identity was not irrational. The chapters that followed outlined and tried to justify a way of fulfilling this desire. I have called this way Secular Judaism; it is an attempt to combine the already existing Jewish goodness of the Wicked Child with Jewish knowledge, thereby transforming her into the Wise Child, for what is wisdom but the effective union of knowledge and goodness?

Previous chapters have sounded all the themes of Secular Judaism. It is now time to play them together and hear what sort of composition they make. But first we must rightly understand the genre. The approach described in this book is *a* philosophy of Judaism; it describes a way of being Jewish and a rationale for being Jewish in that way. It is not a Jewish philosophy; it does not describe a total orientation to life from a Jewish perspective. It does not address many of the most enduring or basic human issues. Nor does it prescribe a complete code of conduct. Crucial moral and aesthetic questions are left open. No "philosophy of life" is offered here, no concept of the good life viewed whole. In its teleological modesty, Secular Judaism is in the mainstream of classic liberalism, wherein each individual is meant to find her own good in her own way. Secular Judaism is also a liberalism because of the fundamental values it endorses: universal human equality and belief in the possibility of moral progress. There are other values extolled and recommended in this work, but, insofar as these things can be neatly ordered, the liberal values are given first rank. They command the deepest loyalty.

Because Judaism *has* been a comprehensive approach to life and has not explicitly (or, arguably, implicitly) valued equality and moral progress above all, it may appear that Secular Judaism, while a liberalism, is no *Judaism* at all. But this appearance fades when viewed against an understanding of Judaism as a dynamic historical culture whose main "story line" is reasonably construed as a people's quest for universal justice. Secular Judaism is, in many ways, not what Judaism has always been — but no Judaism ever was. And if Judaism has not been liberal throughout the millennia, there is no cause to disbelieve that liberalism might yet be Jewish. More of this anon.

As chapter 2 makes clear, none of this is new. Reducing Judaism to morality and "peoplehood" is the central insight of modern Jewish movements. Reform made the moral mission the essence of Judaism, and the "historical" schools understood Judaism as a historical creation of the Jewish people. But although Secular Judaism is made out of different modern Jewish ideologies, including Socialist Yiddishism,[1] and the modern liberal religious movements, it aims beyond pastiche and aspires to fusion into a (not *the*) coherent contemporary Judaism. Its coherence seeks to encompass three realms: the millennia of Jewish traditions, American nationality, and the progressive values of Enlightenment liberalism.

The Content of Secular Judaism
Shtetl Jews

Secular Judaism should try and forge connections to the entire Jewish tradition though not in equal degrees to all of its parts. Some aspects should be treated as archaic or reactionary, practices that we remember

---

1. Humanistic Judaism has not been discussed in this work. It is, and always was, a very minor formal tendency among American Jews, although its sentiments, many of which overlap with Secular Judaism, are widespread among American Jews. The Society for Humanistic Jewry represents the formal movement in America. While I will not analyze the movement, suffice it to say that, though it has strengths that I hope are incorporated into Secular Judaism, it has weaknesses that I believe Secular Judaism overcomes.

but reject, such as animal sacrifice and obedient wives. Other aspects should be studied as the crucial background to our self-understanding. Much of Jewish ritual, mythology, and history, from Shabbes to Shavuos, from the Bible to the Bruriah, would fall in this category. But Secular Judaism should find its immediate origins and main content in the Jewish culture of Eastern Europe and, particularly, in the political and social story of that culture's move to America. Therein lies the "Jewishness" of most American Jews. Socialist Yiddishism proved ephemeral because it believed that this aspect of our Jewishness could be cut off from the rest of Jewish tradition and, as a result, from all ideologically different Jews.[2] In America the demise of Socialist Yiddishism was hastened by a failure to appreciate the process of Americanization and the effect it would have on the children of Yiddish speakers. But although it alone cannot be the totality of a viable Jewish identity, Yiddish and the culture of the Eastern European shtetl Jews should play a very prominent role in Secular Judaism.[3] For it is here that we find most strongly the Jewishness that the Wicked Child is loathe to abandon.

Insofar as nostalgia holds many nonreligious Jews to Jewish identity, it is the shtetl culture and its offspring that they are nostalgic about. Nor is this misplaced sentiment; American Jews correctly recognize themselves more in nineteenth-century Minsk than in second-century Yavneh or sixteenth-century Safad. The search for self-understanding through an appreciation of one's origins is a significant rationale for Secular Judaism (see chapter 1). In spite of the paradoxical flavor, in cultural matters, the most recent origins are the most telling ones. Early features of a culture, if they are to have any effect on the present, must pass through the more proximate traditions. So a focus on the near past does not ignore the influences of the distant past and, in fact, describes the actual form in which the distant past became influential. While early origins give a kind of depth to our self-understanding, they lack the explanatory richness and detail afforded by closer sources. American Jews get an insight into their family dy-

2. Of course Hitler's murders and Stalin's repression, and the subsequent discrediting of socialism, also contributed to the failure of Socialist Yiddishism.

3. I use the term *shetl Jews,* quite imprecisely, to refer to all of the nineteenth- and twentieth-century Jews of Eastern Europe, whether in towns, villages, or cities. I also include those who emigrated and the émigrés' immediate offspring.

namics, speech patterns, senses of humor, mannerisms, social attitudes, and customs through the study of Eastern European Jewry. Saducee influence is pretty well attenuated by now. It may still be there (Pharisical influence certainly is) and identifying with it is spiritually enlarging (see chapter 3). But it is unlikely to shed much light on the Jewish nature of your tastes, habits, fears and aspirations. Did the Saducees fuss greatly over children? Did they love debate? Were they inclined to ironic commentary? These traits, still common among American Jews, have shtetl antecedents, as do many of the characteristics of American Jewry.

It is not simply that we are nearest to the shtetl Jews; much of what we most like about ourselves is their legacy. As traditional cultures go, Eastern European Jewry had a humane one. Without romanticizing it into some *Fiddler on the Roof* idyll, we can still discover there a culture with a moral ideology worth admiring. Granted it was patriarchal, hierarchical, narrow, and rigid, especially compared to a modern liberal society. But its disdain of violence, its praise of mutual respect, compassion, charity, and solidarity were the seedbed of values that flowered when these Jews emerged from the shtetl.

Nor is it only their moral style that we admire. We like their sharp tongue and satirical panache; their self-deprecating humor, skill at subtle dialectics, and flair for the (melo)dramatic; their verbal directness and organizational adeptness. Insofar as we find these stereotypically Jewish qualities in ourselves and like them, and to a great extent we do find and like them in ourselves, it is the shtetl Jews that we have to thank.

Jewish progressive politics, the heart of Secular Judaism (see chapter 4), had its birth in the Enlightenment emancipation — which made Western European Jews liberal — but it was bred in Eastern Europe, where Jewish radicalism and socialism were spawned. If we want to intertwine our children's Jewish education with progressivism, no period of Jewish history serves as well as that of the Eastern European Jews in the nineteenth and early twentieth centuries. Here is oppression and resistance, trade union activism and class consciousness, radical social theory and engaged intellectuals, progressive journalists and left wing artists, nascent feminists and civil libertarians, anarchists and internationalists, secularists and a full spectrum of socialists. It was a time when Jews were a people of the left. We can find progressive strands throughout the Jewish tradition going back to the Pentateuch and Prophets. We can make a plausible case that this progressive strand contains the essence, or is at least a dominant motif, of Judaism throughout the ages. Within the bounds of honest history, Secular Judaism ought to make that case. But in Eastern European Jewry we have the self-conscious emergence of the progressive Jewish people.[4]

For Secular Judaism, Eastern European Jewry also holds special interest as the homeland of Jewish secularisms. The secularization process began in Western Europe with the emergence of liberal Judaisms. But neither Reform nor Conservatism made the transition to a fully secularized version of Jewish life. But in Dubnow's nationalism, Zhitlowsky's Yiddishism, the Bund's Jewish socialism, and the dominant forms of early Zionism, Secular Judaism found in Eastern Europe a strong and varied tradition of Jewish secularisms.

A central thesis of this book is that all of Jewish history and culture funnels into Secular Judaism, and it should all be grist for the curriculum of Secular Jewish schools. But starting with the reign of Czar Nicholas I, the Secular Jewish curriculum should concentrate on the details of shtetl Jewish history: daily life in the Pale, cantonists, *numerus clausus*, particular pogroms, varieties of Jewish nationalism and socialism, emigration — all should be taught. Individual figures should be spotlighted, like the Zionist Leon Pinsker and the Bundist Vladimir Medem. Even more attention should be given to the American part of the story. Secular Jewish students should learn about the *Forverts*, the Henry Street Settlement, the ILGWU, the Triangle Fire, the Artef, as well as sweatshops and *landsmanshaftn*, Ellis Island and the *Arbeterring*. They should become familiar with the names and deeds of Abraham Cahan, Clara Lemlich, Morris Hillquit, David Dubinsky, Jacob Adler, and Lillian Wald.

In sum Eastern European Jewry and its immigration to America should be the main chapter in our curriculum, for it elicits our affection and aids our self-understanding. It grounds Jewish progressivism and secularism, and it allows us to highlight much of what is best in us.

---

4. I say Eastern European because that is where the bulk of Ashkenazic Jewry lived, where the bulk of American Jews come from, and where leftism first became a mass Jewish phenomenon. But Western European Jewry also played an important part in Jewish leftism — through both its thinkers and its institutional organizers.

Yiddish

It is a truism that the spirit of a culture is best embodied in its language. Observers of Eastern European Jewry are made keenly aware of the truism's truth.[5] Yiddish, the *mama loshn,* "mother tongue," of more generations and greater numbers of Diaspora Jews than any other language, the only language of the Jews that they called *Jewish,* is a cardinal component of the Eastern European shtetl culture. It should play a primary role in a Secular Jewish curriculum. Although universal competence among Secular Jews is both an unrealistic and counterproductive goal, a strong sense of the language can be usefully conveyed to American Jews. Songs and short poems can be taught and memorized without any systematic language instruction. Colorful expressions can be examined and discussed and may form the basis of various games. Holidays and rituals that are studied must be named; they should be named in Yiddish. The language of a Secular Jewish school should consist of *Shabbes,* not *Shabbat* or *the Sabbath.* It should explain what a *bris* is, not a *brit milah* or a *ritual circumcision.*

Lists of Yiddish words that have become current in English can be composed. Pupils should know that *shmatte* and *shmaltz* were not originally technical terms devised in the garment and film industries. More extensive lists of the Yiddish of American Jews should also be taught. There are many American Jews of the Wicked Child's generation who neither understand nor speak Yiddish but who, nonetheless, have fairly large Yiddish vocabularies. These vocabularies often came from parents who did not speak Yiddish to their children but were merely using the best words available to communicate certain thoughts and feelings. Substituting English words, at best, would have lost precision and nuance. Emotional, aesthetic, and moral connotations would have been most sacrificed. So Yiddish survived in the language of English-speaking American Jews. Without the conscious intent of perpetuating culture, important elements of Yiddish were passed on.

Obviously a supplementary school has neither the time nor the occasions that are available to a family. But it can still introduce and employ words that are useful as conveyors of the values of the shtetl Jews and that are irreplaceable expressions in their own right. Restricting our-

---

5. See Landis 1981.

selves to a few well-known items in the *M* section, consider *macher,*
machetayneste, mashiach, mavin, mazel, megillah, mensch, mitsieh,
minyan, mishegoss, mitzvah, and the English words, or short phrases,
that are the closest equivalents: *big shot, mother-in-law of my child,*
messiah, expert, luck, story, human, bargain, religious quorum, crazi-
ness, commandment. Note, first of all, that most Jews over forty will
recognize most of the Yiddish terms — indeed, many Yiddish words
have been fairly well preserved as *active* vocabulary in a generation of
non-Yiddish speakers; their preservation attests to their utility. Those
that have a specifically Jewish meaning provide lessons in Jewish tradition. The notion of a *mitzvah,* fully elaborated, contains a wealth of
information about the Jewish religion. But the usefulness to American
Jews of many Yiddish words is quite independent of any explicitly
Jewish content. The words incarnate an attitude and understanding.
How inadequately the translations reveal the sentiment and subtlety of
the Yiddish. That same *mitzvah,* used in secular contexts, besides reminding us of the role, nature, and imperative that good deeds had for
shtetl Jews, is of service in explaining our own sense of right conduct.

More ambitious and creative than lists of words, but still short of instruction aimed at fluency, educators have developed a range of programs to introduce children to the sounds, characteristic modes, and
"feel" of a foreign language. These programs vary from modest attempts to do little more than make a child aware of the existence of a
language, by exposing her to a few samples, to those that lay a substantial basis for ultimate fluency in the language. The supplementary
school can choose the program suited to its interests and resources.[6]
The experience and language of shtetl Jews should also be transmitted
through translations of Yiddish literature. I. L. Peretz and Sholom
Aleichem, even when translated into English, re-create the shtetl
world; and their ideas, dialogue, and descriptions evoke the flavor of
the original Yiddish.

Yiddishism, the ground of secular Jewish identity, was an ideology
forged in a world that had not yet experienced the Holocaust, the establishment of Israel, the advanced assimilation of American Jewry, and
the demise of Yiddish as a spoken language. The Yiddishist vision of a

---

6. See Curtain 1994 and Kennedy 1985 for descriptions of these "Foreign Language
Experience" (flex) programs. I am grateful to David Goldberg for pointing them out to me.

nonreligious Jewish identity needs new content. But that new content should not exclude Yiddish. It can no longer be the whole story (if it ever could), but it can still be an important and beloved character in it.

Socialism

In chapter 4 I argued that Secular Judaism requires a conception of the *good* and that none will serve it as well as progressive politics. Progressive themes throughout Jewish history should be emphasized, and, as I have stated, the prominence of these themes in the heyday of Eastern European Jewry is an important reason to focus on this period. The progressive politics of that epoch was socialism, and, for that alone, socialist history and values merit a place in the Secular Jewish curriculum. But there are reasons independent of the shtetl connection. Granted socialism may no longer capture well or fully the progressivism of contemporary progressive secular American Jews, who, for example, give high priority to some principles not traditionally thought of as socialist planks — such as anti-homophobia — and who, in contrast to classical socialist positions, may see the practical and moral value of markets. But socialist thought and movements were the concrete historical manifestation of the progressive impulse during the last century and a half. To fail to teach about socialism is to suppress the real career of progressive values. It is to make these values bloodless abstractions or empty platitudes. And it is to avoid coming to grips with the historical entanglement of these values with tyranny and oppression.

The Secular Jewish school has at least two fish to fry. It actually does not fry them so much as it cooks them together in a savory paella, where the flavor of each complements the other. On the one hand, it gives content and meaning to Jewish identity. On the other, it provides moral and political education. In this latter task it is not unlike all standard Sunday schools. People send their children to Sunday schools because, quite properly, the public schools cannot be relied on to teach children the moral/religious values of the parents. Well, the public schools certainly cannot be relied on to teach the moral/political values of secular progressives. Insofar as socialist history is taught at all in the public schools, Stalinists are presented as its champions, not its betrayers; the apotheosis of the state is portrayed as socialism's essence, not its corruption. The Secular Jewish school should reclaim the progressive achievements of the socialist movement, both from their misrepresentation in capitalist description and their perversion in Leninist application. Socialism is too rich in valuable progressive ideals to permit its loss to progressive tradition. In the story of socialism, a fullbodied egalitarianism can be taught along with the virtues of liberty, solidarity, and internationalism. The study of socialism can illustrate that these values can be made part of struggles for specific ends; antimilitarism in World War I; civil liberties during the Red Scare and McCarthyism; union rights during the Depression; and health care, education, and employment rights today. The biographies of conspicuous Jewish figures in the general history socialism, Moses Hess, Karl Marx, Ferdinand Lassalle, Eduard Bernstein, Julius Martov, Leon Trotsky, Rosa Luxemburg, Victor Adler, and Leon Blum among others, can serve as a natural gateway to the study of socialism in a Secular Jewish school. Even the rejection of Jewish identity on the part of many of these socialist figures and the borderline anti-Semitism of some of them would prove instructive.

As important as it is to commend the progressive values in the socialist movement, it is equally important to disentangle progressive ideals from the misguided, sordid, and reprehensible deeds done in the name of socialism, lest our children throw out the ideals of economic justice and human solidarity with the sewer water of one-party states and reeducation camps. Moreover, in the hope that our children will be progressive activists, there is much to learn from the defects, delusions, and defeats of past progressive movements. The nationalist undoing of German Socialism at the outbreak of World War I, the transition from Leninist "hardness" to Stalinist butchery, the romanticization of the Cultural Revolution — all are morally edifying. More morally neutral, but still highly practical, lessons may be learned from the destruction of the Paris Commune, the record of failed utopian schemes, and the inefficiencies of some state industries. How much of this can be taught in a children's supplementary school will be a function of the students' ages and the available time. Here I only indicate the potential for the study of socialism in the Secular Jewish school, even though all of this potential is unlikely to be exploited.

Secularism

Even at this late stage of the book, the reader may still question the need for a *new* brand of Judaism based on progressive morals and an identification with the Jewish people from the vantage point of another national identity. Is this not the program of classical Reform as modified by the Historical School? Don't Reform and Conservative (and indeed Orthodox) Jews maintain their American nationality? Doesn't Reform make the pursuit of universal justice the linchpin of its Judaism, and doesn't a sense of historical continuity play a similar role in Conservatism?

All of this is so. And while contemporary Reform has lost some of its social activist élan and Conservatism some of its historical consciousness, there is hope that they might be reinfused with their original spirit. Then how does Secular Judaism advance or alter the initial response of Diaspora Judaism to its confrontation with modernity? The answer is principled secularism. The classical liberal Judaisms, like the liberal Protestantisms, emerging in the nineteenth century have not completely dispensed with what Mordecai Kaplan called, "the God idea." Though not dogmatic enforcers of any theistic creed and though replete with atheistic congregants, the classical liberal Judaisms have filled their ritual and liturgy with God talk that, except in some rarefied sermons and theology, has been bandied about and allowed to pass uninterpreted, at face value. Even Kaplan, who explicitly rejected any supernaturalism as incompatible with modern consciousness, could not give up God talk. He made of God "the power that makes salvation possible." The Reconstructionist movement, inspired by Kaplan's thought, has deemphasized his naturalism, and God talk appears in their congregations as unglossed as it does in the other liberal religious movements. Whatever their official theology, anyone who has spent any time in Reform temples, Conservative synagogues, or Reconstructionist minyanim knows that God permeates the proceedings, even if He (although in the more liberal of these congregations it might be She) does not dominate them.

I am not so peevish as to quarrel with God's presence in synagogue, and I offer no full brief for atheism. Belief in God may be a good thing, and there are those who, though they cannot literally believe in a godlike being, may still find God a useful symbol for what they do most value. *But, for many Wicked Children, God talk feels hypocritical and participation in it an unprincipled compromise with superstition.* Even if they have no principled objection to religion, they are unable to sincerely mouth its words so, for them, God-laden ritual and liturgy is uncomfortable and alienating. Secular Judaism is the full acceptance of modern naturalism, not only theoretically, but in its actual practice and educational program. There is no back door reintroduction of God by means of some abstract identification of Yahweh with Justice, Compassion, or the Spirit of the People, which, in everyday routine, inevitably would evolve into unreflective theism. Although perhaps not a majority, a good portion of Jews cannot, in good "faith," join religious institutions, no matter how liberal the religion of those institutions' religion. The frank and categorical secularism of Secular Judaism offers these individuals a way to be Jewish.

While I offer no *full* brief for atheism, some considerations in its favor are in order. After all, since so much of Secular Judaism is similar to the liberal religious Judaisms, its separate existence can be justified only by articulating its independent value. Throughout this book I have treated the secularism of the Wicked Child as a given. I have argued that, since she *is* secular, honesty requires that she not participate in a casual and insincere bandying about of God's name. Authenticity remains my primary justification for the secularism in Secular Judaism. But it is no argument for the independent value of secularism, only for its value to people who are already secularists. But is there any reason for, or value to, secularism in the first place? If there is not, maybe secularists should try the oft-prescribed remedy for disbelief — observance without belief — in the hope that faith will follow practice.

But this advice is ill advised if there is value to secularism. Although hardly conclusive (it would indeed be a surprise if I could produce a conclusive argument for atheism in this paragraph), I suggest the following: The rationale and value of secularism in the modern world is epistemological and pragmatic; supernaturalism is incompatible with all other modern beliefs and contradicts the basis of all rational, modern action. Granted, if one is attached to God language there are ways around this (hence the field of "Naturalistic Theology"), but they usually involve emptying "God" of all the historical traits that made Him worshiped by Jews, Christians, and Muslims. Modernity may still leave the emotional rationale for theism in place — God is certainly a comforting thought, and the debate about the moral value of theism is still wide open. But I think it clear that we have no metaphysical or practical (except insofar as the emotional and moral issues are also metaphysical and practical) place for God in our world.

This position will strike many as vulgar, literal-minded, and philistine. God language certainly provides the vocabulary that often seems most adequate for describing our ultimate concerns and deepest feelings. It allows us to allude to that which our naturalistic concepts fail to fully capture. God's history carries with it connotations, associations, and images that no single concept or symbol can replace. These are good reasons to retain God in our poetry, and, for many who feel that poetry is our best language, this is reason enough to believe in God. Here I only note that few of us are aesthete enough to have poetic power determine metaphysical belief. Beyond aesthetics the only argument for belief in anything remotely like a traditional God is an argument from authority: although unable to rationally and publicly justify their beliefs, it seems to me that the most admirable people in human history had a deep and unshakable conviction in what they unhesitatingly called God. One hesitates to conclude that one's insight into reality is sharper than Gandhi's, Einstein's, or King's. I suspect they had moved beyond the distinction we secularists maintain between poetry and metaphysics.

But, in any event, a theoretical defense of atheism is of less relevance to Secular Judaism than is a justification for principled secularism at the level of popular practice. And here the claim is simply that *God* is heavily weighed down with distasteful and misleading ideas. The term has too much baggage for modern liberals to carry. The counterclaim, that the bags contain riches too valuable to sacrifice, is also plausible. But this book attempts to clear the path for American Jews who choose not to schlepp the divine weight.

In the past, principled secularists have misunderstood the implications of their principles. For those who could not imagine Jewish identity without religion, assimilation was the alternative. Others, who believed that there was enough in Jewish culture outside of its religious trappings to maintain the identity, dispensed with nearly all ideas and practices related to religion and attempted to build on the remains.[7] But the remains were too flimsy a foundation on which to build. Emancipation doomed Yiddish, and murder hastened its demise. The Yiddishist Jewish nationalists lost the glue holding together their nation. Humanist secular Jews found that moral ideals and values abstracted from Jewish sources were too slender and promiscuous to define and hold together a distinctively Jewish community. Jewish secular humanists have tended to merge with Ethical Culturists and Unitarians.

But principled secularism need only avoid *faking* religion; it need not fear contact with it. All Jewish groups with a chance of long-term survival will have many points of contact with religion, for almost all of Jewish civilization has religious origins or potential connotations. But original meaning does not have to be the same as current meaning. Our contemporary American Halloween routine is not insincere or compromised because we no longer explicitly acknowledge its pagan- and saint-honoring lineage. Religious Jews have many practices that hearken back to animal sacrifice without thereby making their synagogues the home of real or symbolic bloody altars. Meanings change and the evolved meaning can be as meaningful as its progenitor.

Not only do meanings change, they branch out. Most branches of the Jewish tradition remain religious, but that does not preclude other branches from secularizing. Although a secular branch is in some ways more unlike the trunk than the religious branches, a secular branch can be just as authentic a limb of the tree. It is rooted in the same soil and shares the same past as the religious branches. And its fruit can be just as nourishing. As I argued in chapter 3, drained of religious significance, Jewish rituals do not necessarily become pale, for rich *historical* and *national* meaning flows through them. While they may not provide the ultimate succor that their religious analogues do, they need not want sincere emotion and genuine "historicist" spirituality.

Of course, what something once meant, and what it means to others, hovers over what it now can mean to us. But it does not fix our

---

7. I say *nearly* because it proved impossible for even the most rigid of secularists to devise any practice or ideology connected to the Jewish tradition that was completely unrelated to the Jewish religion. At best they could restrict themselves to areas where the religious element was not prominent or obvious.

understanding. To a learned or close listener there will always be an echo of "God-belief" in Jewish rituals, an echo that will be amplified as long as those rituals hold their religious meaning for some practitioners. But even if the religious echoes of fathers and cousins thunder, a community can still give its own voice to the old music. Jews may have originally circumcised their sons at God's command, and many may continue to do so, but my son's bris need not signify obedience to God. I can make the event a pact with history, a mark of kinship, a defiance of Jew hatred — and leave God out of it. Hence, the secularized rituals I recommended in chapter 3 are importantly different from the rituals of liberal religious Judaism. Liberal Judaism only reinterprets God, when the point is to abandon Him. At least that is an important point for a secularist. Yet Secular Judaism also differs consequentially with standard secularisms, for it understands that abandoning God does not mean abandoning the history and traditions of this once God-obsessed people. This distinguishes Secular Judaism from the traditional "Jewish" secularisms that felt contaminated by anything that *others* might see as religious. It is true that we are not free as individuals to unilaterally determine meaning à la Humpty Dumpty. But by developing a language and practice of Secular Judaism, Secular Jews can converse with the tradition and enlarge it so that we too are comfortably encompassed by it.

An American Judaism

While something very like Secular Judaism may fit the needs of other Diaspora Jewries, it is presented here as an identity for secular Jewish Americans. In chapter 1 I spoke of the "thinness" of unsupplemented American ethnic identity. But I do not mean to deny that "American" is a genuine ethnic identity and one to which American Jews fully, if somewhat atypically, belong.[8] Nor do I claim that Jewish participation in American ethnicity is lamentable. Limited though the culture is, it is good to be an American, and I like being one. Secular Judaism is con-

---

8. Michael Lind does a good job of describing the evolution of American ethnic identity and its current content. See especially Lind 1995, 266–8. In this book he casts doubt on the possibility of a national identity separated from a territorial base: "A people united by an idea must have an address" (p. 362). Jews, obviously, are a famous counterexample to this claim.

ceived as a supplement to American ethnicity, not a substitute for it. As a supplement it does not lead to biculturalism. Secular Jews do not have dual cultural nationality in the way one may have dual citizenship. "Secular American Jew" is not a condition of cultural redundancy; it is not having the same sort of thing in two different formats. It is more of a hybrid. The Secular Jew has mixed parentage — which does not give her a Jewish lung and an American lung, a Jewish kidney and an American kidney. The entire body is Jewish American. Although her heart might more resemble her Jewish mother, her hands her American father, the hybrid is a single integrated organism. She inhabits a functioning, coherent culture descended from the marriage of Jewish and American civilizations.

But my use of the term *supplement* does not indicate that the "Jewish" in Secular Jews is intended only as a minor adjunct to their ethnic identity. True, in some ways American features dominate. English is the native tongue and the minutia of daily life is mostly constructed out of the manners and mores common to the American people. The public life of the Secular Jew, and the public imagery that informs her imagination, will be American: Gilligan's Isle, the Superbowl, the O. J. trial, Clint Eastwood, *Roe v. Wade* — these are her publicly made mental icons. The way she banks, shops, cleans house, tips waiters, buys theater tickets, and commutes to work are also in the American mode. She lives according to American laws and gets the bulk of her education in American schools where she not only picks up her basic cultural skills — such as reading, writing, computing, "behaving" — but also learns the current standard American account of America and is exposed to a modicum of its high culture. And it is here that she imbibes her fundamental political liberalism — Jefferson, Madison, Lincoln, Douglass, Anthony, Roosevelt, King.

This is an extensive cultural endowment — enough perhaps to get by on. But the more limited Jewish cultural contribution can be of equal weight, for it is the locus of the special and the more personally and communally meaningful. Here are the holidays that light up winter and welcome spring, the occasions that bring the family together, the meals that celebrate the weekend's arrival, the milestones that mark transitions — birth, adulthood, marriage, and death. These are the annual and life events that standard American culture largely marks through its Christian supplements. But most important, through Secular Judaism one can create the political and moral projects that make life meaningful. And though this can be done exclusively through one's American political heritage, such projects take on a greater spiritual dimension (in the sense discussed in chapter 3) by virtue of being created and pursued within the context of an ancient history and a millennia-long tradition. Further, Secular Judaism provides vehicles for the expression of these moral/political projects, vehicles that reverberate with the abundance of Jewish memory.

Finally, in Secular Judaism one finds the basis for a community of shared social values. America teems with associations and groups that are formed to pursue specific common ends or to share specific interests. But aside from religious organizations, communities of shared social values—which are very different from bowling leagues, PTAs, and political parties—are hard to find. Sometimes aggregates of friends fuse into such a community, but usually one's friendships are a collection of mostly separate relationships that do not make a community. And even when they do, there are no shared practices and rituals to manifest common beliefs and purposes.

So in spite of living a mostly American life, much of life is *about* being Jewish. This aboutness can enable one to forge an emotional bond to one's Jewish heritage that rivals the one produced by the immersion in Americana. But there is no rivalry. Culture and ethnicity, unlike sports fanaticism, demand no ultimate loyalties. Deciding whether one is a Jew or an American is never an issue. One is both. Jewish is the type of American one is; American is the type of Jew. One is not less American or less Jewish for the blending. In moral action both identities are united in an underlying commitment to truth and justice, which, after all, as Superman has pointed out, is as much an American inheritance as a Jewish one.

American Jews, especially secular ones, should seek no charter from the state. The preservation of Jewish culture is the work of Jews. It is enough that the state remain thoroughly liberal and place no bars on free and voluntary efforts to be Jews, and to be Jews after our own fashion. If the United States were to issue cultural charters and Jews managed to qualify, secularists would not get control of the franchise. The Orthodox rabbinate got the official Jewish franchise in Israel (where it is the plum one) to the detriment of the majority of non-Orthodox Israeli Jews. If the American government were to go into the business of recognizing cultures, Conservative rabbis, in the pay of Jewish businessmen, would be granted the official leadership.[9] Their lack of Jewish confidence would cause them to share resources and power with Orthodoxy, and, because they are American Jews, their pluralistic liberalism might cause them to include Secular Jews as equals in the community. But, then again, the same lack of Jewish confidence that would incline them to indulge Orthodoxy, combined with the conservative politics natural to the oligarchic leadership, could lead them to fearfully exclude Secularism. Hence, interest and principle make Secular Jews staunch defenders of a liberal America that protects individual rights and allows individuals to make, un-make, and remake their culture as circumstances, intelligence, and desire permit. This staunch *individualism of legal rights* is a final an-choring of Secular Judaism in American identity.

Klal Yisroel

Secular Judaism makes no claim to be the one true church. Indeed our secularism is most naturally coupled with a principled pluralism. This pluralism moves beyond a tolerance for other cultures to an acceptance that these other cultures also offer valuable ways of being human.[10] It is commonly observed, but nonetheless ironic, that this sort of pluralis-tic acceptance is often most difficult to extend to nearest neighbors and kin — notoriously difficult among Jews.[11] The story is told of a Jewish Robinson Crusoe who, upon being found, gave his rescuers a tour of his island, proudly pointing out all he had built for himself during his

---

9. A harsh generalization not meant to impugn the integrity of the Conservative rabbi-nate but merely to indicate the structural realities of organized Jewry in America.

10. This pluralism is not tantamount to relativism. I believe that it is a deep empirical truth that no culture is bad (although most contain bad features and some may have lots of bad features) but not because I think there are no conceptual grounds for evaluating a culture. Still, Secular Judaism's attitude toward other cultures should not be primarily eval-uative. Secular Judaism should support the contemporary "multicultural" movement in America to the extent that that movement fosters intercultural respect and encourages inter-cultural knowledge. However, as I have stated, I think Secular Judaism should part with "multiculturalism" if its program were to call for coercive state action so as to maintain cultural forms.

11. Comparatively speaking, however, the family and civil strife of postexilic Jews, with a few notable exceptions, has been less bloody than those of other peoples. But perhaps this is because we did not have the weapons during most of our history or because the common enemy always disallowed the worst disunity.

twenty years in isolation. He showed them a bedchamber, garden, dining area, and synagogue. As he continued the tour, he led the rescuers to a pantry, a lookout, and a second synagogue. "But why did you need two synagogues?" he was asked. "Ha! You don't think I would pray at *that* synagogue!"

Rather than indulge in this sectarian inclination, Secular Judaism is drawn to the better and deeper tradition of embracing all *klal Yisroel,* the entire Jewish people. The embrace embraces in three ways. First, it is respectful and interested in all the ideologicaly different ways Jews have chosen to develop the Jewish tradition. Hasidim, Reform, Conservatives, modern Orthodox — it should be part of our curriculum to understand and appreciate them all. This does not require an uncritical approach, and it certainly should not involve any hint that these communities represent a more authentic form of Judaism. They are simply other ways of being Jewish, and as such they may have something to offer to humanity in general and Jews in particular (they clearly do to those Jews who are their acolytes). Second, we embrace Jews whose Judaism is embedded in non-American cultures. Diaspora Jewries exist on every continent and include peoples from a multitude of cultural settings. Cochin Jews of India, Kaifeng Jews of China, Addis Ababa Jews of Ethiopia, as well as European, South American, and Middle Eastern Jews should be studied in a Secular Jewish school. (In chapter 6 I've made the case that Israeli culture should get special attention in the Secular Jewish curriculum.) Finally, all past generations of Jews are included in *klal Yisroel.* Time should not alienate us any more than do ideological or cultural differences.

The embrace is not indiscriminate, unmindful of degrees of kinship. I have argued that shtetl Jews, the Jews of nineteenth-century Eastern Europe, should have a privileged place in the curriculum and that the privilege should increase as the shtetl Jews modernize, secularize, radicalize, and Americanize. Our particular Jewish identity is most strongly tied to these, our actual and ideological, immediate forebears. But all Jews should be acknowledged as part of the *ganse mishboche,* the whole extended family, living and dead. So, although the Sadducees may shed little light on the Borscht Belt, and Ibn Gabriol could not find a thing to eat at Zabars (actually anybody could find *something* to eat at Zabars), the Secular Jewish program appropriates them all.

The special interest, affection, and concern of Secular Judaism for

Jews is not a nationalistic retreat from a universalistic morality. My special feelings for, and involvement with, my own children do not downgrade the moral status of my neighbors' children. My particular relationship with my children does have important moral implications, but none of them are that I must think other children are inferior in value or dignity. Nor do special obligations to my own children mean that I have no obligations to other children; nor do they preclude me from treating other children with as much love and kindness as I can muster. Most significant, my universalism, though not requiring that I be a good parent to all children, does give me reason to promote the existence of good parents for all children.[12] So it is with Secular Jews, *klal Yisroel,* and all of humanity. We treat all Jews as family. Some relatives are closer than others, some we have more affection for, some mess up and lose our admiration or approval, some we grow distant from. But as family members they all have a special status. Their special status as family members does not mean we like them more than all nonrelatives, spend more time with them, or even that, all things considered, we necessarily have more in common with them than with individuals in other groups we belong to. Secular Jews, in general, and individual Secular Jews, in particular, will in many ways feel closer to non-Jewishly defined groups. But that does not vitiate the special connection we have to other Jews as Jews, which in turn does not affect the special connection we have to other humans as humans.[13]

Intermarriage

Secular Jews are among those Jews most likely to intermarry, so Secular Judaism needs to articulate an approach to intermarriage. The mainstream Judaisms perceive intermarriage (which for them simply

---

12. The relationship of rational, objective, universalist morality and the morality of particular personal relations is fraught with theoretical complexities. I believe that the most fundamental moral principles, if they are to be truly rational, objective, and universal, would not take particular relationships into account. Their *application,* not their formulation, would have to take all facts into account, and among the most profound facts of human life is that we have different particular relationships to different people and groups of people.

13. Anthony Appiah (1994, 156) states that "collectives, identities disciplined by historical knowledge and philosophical reflection," would be less unsubtle and altogether quite unlike the chauvinistic ethnic identities we tend to have now. Is not an identity "disciplined by historical knowledge and philosophical reflection" just the kind of identity Secular Judaism would try to promote?

means the marriage of a Jew and a non-Jew) as a misfortune and a threat. It is a misfortune because it dilutes the Jewish heritage for future generations, and it is a threat because its spread betokens the demise of Judaism. For rigid halachists, Jewish law alone decides the case against intermarriage. Conservative and Orthodox Judaisms categorically forbid intermarriage. Their rabbinates are to neither officiate at such weddings nor in any way sanction such unions.[14] These Judaisms demand that the non-Jewish partner to a potential intermarriage become Jewish thereby transforming the marriage into an all-Jewish affair. Conversions are lawful and acceptable; intermarriage is not.

Within Reform Judaism there are rabbis who sanction intermarriage in the belief that they are inevitable and that Jewish acceptance of such couples may salvage the Jewish partner and the children for Judaism; it may even bring the non-Jewish partner into the fold. But Reform shares the perception of other Judaisms that intermarriage is a misfortune. It may not be as concerned with the breach of halacha, but, like Orthodoxy and Conservatism, Reform worries that intermarriage tends to undermine Jewish "continuity," that is, the maintenance of Jewish traditions and the cultural survival of the Jewish people. Reform may have a different approach to the problem than the other denominations, but intermarriage is still categorized as a problem that Jewry would be happy not to have to confront.

Unlike mainstream Judaisms, Secular Judaism welcomes intermarriage without hesitation or ambivalence. This is not because Secular Judaism is unconcerned with Jewish survival. Jewish survival is a fundamental raison d'être of Secular Judaism. Nor is it because Secular Judaism believes, along with Reform, that an openness to intermarriage is a more effective tactic for supporting Jewish "continuity" than is an adamant rejection of intermarriage. This is an empirical proposition that I suspect most Secular Jews are inclined to agree with; but warm acceptance of intermarriage by Secular Judaism has a more principled basis than the calculation that more Jews will be held with Manischewitz than with *moror*.

Secular Judaism is morally commited to accepting intermarriage. Its

---

14. A recent survey, however, indicated that up to a third of Conservative rabbis and 10 percent of Orthodox ones will, on occasion, refer couples to a rabbi willing to perform such weddings (*New York Times* 12 October 1997).

doctrines of full human equality, respect for individual personality, the general value of human cultures, and the value of pluralism make the acceptance of intermarriage more than an adjustment to a grim reality. For Secular Judaism, a successful intermarriage is as Jewishly honorable as any family configuration. Willingness to intermarry with another group is the ultimate acknowledgment of social equality. To exclude a group from marriage candidacy is, prima facie, to imply that it is somehow unworthy of us or at least to suggest that it is too *unalterably* different from us to allow for intimate association. On an individual level, relationships are stifled and distorted when the possibility of romance and marriage are precluded. Moreover, when the ban is violated, as it inevitably will be, individuals are treated with contempt, ostracized, or, at best, granted a grudging acceptance — all of which cuts across the bedrock liberalism of Secular Judaism, which enjoins us to honor individual choices, recognize the full, common humanity of all peoples, and accord everyone equal respect. These values are not compatible with not wanting *them* to marry your sister.

Admittedly, the illiberal implications of forbidding intermarriage are only prima facie. There may be reasons against intermarriage that suggest no inferiority or unchangeable otherness of the excluded groups. Perhaps a case could be made that Jewish law embodies divine purposes for strictly separating and rigidly defining human breeding and cultural groupings, and perhaps these God-ordained purposes are not founded on illiberal beliefs and do not serve illiberal ends. Although these divine intentions are mysterious to me, their presumption by traditional halachists, in light, especially, of the theoretical openness of all branches of Judaism to the admission of anyone as a convert, may save the mainstream denominations from accusations of illiberalism. But Secular Jews certainly cannot invoke God's plan in order to escape the illiberal implications of the prohibition of intermarriage. In the absence of morally acceptable reasons for a restriction on intermarriage, Secular Jews must embrace the practice, for unrestricted intermarriage is the symbol and living substance of universal human equality. The question, then, is "Do Jews have *good* reasons to resist or even regret intermarriage?" Religious Jews may find that they do, but Secular Jews do not.

This does not mean that Secular Judaism fails to recognize the difficulties in making an intermarriage Jewishly successful, nor does it mean that every intermarriage is equally favored to be the home of Secular Jews. Transmitting culture is problematic in any event, and like any set of circumstances, intermarriage presents its own problems. Moreover some intermarriages may be practically or morally incompatible with the creation of Secular Jewish family life. So a Secular Jew cannot be indifferent to the cultural heritage and commitments of a potential spouse. But potential spouses do not have to be Jewish, and although this is trickier, they do not have to be secular. The liberalism of Secular Judaism should embrace the God loving, even if it has to draw a line at the God fearing.

The first order of business for a Secular Jewish evaluation of intermarriage is the determination of just what counts, for Secular Jews, as an intermarriage. It must be said at the outset that, *abstracting from whatever cultural differences it usually indicates,* "racial" intermarriage presents no *moral* difficulties for *any* Judaism, and certainly none for Secular Judaism. This is not to deny that an "interracial" couple will encounter difficulties in our color-conscious society. Although uncourageous, it may be prudent for a couple to hesitate before marrying across American racial castes. But there are no ethical grounds for such hesitation. Indeed there is something particularly morally admirable when choosing a mate about ignoring the hateful racist disabilities imposed on interracial couples. We can understand the rationality of wanting to avoid these difficulties, but avoidance elicits no moral approval. So when I speak of intermarriage, I am always referring to cultural differences. For our purposes, the marriage of a brown-skinned woman with curly black hair to a pink-skinned man with straight blond hair is not an intermarriage if they were both brought up as Secular Jews in Yiddish-speaking homes on the Upper West Side.

A Secular Jew is intermarried if her spouse is either not secular or not Jewish. Each absence presents its own issues. And depending upon the manner in which the spouse is not secular and/or not Jewish, the issues will vary in difficulty. In spite of the general embrace of intermarriage, some intermarriages will be problematic for a Secular Jew. But, before discussing the sorts of intermarriage that would be problematic for Secular Judaism, I will describe the Secular Jewish ideal for an intermarriage. From this description we will more easily see the constraints that committed Secular Jews would impose on a potential intermarriage.

The Secular Jew married to someone who is not a Secular Jew would raise her children as Secular Jews and as participants in her partner's culture. This would not lessen the children's status as Secular Jews; it would, however, give them an additional cultural identity. Consider the analogy between the multicultural identity here suggested and multilingualism. Speaking a second language causes no lack of fluency in the first. One can be at home in two languages and speak each as well as its respective monolingual speakers. Obviously more language learning must be done to become bilingual, and, similarly, more "cultural learning" is necessary to become bicultural.[15] Granted, complete and equal biculturalism may be a barely possible ideal. More often, given the scarcity of time and energy, one culture in an "intermarried" household may get relative short shrift. But even the short-shrifted culture has an authentic place in the child's identity, and it may serve as a seed, which, though not elaborately tended during childhood, may yet blossom in unpredictable future circumstances.

Full humanity requires culture just as it requires language; language is, in fact, the central component of culture. Acultural child rearing is as unviable an option as alinguistic child rearing. You must provide children with some language and some culture. You can raise a child haphazardly, with a melange of languages. This will result in a child who is not proficient in any one of them.[16] But bilingual child rearing does not result in such unproficient speakers; it results in bilingual ones. The indiscriminate mixing of cultural goods in a home would result in the cultural analogue of unproficient speakers. It is akin to the smorgasbord ideal whose desirability I argued against in chapter 1. But

---

15. A disanalogy between a multilingual and multicultural upbringing is that, though there may be limits, a child can learn more than two languages, whereas a multiculturalism consisting of more than two cultures seems destined to be superficial. But since most children are not raised by more than two live-in parents, and the question of intermarriage in our society only confronts us with the coupling of two persons, this disanalogy seems of little relevance to our discussion. Of more relevance is the fact that, although I have framed this discussion in terms of biculturalism, an intermarriage between a Secular American Jew and another American ethnicity would result in bisubculturalism. It would be a home trying to practice and impart two distinct forms of American ethnicity. I speak of biculturalism because the term *bisubculturalism* is cumbersome, and also because I believe the argument applies to the wider category of genuine biculturalism as well as to the narrower and simpler (for the most part) case of bisubculturalism.

16. The child might be proficient in her own idiolect, but, if she were, it would not sufficiently resemble the idiolects of any broad community of speakers and so would not be a sound vehicle of communication.

a bicultural home can transmit the integrity of each of its cultures. It does not have to provide children with a confused, watered-down concoction of disparate cultures but rather with a multiplicity of coherent heritages, each of which maintains its integrity.

The first requirement that Secular Judaism imposes on intermarriage is that the non-Jewish partner be willing to raise the children as Secular Jews, and from that requirement we derive the corollary that she must be liberal. There are many paths of this derivation and many facets of the liberalism so derived. The cultural commitments that the non–Secular Jew brings to the marriage must be liberal enough to tolerate biculturalism. You obviously can't raise someone as a Secular Jew and as something else, if that something else demands that it be the sole cultural melieu of its members. Hence, at the very least, the non-Jewish tradition must tacitly accept pluralism. But the non–Secular Jew must go beyond a willingness to participate in biculturalism in general; she must be willing to cohabit with Secular Judaism in particular. The relatively undoctrinaire nature of Secular Judaism makes it an easy housemate, but it has its standards. It would be hard to bring up a child as a Secular Jew alongside a tradition that required unquestioning belief in a given dogma — biblical inerrancy, for instance. To meet this compatibility requirement, the non–Secular Jewish culture need not share the modernism, progressivism, or any one of the values of Secular Judaism, but it must allow its members to share them. It cannot saddle them with doctrines that make it impossible to tolerate Secular Jews.

But while the narrow compatibility requirement is met through the limited liberalism that would tolerate Secular Judaism, a fuller liberalism is needed to give reasonable chances of success. The tradition of the non–Secular Jewish spouse ought to embody *some* of the liberal values at the moral core of Secular Judaism. This is no more than what most people take as necessary for a successful marriage and child-rearing partnership; the couple should share some fundamental convictions regarding what is right and what is good. Certainly individuals can bring different senses (so long as they are compatible) of what is valuable to a marriage and parenthood, but unless there is significant overlap, it is hard to see how the couple can uncoercively direct their mutual life or the lives of their children. There must be some common goals if there are to be common, cooperative activities. Neither marriage nor shared child rearing seems plausible without these. So the committed Secular Jew should not unhesitatingly marry a racist or sexist; it would also be hard for her to marry someone with no sympathy for progressive politics. Of course many of the basic values of the Secular Jew will have sources external to her Secular Judaism; as I have said, Secular Judaism is not a comprehensive philosophy of life. And it may be that the overlapping values that a marriage is founded on have non–Secular Jewish sources. Still, since many of her social and political values will be Secular Jewish ones, and since, as a Secular Jew, such values will rank high, it would surely raise difficulties to wed someone indifferent to those values.

I qualify all of these constraints on a secular Jewish intermarriage with terms like "it would be hard," or "could not unhesitatingly," or "it would raise difficulties," out of respect for the complexity and individuality of human relationships and marital arrangements. I am unprepared to say absolutely and a priori that all couplings of certain types are morally obnoxious to Secular Judaism. While the Secular Jew will have moral absolutes, she may, in good conscience, find a way to marry someone who does not share them. Still, it is hard to see how a committed Secular Jew could marry an explicit racist.

Could a Secular Jew marry a religious person? It would depend on the nature of her religiosity. In general, in principle, religious practices pose no problem. My spouse can teach my children to genuflect, confess, chant, meditate, put on tefillin, eat peyote, and fast on Ramadan and Yom Kippur without thereby precluding their simultaneous inculcation into Secular Judaism. But if the religiosity demands dogmatic conviction, it can obviously run afoul of the compatibility requirement. My children cannot be raised as Secular Jews while being told that certain supernatural beliefs are unquestionably true. In other words, a Secular Jew can marry a religious person if she is liberal about her religion, that is, willing to let her children entertain alternative beliefs — in this case, nonreligious ones. Admittedly, this may seem, practically, to preclude marriage to a seriously religious person, since a degree of dogmatism is intrinsic to most religions. But I think this is more a theoretical than a practical preclusion. In America, at least, it is remarkable that so many liberal attitudes have permeated the world views of even some of our most religious citizens. So, while the requisite liberalism will certainly eliminate some religious individuals as good marriage candidates for Secular Jews, and while these candidates will more readily be found among Unitarians and Reform Jews than among Seventh Day Adventists or Mormons, few individuals can be a priori eliminated for nuptial consideration based on their religion. Of course, in some religious groups, Satmar Hasidim and Wahhabi Muslims, for example, the illiberalism is so deep and thorough that it would bar all genuine members from consideration as spouses for Secular Jews. (Mind you, they are not looking to marry us either.)

A final constraint on intermarriage, while not imposed by Secular Judaism per se, might arise from the feelings of many individual Secular Jews. In chapter 1 I said that one of the reasons for raising your child as a Secular Jew would be to give her something you are comfortable with, thereby preempting her embrace of that which discomforts you. Hence a motive for Secular Judaism might be avoidance of having a Christmas tree in the house. Clearly a Secular Jew who refuses to countenance a Christmas tree in the house should not marry someone whose deep cultural commitments and desires demand old *tannenbaum* in the living room every December. Similarly, she should not marry someone who would have the children wear *payes* (sidelocks) if she finds that practice repellent. But for that matter, you should not marry a committed city dweller if life in the city is unacceptable to you. Some marriages are unsuitable because of differences in personal preferences, and some of these preferences may be cultural. As a philosophy, Secular Judaism is rather broad in the sorts of intermarriages it endorses, but the historically conditioned emotions of many individual Secular Jews would probably make certain couplings personally problematic. As a Secular Jew, I have no moral objections to my children attending church and taking communion, but I do feel a nonrational (although historically understandable) visceral repulsion at the prospect. I could not have married (I don't think — but love is a powerful motive) a person who would have wanted our children to engage in traditional Catholic practices. Although this emotion is clearly connected to my Jewish ethnicity, it has no principled basis in my Secular Judaism, and I accept that other Secular Jews may feel comfortable raising children who attend St. Mary's Church in the morning before they go to the Sholom Aleichem Shule in the afternoon (although scheduling soccer would be a problem. After all, these are all supplements to their American ethnicity).

That there is a wide array of theoretically acceptable intermarriages within Secular Judaism does not imply that they would all be equally easy. Some, such as marriage to a secular non-Jewish African American would be especially easy. Secular Judaism and a secular variant of African American culture seem like complementary traditions that would generate few tensions. Its history as a culture of an oppressed minority would make African American culture a natural vehicle for the progressive values of Secular Judaism. Harriet Tubman stories, it need hardly be said, would make nice companion pieces to progressive renderings of the biblical Exodus tale.

Marriage to a traditionally observant Jew would pose greater challenges. While the practices of a home that was secularly and religiously Jewish might appear a seamless cloth, many common threads would be open to different understandings. Also, practices of each tradition would directly deny the validity of the other tradition. A Secular gloss on a traditional blessing would likely suggest that its religious content is somehow not real. The serious contemplation of the religious interpretation could render the secular understanding otiose or secondary. Here the conflicts may be subtle, but they can run deep.

Marriage to a person of traditional Christian belief and practice will probably raise even more difficulties. While this marriage would not share the problem of competing interpretations of the *same* practices (as arises in a marriage between a Secular and a religious Jew), it would have, as do all marriages between a committed secularist and a religious person of any stripe, the problem of presenting a theistic and a nontheistic worldview so that neither denigrates the other (even if it implicitly denies the full truth of the other.) This would not be a problem in a secular-secular intermarriage where no contradictory metaphysical claims are taught; it would be a problem in all religious-secular intermarriages. But in addition to reconciling godly and ungodly traditions in the same house, a religious Christian and Secular Jewish intermarriage might also be hard pressed to find commonalties of interests, practices, and pursuits that can strengthen and bind a bicultural home. Of course many Christian traditions preach a social gospel that emphasizes solidarity with the poor and oppressed, but there are also Christian traditions in which the social gospel plays a decidedly secondary role. Still, if there exists an openness to Secular Judaism, even a socially conservative Christianity might be able to form a family union with Secular Judaism. Personal tastes may make such a marriage unlikely, and there is a good chance that a socially conservative Christian would adhere to some doctrines, such as the subordinate status of women, that a Secular Jew might find morally objectionable. Also, it is unlikely that a socially conservative Christian would be liberal enough to expose her children in a full bodied way to Secular Judaism. But if none of these probable contingencies apply, a Secular Jew might well find a happy match in this population.

When I compared the bicultural household to the bilingual one, I noted that both the indiscriminate mixing of cultures and the indiscriminate mixing of languages would be impoverishing. Incoherent melanges, whether cultural or linguistic, are inferior specimens of culture and language. Hence, there is value in maintaining the integrity of each culture in a bicultural home. But integrity is a different notion than purity. Denigrating the value of a cultural melange does not disparage the value of new, blended, cultural forms. Just as Yiddish is a coherent language derived from many languages (as, indeed, are most languages), so a culture can be a blend of various cultures (as are most cultures). These new cultural forms have evolved a coherence and an integrity. A living, dynamic culture will, almost by definition, incorporate new cultural goods, as well as invent them from internal resources. In time, communities of similarly bicultural individuals may form, and, out of their biculturalism, a new, integrated culture may emerge. If Secular Judaism is part of the bicultural mix, the emergent culture may become a new form of Judaism. However it is also possible that the Jewish elements could become so transformed or overwhelmed as to make the new culture a non-Jewish one. While this development would defeat one of the rationales of Secular Judaism, its distant possibility does not outweigh the reasons for welcoming intermarriage, especially since the survival of Jews as a distinct ethnic group is only one of the rationales of Secular Judaism. The other rationales, such as understanding your origins, carrying on ancestral traditions, giving ritualistic and communal framework to your values, reinforcing your progressivism, and resisting anti-Semitism, still apply, even if a Secular Judaism tolerant of intermarriage contributes in the distant future to the waning of American Jewish ethnicity.

But even this remote possibility, that Secular Jewish intermarriages will lead to a new, non-Jewish culture, is mitigated when we consider the probable truth of the empirical proposition motivating the Reform movement's approach to intermarriage: Intermarriage will happen anyway, and working with it is more likely to retard Jewish assimilation than is uncompromising opposition. Intermarriage is common among Jews likely to be drawn to Secular Judaism. Rejection by their families will not drive these Jews to Jewish mates, it will drive them and their children away from Judaism. Unlike Reform, Secular Judaism does not present this argument as the basis for its acceptance of intermarriage, but it does recognize the argument's force as a refutation of the case against intermarriage, which is based on a distant worry that intermarriage could foster the emergence of a hybrid culture that would not be Jewish.[17]

The Historical Framework

Jewish history is the Torah of Secular Jewish education; it is not the sole object of study, but it is the backbone of the curriculum. To Jewish history we attach all the flesh that makes up the body of Secular Jewish culture. None of the contents of Secular Judaism fails to find a place in the historical curriculum. As we teach the story of the Jews, we can explain Jewish customs, Jewish languages, Jewish literature, Jewish morals, and the varied fates of Jews. All we wish to teach can be taught as part of the history, and everything we teach enriches the history. Although every human creation has a history and submits to a historical understanding, such an approach is especially compelling for Secular Jewish education because, through it, each of our main concerns can be made part of the same story. Hence, a historically framed curriculum is more than a spacious platform that conveniently accommodates all our topics. It connects our topics to each other and to us. In such a curriculum, Hanukkah is not just a celebration of an isolated event. It is an episode manifesting the ongoing themes of fanaticism, assimilation,

---

17. This whole discussion of the possibility of biculturalism (or bisubculturalism — our particular concern) leading to a new cultural form that would not be Jewish begs the question of what makes a culture Jewish. Initially I am inclined to say that it is Jewish if it thinks of itself as such. But that will not do. It may be a necessary condition, but groups like Jews for Jesus make me question its sufficiency. A certain amount of recognition by the majority of those who call themselves Jews, causal continuity with past Jewish groups, and so forth are probably necessary.

nationalism, and monotheism. Hanukkah customs are seen as evolving over time, in different ways at different places. Hanukkah is a theme in Yiddish literature and folktales. It figures in some Holocaust martyrology. It is what we and many others throughout the world do each December. What is true of Hanukkah is equally true, not only of other holidays, but also of events, individuals, groups, and artifacts. The expulsion from Spain is tied to contemporary Sephardim, who are tied to the great Salonika community, which is tied to the Holocaust and hence to contemporary Jewish politics. Isaac Luria, Sabbatai Zevi, the Chmelnicki massacres, Gershom Scholem, and Zionism can all be wrapped together and linked to our attitudes toward the Middle East. Historical study is the constant forging of connections and in the forging of those connections the goals of Secular Judaism are realized. Our connection to ancestors roots us. Through our connection to other Jews, we experience solidarity. Our Jewish activities — whether festivals, funerals, songs, or Shabbes meals — become elements in a single, complex tale. Instead of teaching a disparate collection of unrelated items, through history we color in and detail the story.[18]

Secular Judaism, not unlike other Judaisms, is about more than affirming ethnic identity. It strives to reveal the meaning and values Secular Jews attach to that identity. We are not interested in a meaningless recital of events. But to gain meaning, the events must be part of a story. It is their place in the story that tells you how to understand Shabbes customs. It is their place in the story that tells you what the Aramaic and Ladino languages have meant to the Jewish people. The significance of Ellis Island requires that you know where the immigrants were coming from and what they were going to. A moral evaluation of Israel cannot be separated from Jewish history.[19] History provides the narrative context required for transmitting meaning and value.[20] Through the study of history, we can best explain what it has meant to be Jewish and why being Jewish has been valued. In this way Jewishness can become meaningful to our children and valued by them.[21]

---

18. Crediting William McNeill for the term, Michael Lind speaks of "myth-stories" as the cement of ethnic identities (Lind 1995, 352).

19. Ultimately Arab history and European history are also required.

20. Alastair MacIntyre elaborates on this theme throughout *After Virtue* (1984).

21. The history alone does not do this. They also need Jewish culture that is fun and rewarding in their daily lives. But this is no more to say than that they must become the living part of the Jewish story, and Jewishness must become part of their personal story.

This web of connections also promotes the spirituality available to a secularist, by making her part of a larger project. Chapter 3 described a mundane spirituality that consists of seeing oneself meaningfully connected to a wider sphere. History extends one's social and temporal connections, thereby creating the secularist's wider domain. You become related to slaves in Egypt, scholars in Vilna, and peddlers in Tennessee. Your struggles for security, knowledge, and freedom are intertwined with the lives of your forebears.

Moreover, in the absence of God, it is history that gives the moral grounding to Jewish traditions and that makes of them a spiritual practice. It is not connectedness alone, but connectedness to a valuable entity or project, to a good, that makes spirituality. The good may not be a single, simply stateable goal or a thing of uniform, unmixed value. But it has to be, all things considered, something of significant value. For many Jews the continued existence of the Jewish people, apart from any other matters, qualifies as a sufficient good. But Secular Judaism, along with religious Judaism, requires that the spiritual dimension of being Jewish transcend mere survival. Religious Jews serve God. Secular Jews serve the ideal of a more just future. But to pursue that ideal, Secular Jews need history. There can be neither progressive ideals nor progressive activity outside of historical understanding. It is no accident that every progressive ideology, every system of beliefs that has looked forward to a better future for mankind, is historicist. The ancient Hebrew faith, with its expectation of the historical redemption of Israel, is arguably the original progressive historicism. Marx's work is perhaps the most notable entry in the progressive historicist catalogue. But all hopes for a different future are built on the possibility of change through time — a reasonably good definition of history. If the different future is potentially a better future — the fundamental progressive conviction — then ultimately the change must have a noncircular direction. Historical sensitivity is the appreciation of noncircular temporal change, and so in addition to serving its practical pedagogical, ethnic, and spiritual needs, the historically framed curriculum animates the progressive heart of Secular Judaism.

As I said above, the historical framing should be built of materials from every era and venue of Jewish history. It should cover the origins of our people in the moral/religious inspiration of an ancient levantine tribe. The evolving legends, rituals, customs, politics, and laws of the Jews should be studied. This would include myths, literature, and history of the Bible; dealings with ancient empires from Egypt to Rome; and the emergence of rabbinic Judaism and Diaspora Jewry. Jewish experience and civilization under medieval caliphs and kings should also be part of the curriculum. As we approach modern times, the curriculum should settle more on the Ashkenazic experience and specifically on what I have called the *shtetl* Jews and their American sojourn. But this settling is a matter of emphasis. It does not preclude the teaching of developments in other branches of Jewry. Two developments not directly part of the American Jewish trajectory — Israel and the Holocaust — merit a substantial presence in the curriculum (see chapters 5 and 6).

The history taught should be chosen to engender Jewish self-respect and love, without hubris or chauvinism. Therefore, achievements and failures are to be included: Maccabean triumphs but also messianic madness (and even the bit of messianic madness within the Maccabean triumphs). The setbacks and advances for progressive values should run like a leitmotiv throughout the curriculum. Hence, for example, the anti-obscurantism of Maimonidean rationalism but also the inegalitarianism of Hasidic dynasticism should both find a place in the curriculum.

The historical housing should be furnished and decorated with the full panoply of Judaica. Indeed many of these furnishings and decorations should be built-in, at times playing structural roles, so that there is little distinction between teaching history and teaching tradition. But unlike an ahistorical teaching of tradition, the historical setting fosters a consciousness of tradition that is pluralistic, secular, progressive, and critical. A historical perspective allows us to see that traditions change, that human actions cause that change, and that it is sometimes possible to influence, and always necessary to evaluate, the change. Historical consciousness is the precondition of a progressive stance.

An important annex to the study of Jewish history should be the study of the history of progressive movements. While much of this will be done through Jewish history, some of it should be done as part of the general story of mankind. Students should understand that many peoples have longed, and fought, for progressive ideals. The humanism, respect for individuals, tolerance, and naturalism of Secular Judaism should be explicitly tied to the European Enlightenment. A Secular Jewish education may seek to find these strands in pre-Enlightenment

Jewish traditions, but it should not downplay the primary Enlightenment role in their formation, consolidation, and introduction onto the world stage. Similarly, the struggle for freedom should be illustrated by Nat Turner's story, as well as Moses'. Exodus may be the achetypical escape from slavery, but the struggle against the American enslavement of Africans is a variation with as much relevance to American Jews and contemporary progressives. Students' anti-militarism should be nurtured by the anti–Vietnam War movement as well as the Prophets, the timelessness of Isaiah made immediate in the more ephemeral verse of Phil Ochs. And, as I have argued, the history of the socialist movement, the grand progressive synthesis and tragic failure, should be a particular focus of the Secular Jewish curriculum. In this way the tradition of progressive Enlightenment liberalism becomes a defining feature of the Secular Jewish creed.[22]

The Institutional Setting

A Secular Jewish community begins with a school. That is why this philosophy of Secular Judaism is cast in the form of a curriculum discussion. A school can be a circumscribed institution, but it can also become the basis of a community, and it can do this more readily than most other institutions. The commitment to our children's school is a natural extension of the commitment to our children. Secular Judaism is a Judaism for the Wicked Child. There is nothing in it to which she will have a principled objection, and there is much in it that will attract her. Still, much of Secular Judaism may be awkward and unfamiliar to the already quite assimilated Wicked Child. But involvement with the awkward and the unfamiliar is routinely done for the sake of children. We participate in embarrassing PTA fund raisers, we socialize with strangers at school picnics, we sit through school concerts and plays that might otherwise not meet our aesthetic standards. Indeed, in the course of our children's education we transform our homes: second-grade artwork festoons our refrigerators, fifth-grade science projects take over our kitchens, kindergarten classroom hamsters become our houseguests during school vacation. The notion that our children's

---

22. Many possible curricula meet these criteria. In appendix A I provide one model.

education should extend into our home, and that "extracurricular" activities are part of their education, is widely accepted. The most natural way for Passover customs to enter the Wicked Child's home is through her child's homework assignments. A Rosh Hashanah service as a school event might pull in a parent otherwise disinclined to bestir herself for the Jewish New Year. Songs in praise of Shabbes before the Friday night meal are more easily imposed on parents by children than the other way around.

In time, because the Passover customs, the Rosh Hashanah service, and the Shabbes songs are not only free of the moral and metaphysical matter the Wicked Child has disdained, but are actually supportive of her values and nourishing to her residual Jewish attachments, they become cherished customs to her and her family and not just a sop to the children's school. Once insinuated into her life, the compatibility of Secular Jewish traditions with many of the needs and values of the Wicked Child, allows for a gradual blending. These Jewish traditions become her Jewish traditions.

School functions can evolve into community events. Folk dances taught at school create a need for school dances. Accompanying parents quickly are seduced by the joys of dancing, and before long community dances are arranged. The school *Purimshpiel* may be a prelude to community Purim celebrations. What were originally only school events for children evolve into community events in which both children and adults have primary place. In fact, through school wholly adult activities can ensue. Study and discussion groups, adult sings, lecture series — all might occur naturally among parents who are sufficiently ideologically akin to have chosen to send their children to a Secular Jewish school. Finally, the school can become the organizational means of communal social action. The classes would have their social action projects, and nothing would be more natural than a school committee devoted to organizing some of the parents' activist energies as well.

Thrown together initially to educate their children, Secular Jews find companions with whom to celebrate holidays, to dance, to sing, to party, to reflect, and to work for justice. Friendships will likely follow. Voilà, community! — not willed into being but growing out of shared activities that are outgrowths of the basic decision to give your child a

Jewish education.[23] This is unsurprising, for no individual decision has more communal meaning than the one to educate children, especially the decision to educate them in the ways of a minority subculture.

The school in which these communal activities begin may prove structurally inadequate for their fullest development. The Secular Jewish community that begins with a school may need to form new bodies structured to give scope to the community's ambitions. Eventually the school may be only one element in a multifaceted Secular Jewish community organization. With a school as the germ of a community, possibilities expand. Leonard Fein has described Jewish communities that have developed

> *bikkur cholim* — visiting the sick — into a virtual art form, a voluntary but highly organized program to ensure that the dislocation that attends serious illness will be minimized [and] *Cheva kadisha* — burial societies — composed of barely observant Jews [that] become expert not only in the traditions of burial but also in the literature of bereavement and comfort. Here a synagogue has become a shelter for the homeless; there so many Jews volunteer to staff soup kitchens on Christmas day that there is a waiting list for participation.[24]

Ultimately a Secular Jewish organization may choose to affiliate with the umbrella Jewish organizations in the area. In the same way that a viable Secular Judaism cannot rigidly cut itself off from all religious nuances in its customs and rituals, a vibrant Secular Jewish community should not cut itself off organizationally from other Jews. To be sure, the affiliation with other Jews must be principled and not require that Secular Jews compromise their political or (non)religious integrity. But swimming in a JCC pool and playing in a JCC basketball league is not reactionary. Cooperating with local synagogues to reduce world hunger requires no insincere praying. Secular Jewish organizations can fight for the democratization of the Jewish umbrella groups and add their voices to the definition of American Jewry from within the larger

---

23. Of course some individuals can resist the natural draw to community that a school exerts, and if there happen to be enough such individuals in a school, that school may never become the seed of a community. This may be a particular danger for a secular Jewish school because so many Wicked Children enter the arena of Jewish affiliation with great ambivalence. It may be all they can do to bring their child to school at the designated class times.

24. Fein 1994, 47.

community. Who knows, there may be so many Wicked Children floating about that, once organized, they would become the mainstream of American Jewry.

The Prospects for Secular Judaism

Jews can lay a fair claim to having invented God, and perhaps God could say the same about Jews. Undoubtedly God will do quite nicely after a divorce, but we might wonder about the Jews. Can secularized Jews be a lasting phenomenon? For thousands of years, through territorial dispersion, language change, political upheavals, economic revolutions, persecutions, and a wide array of host cultures, it is plausibly argued that Jews have remained Jews because of their adherence to laws commanded by God. Can a Jewish identity long exist emptied of its devotion to, and belief in, divine commandments?

I do not know. I hope to have shown that for the current generation of American Jews there can be a rich Jewish life without God. But it is reasonable to doubt that a Godless Judaism can be passed on from generation to generation. But even if it cannot, Secular Judaism has a valuable role to play in our lives. At the least, it can be a halfway house on the road to total assimilation. As such, it would fail in most of the goals I have set for it, but it could still serve as an untraumatic way for individuals to leave Jewish life. Secular Judaism might be a kind of ethnic methadone so that Jews, addicted to a tribal identity for thousands of years, would not have to go cold turkey and suffer the withdrawal symptoms of guilt and family alienation.[25]

---

25. Joel Greifinger suggests that the appeal of Secular Judaism will lie mostly in the low level of commitment and knowledge it requires. I believe that this is its appeal to some in current secular Jewish institutions. However, if this is the appeal of Secular Judaism to most Secular Jews, then it is indeed doomed to a short life as a way station to total assimilation. But I think that, as practiced, the liberal religious Judaisms can be as undemanding as anyone might wish, and they are able to sustain their existence with a large segment of barely committed, ignorant adherents. The conventionality of the religious aspect provides a certain stability. The liberal religious Judaisms will be the natural homes of lazy Jews (which is not to deny that they will also be the home of extremely dedicated Jews). But Secular Judaism will not last if a high percentage of its members are minimally committed to its existence and minimally knowledgeable with regard to Jewish traditions. If it is to be at all, its ultimate appeal cannot be that it asks little. And if Secular Judaism does require a serious commitment, indeed if any liberal Judaism, religious or otherwise, requires a serious commitment, then the charge of fostering assimilation that Orthodoxy hurls at liberal Judaisms becomes highly dubious. Statistics may show that after a few generations Reform Jews, for instance,

A slightly more elevated career for Secular Judaism would be as a transitional institution. Secular Judaism would ease Wicked Children, or at least the children of Wicked Children, into the ranks of liberal religious Judaism. Reintroduced to Jewish history and customs through Secular Judaism, Secular Jews might find that, not only do they want to be Jews, they even want to remarry the God of the Jews. Reconstructionism and Reform share so much of the Secular Jewish agenda that it would take relatively little for many Secularists to merge with these mainstream groups. In this scenario, Secular Judaism would have been a salvage operation, saving Judaism for many Jews who weren't prepared to take it straight at first and, from the point of view of the larger Jewish community, saving many Jews for Judaism.

But there are two more promising possibilities for Secular Judaism: one is as a peripheral but permanent, or at least long lasting, form of Judaism. Some reform movements in Jewish history have resulted in sectarian splits wherein one sect stops acknowledging the Jewish identity of the other or one of the sects stops identifying itself as Jewish. However it happens, the result is disaffiliation with the Jewish people. Christianity comes to mind, as do more borderline cases: Samaritans, Karaites, Sabbateans. But sometimes the new sect, even if bitterly denounced at first, is accepted as a way of being Jewish. The established rabbinate of Eastern Europe reviled and rejected Hasidism for decades. These *mitnagdim,* opponents of Hasidism, which included the most revered and orthodox of traditional rabbis, did all they could to delegitimize Hasidism. They even went so far as to enlist Gentile state power in their fight against the new sect. But Hasidism not only flourished, it flourished as a Judaism; and in popular Gentile and Jewish opinion, it flourished as the paradigmatic Judaism.

Liberal religious Judaisms are often viewed by the Orthodox as wayward forms of the faith; neglectful of essential duties, they hardly qualify as Judaisms. Indeed the Orthodox position is that there are no "Judaisms," only Judaism, an invariant religion. But still, Conserva-

---

are more likely to assimilate than Orthodox Jews (although one can question the validity of extrapolating current data), but that may only show that Reform Judaism attracts more uncommitted Jews than does Orthodoxy. It does not show that Reform, per se, leads to assimilation, or that Reform causes a lesser commitment. The key to fostering "Jewish continuity" is commitment, not what one is committed to. The question then is "is secular Judaism capable of eliciting commitment?"

tive, Reform, and Reconstructionist Jews are widely considered Jews. They are represented in (and often dominate) local, national, and international Jewish organizations. They are considered Jews by the media and politicians. They are subject to anti-Semitism. They are enmeshed in Israeli politics. And although, in principle, most Orthodox consider them Jews by birth and not by practice, in practical terms, even the Orthodox relate to the liberal religious movements differently than they relate to fully assimilated people whose Jewish ancestry plays absolutely no role in their lives. While there is debate over whether liberal religious Judaisms can endure, there is no debate about their Jewishness. Complex historical, sociological, and political factors determine the Jewish fate of a new sect within Judaism. But there are no a priori reasons preventing Secular Judaism from securing a place in the Jewish world. It may find a niche within the Jewish community to the left of Reform and Reconstruction, perhaps at the edge of the recognized Jewish world; but it need be no less Jewish for living close to the edge.

The other promising possibility for Secular Judaism is a future as a (or even the) mainstream Judaism of America. Improbable perhaps, but not implausible. Judaism, like most other things, changes through time. Ezra, Akiva, Rashi, Caro, Maimonides, and the Vilna Gaon, all fairly mainstream fellows, had differences in practices and beliefs. Their common Judaism was ever evolving, and the dominant form in any given epoch was the momentary result of that evolution. Although they may have thought of themselves as defined by the tradition, it is clear that they were doing much of the defining. Whatever pretensions some have had, or may still have, to being implementers of the uninterpreted, literal word of God, most Jewish tradition implicitly acknowledges the centrality of human input into the fashioning of the tradition. With the advent of liberal religious Judaisms, this acknowledgment has become explicit, and the fashioning has become a conscious activity. The capacity to evolve consciously has served as a strength that has helped liberal Judaisms dominate organized religious American Jewry. It would be an even more prominent strength of Secular Judaism, which would be freed of the conservative effects of a tradition with divine entanglements and would also, given its essential politics, probably be unencumbered by the conservatism of oligarchic leadership. Secularism could honestly develop keeping in mind the needs of American Jews as American Jews.

There is reason to believe that the profile of most American Jews who share the humanistic mindset of liberal religious Jews is even closer to our Wicked Child than to the solid citizen of a Conservative congregation. If Secular Judaism really could appeal to Jews on the verge of assimilation, and this is where a plurality of Jews are, then perhaps Secular Judaism could be more than an exotic denomination for marginal Jews. Indeed, as true heirs of the Enlightenment, Secular Jews can reasonably believe that it is natural that Secular Judaism be the wave of the Jewish future. After all, people are rational, and reason should ultimately reveal the truth. Secularism, liberalism, progressivism, and Jewish traditionalism are, to Secular Jews, the right way, the most truthful and moral way, of being Jewish. Being true and good is hardly a guarantee of success. But are we so cynical as to think it of no help in making a worldly career?

If the appeal to truth and goodness, as grounds for the good prospects of Secular Judaism, is too absolutist and intolerant-sounding for a movement that is deeply liberal and historicist, then we can say that the Secular Jew believes that Secular Judaism is the most viable form of Judaism given the zeitgeist. Although our advances have been erratic, modernity tends toward naturalistic belief and egalitarian, democratic politics. Secular Judaism is the modern form of Judaism.[26]

---

26. I am aware that an equally strong, maybe stronger, case can be made that rationality is a minor feature of modernity, that fundamentalism, mysticism, and obscurantism are on an upswing; that democracy and egalitarianism are discredited and in decline; and that being true or morally correct is no predictor of success. This is why I claim that a major role for Secular Judaism is plausible, not that it is probable. Moreover, while mainstream Judaism has changed significantly over the ages in its beliefs and practices, it is arguable that the Jewish *belief* that they, the Jews, were living according to rules eternally fixed by the Torah was essential to Jewish survival. In this view, liberal religious Judaisms, let alone Secular Judaism, have no long-term prospects: Compromise regarding halacha is an inevitable prelude to assimilation. Only Orthodoxy will keep the Jewish people a people. The nearly two hundred years of liberal religious Jewish identity is dismissed as gradual assimilation and not taken as evidence for the possibility of Jewish survival in liberal guises.

But this view fails to take into account the fundamentally new environment modernity has brought to Jewish existence. Belief in the absolute, unchanging validity of the Torah may have been required for Jewish cohesion and survival when all life was communal and no community was liberal. A questioning of Jewish tradition was tantamount to endorsement of Christian or Muslim traditions. But now the inflexibility of its self-understanding may make Orthodoxy the form of Judaism most ill suited to survive in the modern world. Bershtel and Graubard (1992, 300) argue that there is no escaping for Jewry, of the modern condition: Judaism is now an individual choice, and even the most Orthodox are aware that they have other possibilities. I think Bershtel and Graubard overstate the case. The world changes, and the environment fostering liberal, individual choice may not prove enduring. Moreover, even

Norman Cantor has argued that modernity and its defining ideas are substantially the creation of Jews. He mentions Marx, Einstein, Freud, Durkheim, Wittgenstein, Lévi-Strauss, Boas, and Chomsky to make his case.[27] Even if Cantor's assignment to Jews of the responsibility for modernity is overblown, it is indisputable that westernized Jews were deeply involved in the shaping of the modern world. Surely a Judaism that is fully at home — in a modern world to which Jews have significantly contributed — has as good a chance of flourishing in that world as any other Judaism.

The Internal Stance

Part of what estranges the Wicked Child from her Jewish identity is her attachment to the ideal of Enlightenment rationality. Not only does the ideal, in her view, require the rejection of the supernatural, divine basis of Jewish religion, it also demands an objective look at Jews and Jewish history. What does unbiased historical scholarship tell us about the Jewish past? What does cool sociological analysis reveal about their present? What would a neutral moral assessment say about the value of Jewish culture?[28] The Wicked Child concludes that the Jews are a group, and, like other groups, they are buffeted by circumstances and have the full human range of motives and interests. She would ac-

---

in a liberal society, individual cultural choices are not as unconstrained as Bershtel and Graubard suggest. Still, I think they are correct that current American conditions create a new atmosphere for Jewry in which Judaism must survive: ingrained liberalism. I think that the thoroughgoing liberalism of Secular Judaism is a strength in this regard. It also offers another option to American Jews in a situation where Jewish identity will exist only as an option.

27. Cantor 1994, 301–5.

28. These are deep and murky epistemological waters. The suggestion that historical or sociological enquiry can be unbiased is controversial. Much depends on the definition of *bias*. Rather than argue for it here, I baldly state my position: Objectivity is an unreachable goal that one approaches by taking more and more perspectives into account. No perspective is intrinsically privileged, although some perspectives have more features in common with others, and some perspectives prove especially useful for some purposes. The notion of a "neutral moral assessment" raises some special problems, but I think with appropriate adjustments we can render the same sort of objectivity for morality that we do for other domains of knowledge. The question of the objectivity of knowledge, and especially that of moral knowledge, has been a perennial of Western philosophy, but in the last few decades it has received more attention than ever. Feminists, deconstructionists, analytic relativists, neopragmatists and postmodern philosophers of all stripes have either challenged or reconstructed the notion of objectivity. For a careful and, I think, largely successful attempt to take all of the critiques into account and rescue an idea of objective knowledge, see Haack 1995.

knowledge that Jewish history is more colorful and dramatic than that of most people and that (due to understandable historical causes) the achievements of individual Jews, scientifically and culturally, are disproportionate to their numbers. But she would also note that Jewish culture has weaknesses and unattractive features, and that Jewish history records its share of unheroic and selfish Jewish activity.

But the facts of the case are not as important as her orientation to the case. It is an orientation we may call the *external stance*. It is the stance required of science, indeed of all objective rational inquiry and assessment. But there is a long felt, much bemoaned shortcoming to the external stance. It is not the stance of poetry or love. The question posed by the external stance is, "How would this object appear to all observers (or alternatively, to no particular observer)." Alas, no one looks good to all observers (or to no particular observer). As an object of rational inquiry and assessment, neither Jews, nor anyone else, unproblematically stirs the soul or engenders pride. An *object* is studied from the outside. As we would expect, it is cold on the outside; this aids the clarity and dispassion of our judgment. But cold judgments from the outside are not the only valuable ones.

Another orientation is the internal stance.[29] From it, one looks at things from the inside. Here you do not observe and assess Jewry and then, based on your findings, decide to identify as a Jew. Instead you begin with the Jewish identification. You look at things with Jewish eyes and Jewish inclinations. The internal stance discovers a different, in some ways more limited but not lesser, truth than the external stance. It is the truth on which attachment and love feed. How many of us would love our children if we looked upon them only with objective eyes, if we saw only what any observer could see? It is not the facts about our children that make us love them; it is our love that enables us to be endeared by these facts. Of course, we should strive to see our children objectively, too. We do not want our love for our children to obscure for us how they look to others or blind us to the ways they need to and can be changed. We should understand how people outside

---

29. The philosopher Thomas Nagel has done profound and subtle work exposing and exploring the external and internal stances. It is his ideas and terminology that I appropriate here, although not in a version he would necessarily endorse. Most of Nagel's work is relevant to the issue, but see especially Nagel 1986.

the family experience them. Moreover, at times (like coaching your kid's soccer team), you must treat your child impartially, not favoring her interests over the interests of other children. All this requires the external stance. It is a stance that should always be available to you. But by itself, it will never make you part of a family. If this is the only way you can look at your parents, brothers, sisters, and children, you can never truly love them.

In the Passover story of the four children, the Wicked Child is essentially, and perhaps justly, accused of refusing to take an internal stance toward Jews. If she is understood as asking for a purely objective justification for committing herself to the Jewish people, she cannot be answered. Because the rabbis have understood her to be asking her question from an external viewpoint, their dismissal has been just. "God did this for me, not for you," they tell her. But as many commentators have pointed out, the Wicked Child is attending the seder. She does not ask her question as an ethnologist doing field work. She is still sitting at the table. She may be thinking about leaving the house, but she is still on the inside. As long as she is there, a different answer is possible.

Secular Judaism is only for those still sitting at the table. In chapter 1 I spoke of an "already existing inclination," a "gut desire," and an "attachment" as the raw material for the development of Secular Judaism. In other words, candidates for Secular Judaism must still be sitting at the table, prepared to look at the world as Jews; they are those whose commitment to being Jewish is, at least in part, nonrational. They find themselves inside a Jewish identity, and they want to stay there and bring their children inside, too. Secular Judaism provides no independent objective reason for being Jewish. It is built on a preexisting nonrational commitment.

This nonrational commitment is not irrational. If it were we would have reason to overcome it. Some internal stances are irrational in that they conflict with an external stance. It is irrational to have a racist perspective. Racism is objectively false and objectively pernicious. The internal stances that we accept should be compatible with the external stance. Love should not deny reality but should give us another dimension of it. Our internal stance toward Jews and being Jewish must harmonize with an external viewpoint. Achieving this harmony is not easy; things look and feel different from inside than they do from the outside. It is this difficulty in harmonizing the two stances, combined with the Wicked Child's Enlightenment-bred loyalty to the external stance, that tempts her to abandon the internal viewpoint in regard to her Jewish identity. Secular Judaism tries to create a harmony that can overcome this difficulty. It is an effort to build a Jewish home in which the Wicked Child can live because it enables her to go outside and roam around without becoming a different person. She is secular, rational, just, and fair inside or outside of the house. She is unsurprised and knowledgeable about how the house looks from the outside, and she is aware of and concerned with the effects of her home on the neighborhood. She is comfortable out and about. But everybody needs a home, everyone needs to come inside sometimes. And being inside has a feel all its own.

At Home with the Jews

From the Jewish point of view it has always been considered a blessing to be Jewish. An extremely burdensome blessing, but a blessing nontheless. The blessing is of a kind with the joys of belonging to any culture, community, club, or family: It is familiar and comfortable. I have also spoken about other things Jews like about being Jewish: our sense of irony and skepticism, our humor, emotionality, and bluntness. But the core of the blessing, and what has made it burdensome, has always been that Jews have the privilege of serving God by following God's law. The tradition tells of God shopping the Torah about looking for buyers and finding that the Jews were the only takers. Torah was understood as a yoke that ennobled rather than degraded. Torah was replete with restrictions that conferred moral superiority. This feeling of moral superiority is a problem and an opportunity for Secular Judaism. In a brilliant comic passage in his satiric masterpiece *Portnoy's Complaint* (part of which was quoted in chapter 4), Philip Roth expresses the problematic form of this attitude of moral superiority among American Jews of the first half of the twentieth century. Here is a fuller version of the passage:

> Self-control, sobriety, sanctions — this is the key to a human life, saith all those endless dietary laws. Let the *goyim* sink *their* teeth into whatever lowly creature crawls and grunts across the face of the dirty earth, we will not contaminate our humanity thus. Let *them* (if you know who I mean) gorge themselves upon anything and everything that moves, no matter how odious and abject the animal, no matter how grotesque or *shmutzig* or

185

dumb the creature in question happens to be. Let them eat eels and frogs and pigs and crabs and lobsters; let them eat vulture, let them eat ape-meat and skunk if they like—a diet of abominable creatures well befits a breed of mankind so hopelessly shallow and empty-headed as to drink, to divorce, and to fight with their fists. All they know, these imbecilic eaters of the execrable, is to swagger, to insult, to sneer, and sooner or later to *hit*. Oh, also they know how to go out into the woods with a gun, these geniuses, and kill innocent wild deer, deer who themselves *nosh* quietly on berries and grasses and then go on their way, bothering no one. You stupid *goyim!* Reeking of beer and empty of ammunition, home you head, a dead animal (formerly *alive*) strapped to each fender, so that all the motorists along the way can see how strong and manly you are; and then, in your houses, you take these deer—who have done you, who have done nothing in all of nature, not the least bit of harm—you take these deer, cut them up into pieces, and cook them in a pot. There isn't enough to eat in this world, they have to eat up the *deer* as well! They will eat *anything,* anything they can get their big *goy* hand on! And the terrifying corollary, *they will do anything as well.* Deer eat what deer eat, and Jews eat what Jews eat, but not these *goyim.* Crawling animals, wallowing animals, leaping and angelic animals—it makes no difference to them—what they want they take, and to hell with the other thing's feelings (let alone kindness and compassion). Yes, it's all written down in history, what they have done, our illustrious neighbors who own the world and know absolutely nothing of human boundaries and limits.[30]

The chauvinism of this rant, particular to New York Jews in its details, in general form has a long pedigree in Jewish civilization. Throughout Jewish history the doctrine of the chosen people has often had racist overtones at times accompanied by fantasies of eventual domination. The notion that Jews have a special role to play in redeeming the world has seemed to indicate that there is something special about them making them fit to save the world, whereas others were unfit to do so. That Jews would serve as a light unto the nations might imply that the nations are in darkness.

But this feeling of moral superiority is not a hopelessly reactionary attitude that should be swept by progressives into the dustbin of Jewish

---

30. Roth 1967, 81. The wider context of this passage makes plain that Roth is less interested in exposing a sense of moral superiority than in tying it to Jewish repression, guilt, and fearfulness.

history. On the contrary, it can be the key for uniting Secular Judaism with most historical Judaisms. It can be refined into a sense of moral specialness and can become the hallmark of the internal stance for Secular Judaism, as in some ways it has been for Judaism throughout the ages. But first the sense of moral specialness must be separated from any possible chauvinistic connotations. Liberal Judaisms have wrestled with this problem. Kaplan thought that the only way to deal with it was to abandon the "chosen people" and "light unto the nations" doctrines. Reform turned them into a voluntary willingness to follow the moral law and work for the world's salvation. Hence, in the Reform reading, the only special feature of the Jews is that they have stepped forward to carry out God's mission, and, indeed, any human being who steps forward is considered just as special, and any morally laggard Jew not special at all. But, because they have not explained God's role in the election of Israel and why Jews volunteered, Reform has not been completely able to exorcise the background racism in the doctrines of moral specialness.

But Secular Judaism is well suited to adopt and adapt the Reform approach. It can, without any chauvinism, make the central goodness of being a Jew a sense of being morally special. Without God, the sense of moral specialness can be understood as characteristic of Secular Judaism's internal stance. We are not objectively special. No one has chosen us, and our choices have not put us into a special relationship with any being external to us. But our choices, our values, our commitments, and our interpretations of events make us seem morally special to ourselves. This is the way we look to us. It is an artifact of our perspective, real because our perspective is as real as any other — of crucial importance to us, because it *is our* perspective. We can acknowledge that from their perspectives, others may look morally special to themselves. And we also see that from an external stance no human group is well situated for moral boasting.[31]

---

31. Charles Taylor argues (1994, 25) that group identity and self-esteem require the recognition of the Other. While I find it plausible that individual identity and self esteem must be recognized by the other to exist, I think Taylor commits a fallacy of composition when he claims that this dynamic applies to groups. Once again Jews serve as an obvious counterexample. For all the self-doubt and Kafkaesque self-denigration associated with Jews, the truth is that, through many centuries, Jews have been widely despised, scorned, and persecuted by host societies, but Jews have, nevertheless, thought quite highly of themselves.

Although it is *objectively* absurd to have universal specialness, there is nothing paradoxical about all groups being special to themselves. In fact, don't we now strive to raise every child so that she feels special? Just as we point out to our children all of their features that should make them beautiful to themselves, so we should teach our children to love their *Yidisher kop* and *Yidisher harts*. There is nothing wrong with feeling smart and good, feeling that you are especially humane, sensitive to suffering, and morally mature, as long as there is no claim to objective status for your wisdom and goodness, no expectation that others ought to see you that way. The only consequence of Jewish self-esteem should be that, since we see ourselves this way, we should expect ourselves to act this way. The internal stance returns us to the essential Jewish tradition of Torah as a burdensome blessing, as an ennobling yoke to which we have harnessed ourselves. Jewish education has always aimed at getting its children to put on that yoke. Secular Judaism tries to carry that tradition forward, incorporated into the wider human movement for moral progress.

A Liberal Judaism

The liberalism of Secular Judaism rests on two pillars: its faith in reason and naturalism as the source of knowledge, and its devotion to, and belief in, the worth of the autonomous individual and the fundamental moral equality of individuals. A corollary of the second pillar is a decent respect for individuals in aesthetic, political, social, and cultural groupings. This corollary is often viewed as requiring a quietist tolerance as part of the liberal essence. Liberals live and let live. They disapprove of missionary zeal. They do not try to change others, let alone the world. Shouldn't a truly liberal culture seek merely to cultivate its own garden, finding joy and meaning in its communal life without the busybody motive of world moral betterment? Isn't there something deeply *illiberal* about the progressivism at the heart of Secular Judaism? Would Secular Judaism not be better conceived, or at least more liberally conceived, simply as a cultural option for unbelieving Jews?

No. Liberalism contains two opposing dispositions. One is indeed relativist and takes its relativism as implying a "mind your own business" social and political posture. But this is the lesser tradition. The greater liberal tradition believes in universal truths and is meliorist to the bone. This second tradition is the common, unifying ground of the Judaism and liberalism of Secular Judaism. Historical memories and traditional customs will contribute to the Jewishness of Secular Judaism, but its work as a community for world redemption is its ideological link to traditional Judaism. For if liberalism's quest for a better world goes to the bone, Judaism's quest for a better world is in the marrow. Secular Jews are unambiguously in the liberal camp, and although in their own section, they also sing *ani maamin* in the Jewish chorus.

An individualistic communitarianism; a fighting liberalism; a world-weary, near cynical utopianism; an atheistic Judaism — are we not here offered a culture of paradox? One way or another it has never been easy to be a Jew. Why should Secular Judaism be any different?

From Wickedness to Wisdom

In the Haggadah parable the Wicked Child's self-distancing from the Jewish people is inferred from her use of the word "you"; "What is this service to you," she asks, and with this "you" the rabbis determined that she had abandoned the Jews. Incredibly, the Wise Child's question uses the same grammatical form, without rabbinic reprimand, "What are the testimonies, laws, and judgments that the Lord our God has commanded *you?*" The Wicked Child's wickedness rests in a word that is not even remarked upon when found in the Wise Child's mouth. The real difference between their questions, putting aside the pious and formulaic nod the Wise Child makes to "the Lord our God," is in the specificity of their requests. The Wicked Child has questions about the foundations of the entire practice; the Wise Child wants explanations of matters internal to the practice. The Wicked Child's question has a certain logical and moral priority: "First tell me what it's all about, then we can go into details." Once satisfied as to what it is all about, the desire for details will follow. The transition from Wickedness to Wisdom, from estrangement to communion, is a natural one. Having tried to answer the reasonable concerns of our generation of Wicked Children, perhaps we can now move ahead and raise generations of Wise Grandchildren.

Appendix A

THE FOLLOWING is an outline of a curriculum for a supplementary Secular Jewish school. It is based on a curriculum developed for the I. L. Peretz School of the Workmen's Circle of Brookline, Massachusetts. The six-year curriculum is intended for students ages seven to thirteen years old, although parts of it could serve as material for older students as well. It can easily be divided so as to extend over more years of schooling. Still, it is a doable, if ambitious, program for six years of Sunday school. This is an outline of the curriculum, and so provides content rather than form; no preferred pedagogic techniques are described, no model lesson plans given. For the most part, other than maintaining respect for children, I do not see that Secular Judaism has any technical pedagogical axes to grind. A Secular Jewish school movement could be open to a variety of teaching approaches and techniques. At the Brookline *shule,* we strive for what is sometimes called an "integrated" curriculum, whereby the various contents we wish to teach — musical, moral, linguistic, ritualistic, political, biographical, and so forth — are conveyed through exploration of a single topic. After the first couple of years, that topic is usually a historical epoch or event. This historically based approach is argued for in the text (chapter 7), and, indeed, an acute historical consciousness is part of the ideological core of Secular Judaism. Nevertheless, a sound Secular Jewish historical consciousness might well be conveyed through a curriculum that does not use history as its organizational framework. The one pedagogic principle that I cannot imagine a successful Secular Jewish curriculum dispensing with is the encouragement of significant family involvement with the pupils' schoolwork. The schoolwork should therefore include activities that extend into the student's home life and that require parent participation.

The lists of general resources emphasize children's books, though some books for adults are cited, as background for teachers. A few useful videos are also indicated.

Judith Katz-Levine, Marjory Rome, and Abbie Fennell helped devise and flesh out the primary year curriculum.

Curriculum for a Secular Jewish Sunday School
The Primary Year

Objective

The goal of this year is to introduce the children to some basic Jewish customs primarily, but not exclusively, related to the Jewish holidays.

Brief Outline

The curriculum for this year is closely tied to the Jewish Calendar. Songs, stories, crafts, and cooking take the children from Rosh Hashanah through Yom Kippur, Sukkas, Simchas Torah, Hanukkah, Tu b'Shevat, Purim, and Passover. Some non-"holiday" traditions are also covered, such as Shabbes and giving *tsdukah*. Songs expose the children to the sounds of Yiddish and Hebrew. Picture books and actual examples expose them to the sights of traditional Jewish objects.

Issues, Items, and Ideas That Should Be Covered

Family, celebrations, the seasons, history, heritage, religion, legends, God(s), peoplehood, shofar, harvests, Rosh Hashanah, Yom Kippur, Sukkas, a sukkah, Simchas Torah, the Torah, Hanukkah, menorah, *chanukiot,* the Maccabees, dreidel, oppression, fairness, tolerance, homelessness, poverty, *tsdukah*, mitzvah, nature, Tu b'Shevat, the environment, Purim, megillah, Esther, Mordechai, Haman, hamantaschn, *grogger,* Passover, the seder, the Four Questions, freedom, the Haggadah, pharaoh, Moses, Miriam, matzo, the American Civil Rights movement, Shabbes, challah, and work.

Some General Resources

Apple Blossom, S. Levey Oppenheim
The Big Sukkah, P. Schramm
Cakes and Miracles, B. Golden
The Castle on Hester Street, L. Heller
Chicken Man, M. Edwards
The Creation, O. Sherman
Elijah's Angel, M. Rosen
The First Passover, L. Swartz
The Glass Menorah, M. Silverman
A Holiday for Noah, S. Remick-Topek
A House on the Roof, D. Adler
In the Month of Kislev, N. Jaffe
The Jewish Kids Catalogue, C. Burstein
Joseph Who Loved the Sabbath, M. Hirsh

Mrs. Moskowitz and the Shabbes Candlesticks, A. Shwartz
Oasis of Peace, L. Dolphin
Passover Parrot, E. Busman
Poppy Seeds Two — A Twisted Tale for Shabbat, D. Uchill-Miller
Potato Pancakes All Around, M. Hirsh
A Rosh Hashanah Walk and *Two by Two,* B. Reid
A Seder for Tu BiShevat, H. Appleman and J. Sherwin
The Shofar That Lost Its Voice, D. Fest
The Spotted Pony, Days of Awe, E. Kimmel

Also, many of the Children's Bible storybooks and folktale books listed in the second-year curriculum may prove useful.

The Second Year Curriculum

Objective

The goal of this year is to introduce the students to the history and customs of the Jewish people through Bible stories, folktales, Yiddish literature and holiday traditions.

Brief Outline

The year will cover Bible stories (The Creation, Adam and Eve, Abrahama, Sarah, Isaac, Rebecca, Jacob, Esau, Leah, Rachel, Joseph, Moses, Joshua, Saul, David, Solomon, Deborah, Naomi and Ruth), some classics of Yiddish literature for children. The holidays of Rosh Hashanah, Yom Kippur, Sukkas, Hanukah, Tu B'shevat, Purim, Passover, Shavuos — and folk tales related to the Bible stories or holidays.

Issues, Items, and Ideas That Should Be Covered

The concepts of a myth and a legend, the significance of seasonal change for humans, shofar, fasting, famine, food production, repentance, sukkah, menorah, Torah, temple, synagogue, seder, monotheism, biblical sex roles, Haggadah, mitsvot, *tsdukah,* moral laws. The ideas of courage, heroism, temptation, friendship, loyalty, honesty, forgiveness, *rachmones,* and solidarity. The importance of music, poetry, and nature. A tolerant, respectful, and accepting attitude toward others, including those who are different. A love of freedom and equality.

Some General Resources

The following is a far from exhaustive bibliography. In particular I do not include any books devoted to individual Bible stories or individual holiday tales. There are hundreds of these; many of them are wonderful. Although not listed in the bibliography or in the detailed curriculum below, teachers will probably want to incorporate these books of individual tales into the lessons.

The Bible Story Activity Book, J. Pliskin
Chag Sameach: A Jewish Holiday Book for Children, P. Shaffer
A Child's Book of Midrash, B. Goldin
A Child's Introduction to Torah, S. Newman
The Diamond Tree, H. Schwartz and B. Rush
Does God Have a Big Toe: Stories about Stories in the Bible, M. Gellman
Elijah's Violin and Other Jewish Fairy Tales, H. Schwartz
First Book of Bible Heroes, A. Mailach
Happy Holiday Pop Up, S. Sharfstein
Jewish Days and Holidays, G. Cashman
Jewish Heroes, I. Weilerstein
Let's Steal the Moon: Jewish Tales Ancient and Recent, B. Serwer
One Minute Bible Stories, S. Lewis
Our People in Olden Days, B. Israel
The Picture Book of the History of the Jews, B. and H. Fast
Workmen's Circle Gut Yomtef Booklets, N. Kadar, ed.
Yiddish Stories for Young People, I. Goldberg

The Third Year Curriculum

Objective

To introduce students to East European Jewish life of the nineteenth and early twentieth centuries and to describe Jewish immigration to America from 1880–1924.

Brief Outline

The year begins with the students' personal explorations of the origins of their families. It then turns to life in the shtetl: First family life is examined: Traditional roles within the family, marriage customs, holiday customs, housing and clothing styles are all explored. Next, shtetl community institutions are introduced: education, religious life, community officials and types. Shtetl art, literature, music, and dance are discussed. Anti-Semitism in Eastern Europe — the canton system, the Pale of Settlement, pogroms — are briefly covered. The year then turns to the great emigration from Eastern Europe, the passage to and entry into America. American life for Jews, especially on the Lower East Side, is the focus of the latter part of the year. Housing, schooling, music, theater, literature, and a hint of political life are covered. Throughout the year Yiddishism, Yiddish literature in translation, and Yiddish song are emphasized.

Issues, Items, Ideas and Words That Should Be Covered

Shtetl, *zeide, bubbe,* mama, *tata, maidl, yingl, balehbusteh,* Shabbes, kiddush, challah, *chuppe, shadchan, badchan, shteitl,* yarmulke, *tzitzis,* tefillin, shul, *daven,* rabbi, *chazan, shammes,* heder, bar/bat mitzvah, shnurer, tsedukah, *rachmones,* mitzvah, kashrut, *shochet, mazel tov,* Pale of Settlement, czar, cantonists, quotas, blood libel, pogrom, the *goldene medina, fussgeyer,* emigration, steerage, dockside examinations, Ellis Island, greenhorn, Lower East Side, tenement, sweatshop, assimilation, night school, *landmanshaft,* vaudeville, Second Avenue Theater, Catskills, Borscht Belt, Yiddish newspapers, klezmer, unions, Sholom Aleichem, I. L. Peretz, Emma Lazarus, Lillian Wald, settlement houses, peddlers, the Joint, HIAS, the Arbeter Ring.

Some General Resources

A Bintel Brief: Sixty Years of Letters from the Lower East Side to the "Jewish Daily Forward," I. Metzger
Ellis Island, M. Pullman
Fiddler on the Roof (video tape)
The Friendly Society: A History of the Workmen's Circle, J. Shapiro
Holiday Tales of Sholom Aleichem, A. Shevrin
Leaving for America, Holiday Memories of a Shtetl Childhood (audio tape) and *Real American Girl: Stories of Immigration and Assimilation,* R. Bresnick-Perry
Molly Picon: A Gift for Laughter, L. Pere
Selected Stories of I. L. Peretz, I. Howe and I. Greenberg
Selected Stories of Sholom Aleichem, A. Kazin
Wise Men of Chelm, S. Simon
Yiddish Stories for Young People, I. Goldberg

The Fourth Year Curriculum

Objective

The goal of this year is to introduce the students to the cultural and historical development of the Jewish people between the postbiblical and the shtetl periods.

Brief Outline

The year begins with an exploration of Jewish life in Palestine during the Roman occupation. Important figures such as Hillel, Akiva, Bar Kochba are presented. The rise of Christianity and Rabbinic Judaism is discussed; the revolts against the Romans, destruction of the Temple, and expulsion from Palestine are topics. The students will learn about the origins of Ashkenazic

Jewry in the Rhineland and the beginnings of Yiddish, as well as some aspects of medieval Jewish life and the Jewish experience during the Crusades. The origins of Sephardic Jewry in Islamic Spain, the Golden Age, figures such as Maimonides and Judah Halevi, and the expulsion of 1492 are presented. Contemporary Sephardic customs and communities are looked at as are some other non-Ashkenazic Jewish communities, such as the Jews of India, Yemen, and Ethiopia. The year ends with the beginning of the Ashkenazic settlements in Eastern Europe and the Chmelnicki massacres.

Issues, Items, and Ideas That Should Be Covered

Evolution and variations in holiday practices, preservation of ethnic identity, assimilation, resistance to oppression — armed and unarmed; Messianism — religious and secular; commonalities and differences between Judaism, Christianity, and Islam; the variety of Jewish communities; the concept of exile; the plight of refugees; the Torah, the Talmud, and some of the ethical outlooks of these books regarding labor, charity, communal solidarity, foreigners, violence, and sex roles; study, education, knowledge, and the law (halacha) as Jewish values; Tisha B'Av; Tu b'Shevat; Simchas Torah; the forms and growth of Jew hatred; language as a vehicle of culture and ethnicity.

Some General Resources

Eyewitnesses to Jewish History from 586 B.C.E. to 1967, A. Eisenberg, ed.
Great Figures and Events in Jewish History: From the Gaonic Period through the Golden Age, H. Braver
Heritage (video) series, A. Eban
Heroes of Jewish Thought, P. Karp
Jewish Heroes, I. Weilerstein
The Jewish Traveler, A. Tigay, ed.
The Jews, H. Fast
Leaders of Our People, M. Gumbiner
Our People through the Middle Ages, S. Goodman
Poems from the Hebrew, R. Mezey, ed.
The Yiddish Songbook, J. Silverman, ed.
A Young People's Encyclopedia of Jewish History, I. Shamir and S. Shavit

The Fifth Year Curriculum

Objective

This year introduces the students to the Jewish people's experience in the modern world up to the rise of the Nazis. The focus is on the varied ways Jews responded to the dismantling of the traditional world.

Brief Outline

The year begins with the final developments of premodern Jewish life: Hasidism and its traditional opponents. The lessons next turn to the Haskalah, emancipation in Western Europe, assimilation and the rise of racist anti-Semitism. Life in, and the persecutions under, Czarist-ruled Eastern Europe are explored. Most of the year should be devoted to the Jewish involvement in, or creation of, various social movements: Zionism, socialism, Yiddishism, and trade unionism. These studies seek to give the students a sense of the history of these movements and their cultural manifestations.

Issues, Individuals and Ideas That Should Be Covered

Ba'al Shem Tov, Rebbe, Hasidism, Mitnagdim, Vilna Gaon, Jewish pluralism, Haskalah, Mendelssohn, the French Revolution, human rights, Heine, emancipation, racist anti-Semitism, American racism, Dreyfus, Pale of Settlement, pogroms, *numerus clausus*, Beilis, Protocols of the Elders of Zion, Pinsker, Herzl, Zionism, Gordon, Labor Zionism, Ahad Ha'am, aliyah, kibbutzim, Arab nationalism, Palestinian nationalism and culture, Ben Yehuda, Bialik, socialism, Marx, LaSalle, Rosa Luxemborg, Trotsky, the Bund, Communism, Emma Goldman, immigration, landsmanshaft, unions, organizing, the Workmen's Circle, Cahan, *Forvarts*, Freiheit, the labor poets, Hillquit, strikes, union solidarity, scabs, Dubinsky, Hillman, the ILGWU, the ACW, tenements, sweatshops, the Triangle fire, Lemlich, Yiddishism, Zhitlovsky, Mendele, Peretz, Sholom Aleichem, the Yiddish theater, the Balfour Declaration, the Arab Revolts, Henrietta Szold, Judah Magnes, Ben Gurion, Soviet Jewry.

Some General Resources

Peddlers and Dreamers, M. Rosenfeld
A Picture Parade of Jewish History, M. Epstein
Rooftop Secrets and other Stories of Anti-Semitism, L. Bush
Sholom Aleichem Holiday Stories, A. Shevrin
Stories for Children, I. B. Singer
A Treasury of Yiddish Stories and *World of Our Fathers*, Irving Howe
Yiddish Stories for Young People, I. Goldberg
A Young Person's History of Israel, D. Bamberger

The Sixth Year Curriculum

Objective

The goal of this year is to introduce the students to the basic history of the Holocaust and to the racist and reactionary ideas that made it possible.

Brief Outline

The year begins with a look at race relations in our contemporary lives. It then examines Jewish life, between the wars, in Germany and Poland; the history of anti-Semitism; the rise of the Nazis and their particular ideology (especially its racist, sexist, homophobic, and antidemocratic elements); and the murder of Europe's Jews. Other genocidal historical episodes are looked at (such as that of the Armenians in World War I). The year concludes with the founding of the State of Israel and contemporary Middle East politics.

Issues, Ideas, Individuals, and Events That Should Be Covered

Nazis, Hitler, Himmler, Goebbels, Weimar Republic, Brownshirts, racism, anti-Semitism, master race, subhumans, Aryan, scapegoating, Nuremberg Laws, Kristallnacht, voyage of the St. Louis, ghettos, Final Solution, genocide, special action (Einsatz) groups, Babi Yar, transports, Korshak, Judenrat, SS, concentration camp, Dachau, extermination camp, selections, kapo, Auschwitz-Birkenau, Treblinka, Theresienstadt, the persecution of Roma and Sinti (Gypsies), gays, socialists, dissidents, occupation, resistance, underground, partisans, ZOB (Jewish Fighting Organization), Warsaw Ghetto Uprising, Ringelblum, Senesh, Anielewicz, Wittenberg, Sobibor Revolt, Hirsch Glick, righteous gentiles, Bonhoeffer, Scholls, Denmark rescue, Le Chambon, Nuremberg Trials, displaced persons camps, White Paper, United Nations partition vote, Ben Gurion, Labor Zionist, Revisionist Zionists, War of Independence, Six Day War, Intifada, PLO, Jim Crow, Ku Klux Klan, lynchings, SCLC, NAACP, SNCC, Fannie Lou Hamer, James Bevel, Robert Moses, Goodman, Schwerner and Chaney, Freedom Rides, sit-ins.

Some General Resources

And the Violins Stopped Playing: A Story of the Gypsy Holocaust, A. Ramati
Arabs and Jews, D. Shipler
Ben Gurion: The Burning Ground, S. Tevet
The Birth of the Palestinian Refugee Problem 1947–1949, B. Morris
Border Street (video tape)
Children of the Holocaust, H. Epstein
Clara's Story, C. Isaacman and J. Grossman
The Courage to Care: Rescuers of Jews During the Holocaust, C. Rittner and
    S. Meyers
Diary of Anne Frank (video tape)
Europa, Europa (video tape)
Eyes on the Prize (video tape)
Father of Orphans: The Story of Janusz Korczak, M. Bernheim

Genesis 1948, D. Kurzman

A History of Israel, H. Sachar

A History of Zionism, W. Laquer

Hitler's War against the Jews — The Holocaust: A Young Reader's Version of the War against the Jews, 1933–1945, by Lucy Dawidowicz, D. Altschuler

The Holocaust: A History of Courage and Resistance, B. Stadtler

The Holocaust: The Fate of European Jewry 1933–1945, L. Yahil

I Am a Star: Child of the Holocaust, I. Auerbacher

I Never Saw Another Butterfly, H. Volavkova

In Kindling Flame: The Story of Hannah Senesh, L. Atkinson

Intifada, Z. Schiff and E. Ya'ari

Lest Innocent Blood Be Shed, P. Hallie

Maus, A. Spiegelman

The Nazi Seizure of Power, S. Allen

Never to Forget: Jews of the Holocaust and *Rescue: The Story of How Gentiles Saved Jews In the Holocaust*, M. Meltzer

Night, E. Wiesel

The Other Victims: First Person Stories of Non-Jews Persecuted by the Nazis, I. Friedman

The Pink Triangle, R. Plant

The Question of Palestine, E. Said

Rescue in Denmark, H. Flender

Shoah (video tape)

The Story of Carl Stojka: A Childhood in Birkenau, publication of U.S. Holocaust Memorial Museum

The Struggle for Palestine, J. Hurewitz

Survival in Auschwitz, P. Levi

The Survivor, T. Despres

Tell Them We Remember, S. Bachrach

Their Brother's Keepers, P. Friedman

They Fought Back and *Uncle Misha's Partisans*, Y. Suhl

They Thought They Were Free: The Germans 1943–1945, M. Mayer

The Wall, J. Hersey

The White Rose, I. Scholl

Witness to the Holocaust: An Oral History, R. Lewin

The Yellow Wind, D. Grossman

The Zionist Idea, A. Hertzberg

Appendix B

THE FOLLOWING is most of the Rosh Hashanah service and some selections from the Yom Kippur service of the I. L. Peretz Shule of the Workmen's Circle in Brookline, Massachusetts, for the year 5758 (October 1997). There were approximately four hundred people in attendance. These services have been fashioned over the years by parent groups of the *shule*. Wayne Lencer, Phil Brown, Alice Rothchild, Steve Vogel, Jack Needleman, and Karen Klein have been particularly active in their development. Their efforts were aided by the work of Dick and Paula Belsey and especially by the work and ideas of Rabbi Al Axelrod.

Many of the people drawn to Secular Judaism have little knowledge of Jewish traditions. The following services address that ignorance and therefore combine didactic with ritualistic and celebratory elements. It is conceivable that in time a stable, knowledgeable Secular Jewish community will create services and rituals that do not need to contain such large sections of instruction. Still, as they stand, these services already illustrate the potential that Secular Judaism has for employing and transforming rituals from the religious Jewish traditions. The services include ancient prayers and formulas, but they also contain old and new folk songs, classic Yiddish and Hasidic tales, poems by well-known artists, and poems and reminiscences of community members. While initially each Secular Jewish community will create its own service, perhaps, in time, there will be a convergence in form and content. This convergence would not eliminate the particularity of the services of each community; there should always be space for members' personal, spiritual, and artistic expression. But in time the elements particular to one community may begin appearing in other communities. Subsequent standardization may enable the emergence of a traditional Secular Judaism.

The services are works in progress. The evolution I urge would incorporate ever more material, meaningfully secularized, from the traditional High Holiday services. I also hope for an expansion of the Yiddish and Hebrew portions of the service.

The Rosh Hashanah Service

Greetings Welcome to the new year.

We will now sing in Hebrew and Yiddish verses "Haveynu Sholem Aleichem," the welcoming song that so often opens our meetings and events.

HAVEYNU SHOLEM ALEICHEM
(May we greet each other with peace and good will.)

Haveynu sholem aleichem
Haveynu sholem aleichem
Haveynu sholem aleichem
Haveynu sholem, sholem, sholem aleichem.
Mir vilm ale nor sholem
Mir benken ale nokh sholem
Mir zingen ale far sholem
Mir rufn sholem, sholem
Sholem oyf der velt

Haveynu sholem aleichem
Haveynu sholem aleichem
Haveynu sholem aleichem
Haveynu sholem, sholem, sholem aleichem
(Translation:
All of us want peace
All of us yearn for peace
All of us sing for peace
We cry peace, peace
Peace to all the world)

For thousands of years the Jewish people have celebrated the New Year with joy, hope, and thoughtful reflection. The holidays of Rosh Hashanah and Yom Kippur presented our ancestors with time and space for self-examination and personal judgment. For religious Jews, these traditions are carried out through prayer.

But what do Rosh Hashanah and Yom Kippur mean to a community of secular Jews and our families? Today we will explore this together in our community.

Candlelighting

Traditionally each holiday begins with candlelighting. This custom has social meaning in that it engenders feelings of happiness, warmth, and a sense of unity with our sisters and brothers throughout the world with whom we are celebrating Yom Tov. It represents bringing light into darkness, hope into despair.

בָּרוּךְ אַתָּה יְיָ אֱלֹהֵינוּ, מֶלֶךְ הָעוֹלָם אֲשֶׁר קִדְּשָׁנוּ בְּמִצְוֹתָיו,
וְצִוָּנוּ לְהַדְלִיק נֵר שֶׁל־(שַׁבָּת וְ) יוֹם טוֹב.

Boruch atah Adonoi Elohenu Melech ha'olom
asher kedshanu b'mitzva so vetsivanu l'hadlich ner shel Yom Tov

Read together:

> With these lights
> We welcome the Yom Tov.
> In their glow of contrasting colors
> We discern
> The light and dark of our days.
> We recall
> All the disappointment and joys we have shared,
> And the hopes and intentions
> We now nurture for the New Year.

The History of the Holiday

Rosh Hashanah is, for the Jewish people, the beginning of a chain of harvest-time holidays. Rosh Hashanah, the New Year, marks the beginning of the Ten Days of Awe, and Yom Kippur marks the end. Four days later is Succos, when people eat meals in a *sukka,* a hut covered with materials grown from the earth. This is to remember the wandering through the desert when the Jews escaped from Egypt. Shemini Atzeret is the eighth day of Succos, when Jews pray for rain. This is followed by Simchas Torah, when the yearly cycle of Torah reading is concluded, and the congregation joyfully dances in the streets to celebrate that accomplishment.

In Jewish religious teachings, God created Adam and Eve on Rosh Hashanah, and hence it is the birthday of the world. Other momentous things happened on Rosh Hashanah: The patriarchs Abraham and Jacob were born; the matriarchs Sarah, Rachel, and Hanna gave birth to Isaac, Joseph, and Samuel; Joseph was freed from an Egyptian prison; and later, the Jews in Egypt stopped their slave labor and started the rebellion that would lead to their liberation from Egypt.

Reader: This is the first day of the Jewish New Year — a day when we come together to remember the year just past and to plan the year to come.

This is a day of joy: We are thankful for life; for the health and happiness that make life bright and good; for our dear families and for all the rich blessings that we enjoy every day.

This is a day when we express our hope that we shall be blessed with continued life, happiness, and peace. Welcome to a New Year!

Children: But how can this be a new year? It is still the old year on the calendars on our walls.

Reader: This is the new year of the Jewish calendar. This is a holiday that Jews all over the world celebrate together. In many countries, Jewish families come together to celebrate this very old holiday.

Children: But why does Rosh Hashanah happen in the fall of the year?

Reader: Thousands of years ago, the Jewish people were farmers. They decided to have a religious holiday after the fall harvest. That holiday became a new year's celebration because fall is the end of the farmer's year of work.

After the crops were harvested there was time to think about the way people were treating each other and whether their actions were right or wrong.

After several hundred more years, by the time of the Romans, the holiday became known as *Rosh Hashanah* and was thought of as the time of year when God judged the behavior of each person during the past year.

Children: But is it a good idea that we, too, celebrate our new year in the fall?

Reader: Fall is a good time for us to start a new year. The last few weeks of summer are a quiet time; vacations are over and school is just beginning. We have had time to think about the past year, to decide what was good and bad about it, and to start to make our plans for the year to come.

Children: Why do we speak and sing in Hebrew and Yiddish when we cannot always understand the words?

Reader: The Jewish people are an ancient people, almost six thousand years old. We have a rich heritage that spans all those years in many different countries. Speaking and singing in Hebrew and Yiddish helps us to remember our heritage.

He Na Ma Tov
(How Good and Pleasant It Is for People to Live Together in Unity)

He Na Ma Tov u-ma-na-im
Shevet achim gam ya-chad
He Na Ma Tov u-ma-na-im
Shevet achim gam ya-chad

He Na Ma Tov
Shevet achim gam ya-chad

He Na Ma Tov
Shevet achim gam ya-chad

Oy vi gut un vi voyl es is
Brider un shvester tzuzam

The Names of the Holiday

The holiday we are celebrating today has different names. The most familiar, of course, is Rosh Hashanah. The name *Rosh Hashanah* means the "head" or "beginning of the year." We say good-bye to the old year and welcome to the new year.

Another name is *Yom Hazikaron*, the Day of Remembering. Here the focus is on gratefully acknowledging all that the past year has brought us of life and health, of love and joy, of beauty and truth, of strength and courage. Whatever good we have known this year, we reflect upon in joy. Yet in this hour, we also reflect upon our sorrows, failures, and disappointments.

A third name for the holiday is *Yom Hadin*, the Day of Judgment. This means we have an opportunity not only to examine, but also to evaluate, our lives.

A fourth name is *Yom Teruah*, the Day of the Blowing of the Shofar. On this day the shofar is sounded to welcome in the new year.

UNETANAH TOKEF

One thousand years ago a prayer, central to the meaning of Rosh Hashanah and Yom Kippur was written. It is called "Unetanah Tokef" and is found in the traditional *machzor,* or High Holiday prayer book.

Read together:

On Rosh Hashanah it is written,
And on Yom Kippur it is sealed:

How many shall leave the world and how many shall be born,
Who shall live and who shall die,
Who shall rest and who shall wander,
Who shall be humbled and who exalted.

But
teshuvah, tefillah, tsdukah
can remove the severity of the decree.

"Unetanah Tokef" tells us that what we are shapes what we become — the child is parent to the man and woman. But it also says that we are capable of changing the outcome and that this is done by tefillah, teshuvah, and tsdukah.

Tefillah, commonly translated as "prayer" is really derived from the word for "honest self-judgment."

Tsdukah, commonly translated as "charity," is derived from the word *tsadik,* "a just person." It means justice to others.

Before we discuss *teshuvah* we have to know the meaning of the word *chet,* usually translated in English as "sin." *Chet* has its origins in archery, and the term is used to indicate "missing the mark."

Such is the Jewish concept of sin — missing one's goal and losing sight of the important things in life.

Finally, then, *teshuvah,* commonly translated as "repentance" really means "turning," turning to hit the mark.

These images — honest self-judgment, justice to others, and turning — form the central theme of our *machzor* today.

In keeping with Jewish tradition, on Rosh Hashanah and Yom Kippur we ask ourselves if we have hit the mark — as people, as families, and as a community. Whether we look for answers through prayer, as our religious brothers and sisters do, or as members of a progressive secular Jewish *shule,* the question remains important and relevant. By joining together today — different people, different families, different generations — we embrace a tradition over three thousand years old, and we benefit from a conviction that the new year can be a creative moment. Together we help each other find the courage and time to "turn."

Read together:

> It takes an act of will
> For us to make a turn.
>
> It means breaking with old habits
> It means admitting that we have been wrong;
> And this is never easy.
>
> It means losing face;
> It means starting all over again;
> And this is always painful.
>
> It means saying: "I am sorry."
> It means admitting that we have the ability to change;
> And this is always embarrassing.
>
> These things are terribly hard to do.
> But unless we turn, we will be trapped forever
> In yesterday's ways.

Turn! Turn! Turn!

Chorus:
To everything, turn, turn, turn,
There is a season, turn, turn, turn,
And a time for every purpose under heaven.

A time to be born, a time to die.
A time to plant, a time to reap.
A time to kill, a time to heal.
A time to laugh, a time to weep.
(Chorus)
A time to build up, a time to break down.
A time to dance, a time to mourn.
A time to cast away stones
A time to gather stones together.
(Chorus)
A time of love, a time of hate.
A time of war, a time of peace.
A time you may embrace.
A time to refrain from embracing.
(Chorus)
A time to gain, a time to lose.
A time to rend, a time to sew.
A time to love, a time to hate.
A time for peace, I swear it's not too late.
(Chorus)

Adapted by Pete Seeger from the Book of Ecclesiastes*

A Community of Memory

One name for this holiday is Yom Hazikaron, the Day of Remembering. Our common memory holds us together, despite war, persecution, and diaspora.

I. L. Peretz, the leader of secular Judaism for whom our *shule* is named, wrote "A people without a memory is like an individual with amnesia."

We Jews are a community by virtue of historic memory. We have been held together and upheld by common remembering. Memory performs the impossible for us; it holds together the past and present and gives continuity and dignity to human life.

---

*TRO © 1962 (Renewed) Melody Trails, Inc. New York, N.Y. Used by permission.

Read together:

> We live at any moment with our total past.
> We hate with all our past hatreds.
> We love with all our past loves.
> Every sunset we have ever seen has formed our sense of the beautiful.
> Every bar of music we have listened to is included in our response to
>   the melody which now rings in our ears.
> That is why it is so important to be cautious in what we make of each
>   day.
> It will live with us always.

Ben Zion Bokser

A Secular Amidah

The "Amidah," also called the *Shemoneh Esray,* or *Eighteen Blessings,* is the central prayer in the traditional Jewish service. For observant Jews, it is a series of praises and sanctifications of God; it offers thanks for life; it asks for peace; it asks for help in being kind to our fellow people.

Read together:

> Let us ask ourselves hard questions
> For this is the time for truth.
> > How much time did we waste
> > In the year that is now gone?
> Did we fill our days with life
> Or were they dull and empty?
> > Was there love inside our home
> > Or was the affectionate word left unsaid?
> Was there real companionship with our children
> Or was there living together and a growing apart?
> > Were we a help to our mates
> > Or did we take them for granted?
> How was it with our friends?
> Were we there when they needed us, or not?
> > The kind deed: did we perform it or postpone it?
> > The unnecessary gibe: did we say it or did we hold it back?
> Did we deceive others?
> Did we deceive ourselves?
> > Did we respect the rights and feelings
> > Of those who worked for us?

Did we acquire only possessions
Or did we acquire new insights as well?
    Did we fear what the crowd would say
    And keep quiet when we should have spoken out?
Did we mind only our own business
Or did we feel the heartbreak of others?
    Did we live right,
    And, if not,
    Then have we learned
    And will we change?

A Community of People

Jews band together as a community, so even when they are far from their original home they have a community. On my family's annual trek from Florida to New York, we pass through many small towns along small highways. In South Carolina, in 1962, my parents and I were intrigued by a little sign on a lamppost that directed us to the local temple. How odd to see this sign in such an out-of-the-way place. We followed the sign, located the temple, and entered. I do not know what day it was, but there were nine men waiting for a tenth. What an amazing coincidence. I was thirteen, five months past my bar mitzvah, and I completed the community. In passing we shared with that community, embracing what was something of a patriarchal tradition, and we went on our way. Thirty years later that encounter is still in my heart as a piece of the historic Jewish community.

Rosh Hashanah is a day when the neighborhood resounds with the activity of a community. I remember one New Year in Brighton Beach, going from shul to shul with a woman friend; we were intent on sitting together, even in the Orthodox shuls. All the people in the neighborhood were out and about with no preoccupation other than being together on Rosh Hashanah. As a full-day observance, Rosh Hashanah draws people into the center of observance, even if they participate in no other religious activity all year. The streets pulsed with festivity amid the gravity of the holiday. Apparently Rosh Hashanah can be a kind of street festival.

Phil Brown (1992)

Consider that the Jewish religion does not require an official clergy to lead prayer — a minyan of believers suffices. Thus, it is community that is central to the values and ethics of Judaism. It is immensely important that on the Days of Awe it is not a deity that can give complete forgiveness; only another person can forgive us for the hurt we have caused them. Thus it is the community of people that Judaism embraces; we need no god to create the bonds of life.

Shema

The "Shema" is often considered the singular statement of belief in Judaism. Jews facing their deaths as martyrs struggled to chant the "Shema" so as to make their belief and their community of people endure. During regular prayers, the "Shema" rises up in tremendous strength, loud and full and resonant, summoning the collectivity of the congregation. We may also view the "Shema" in a secular fashion — as a statement of unity.

We, the Jewish people, are one. We, our community of people, are one.

שְׁמַע יִשְׂרָאֵל. יְהֹוָה אֱלֹהֵינוּ, יְהֹוָה אֶחָד.

Shema Yisroel Adonoi Elohenu Adonoi Echad.

A Secular Shema

You who live secure
    In your warm houses,
    Who, returning at evening, find
    Hot food and friendly faces:
        Consider whether this is a man,
        Who labors in the mud
        Who knows no peace
        Who fights for a crust of bread
        Who dies at a yes or a no.

        Consider whether this is a woman
        Without hair or name
        With no more strength to remember
        Eyes empty and womb cold
        As a frog in winter.

Consider that this has been:
I commend these words to you.
Engrave them on your hearts
When you are in your house,
When you walk on your way
When you go to bed, when you rise;
Repeat them to your children.

Primo Levi

At this point in the service, the congregation sings Bob Dylan's "Blowin' in the Wind."

The Shofar

The Jewish people, many many years ago, announced the beginning of the new year by blowing a shofar, a musical instrument made of a sheep's horn. Actually, they blew the shofar to announce the first day of every month, Rosh Chodesh, which always starts when a new moon appears, every twenty-nine days.

But on the first day of the New Year, they blew the shofar especially loud and long. They blew to get the attention of their God, and to ask their God to remember them and be kind to them in the new year. Then they blew it again to tell the people to think carefully about the year just past and to be sorry for the things that they had done wrong.

The shofar call for the New Year has four parts that are repeated several times and that end with a very long blast. They are:

> T'kiah
> Sh'varim
> T'ruah
> T'kiah

> Call out the shofar's notes and it will answer.
> (Shofar blasts)

May the sound of the shofar awaken us to the flight of time,
And summon us to spend our days with purpose.

May the sound of the shofar shatter our complacency
And make us conscious of our weaknesses and our strengths.

> May the sound of the shofar remind us that it is time
> to "Proclaim liberty throughout the land
> and for all the inhabitants thereof."

> (Shofar blasts)

Our Ties to Others

We have come together in our *shule* community to draw strength from our traditions and from one another in order to meet the challenges of tefillah, tsdukah, and teshuvah — of honest self-judgment, justice to others, and turning to better hit the mark.

One of the most compelling aspects of our Jewish tradition is that we are asked to take responsibility for others as well as ourselves.

The great sage Hillel said, "If I am not for myself, who will be for me? But if I am only for myself, who am I?"

read together:

> We must decide for ourselves how to make a better year. We will stop
> and think and begin again.
> Did we love our family?
>> Or did we forget to say a kind word?
> Did we share?
>> Or just think of ourselves?

> Did we help?
>> Or let someone else do the work?
> How about our friends?
>> Can they trust us and depend on us?
>> Do we feel sorry for them when they are sad?
> Were we fair to others?
> Or were we sometimes dishonest?
> Did we decide for ourselves what is right and wrong?
> Or did we just follow what others do?

Making Peace

At all of our holidays, we speak of the desire for peace. Living together in
harmony with all people in the world is central to our ethical framework. We
wish to help heal the wounds and divisions between peoples all over the world.

read together:

> May we see the day when war and bloodshed cease,
> When a wondrous peace will embrace the world,
> When nation will not threaten nation,
> When humankind will not experience war.

> For all who inhabit this world shall realize
> That we have not come into being
> To argue, to hate, or to be violent.
> For we have come into being
> To praise, to labor, and to love.

> Have we paid enough attention to the world around us? Let us begin
>> the new year with our hearts and minds rising to the winds of
>> peace.

>> I had a box of colors —
>> Shining, bright and bold.

I had a box of colors,
Some warm, some very cold.

I had no red for the blood of wounds.
I had no black for the orphans' grief.
I had no white for dead faces and hands.
I had no yellow for burning sands.

But I had orange for the joy of life,
And I had green for buds and nests.
I had blue for bright, clear skies.
I had pink for dreams and rest.

I sat down
and painted
Peace.

Tali Sorek, age 13, Beersheba, Israel

ALE BRIDER
(All Brothers)

This song has traditionally been sung at progressive and secular Jewish gatherings, and is closely associated with the Jewish labor movement. It has become a voice for the unity of purpose and the harmony amongst people. "Ale Brider" is based on the poem "Akhedes," or "Brotherhood," by Morris Winchevsky (1856–1932).

Un mir zaynen ale brider
Oy, oy, ale brider
Un mir zingen freylekhe lider
Oy, oy, oy

Un mir haltn zikh in eynem
Oy, oy, zikh in eynem
Azelkhes iz nito bay keynem
Oy, oy, oy

Chorus

Un mir zaynen ale shvester
Oy, oy, ale shvester
Vi Sore, Rivke, Rut un Ester
Oy, oy, oy

Un mir zaynen ale eynik
Oy, oy, ale eynik

Tzi mir zaynen fil tzi veynik

Oy, oy, oy

Chorus

(Translation: For we are all brothers and sisters and sing happy songs. We stay together, like nobody else does. We are all sisters like Sarah, Rebecca, Ruth, and Esther. We are all united, whether we are many or few.)

Yizkor

One of the most moving hours of Rosh Hashanah and Yom Kippur is the time set aside for remembering the dead. We recite "Yizkor" to remember those who have gone before, to remind ourselves how we should live.

Read together:

> This is the time we remember
> Those who gave meaning to our lives.
> This is the time we remember
> The bonds that tied us together,
> The love that we shared,
> And the memories that remain with us still.

We all rise and take this time to share the memory of family or friends who have passed away.

Where Will I Be?

> Do not come when I am dead
> To sit beside a low green mound,
> or bring the first gay daffodils,
> Because I love them so,
> For I shall not be there.
> You cannot find me there.
> Where will I be?
> I will be reflected from the bright eyes of little children;
> In the smile of a bride under the chupah;
> In the flames of Shabbat candles at the family simcha.
> I will warm your hands through the glow
> Of the winter fire;
> I will soothe you with the drop
> Of the rain on the roof;
> I will speak to you out of the wisdom
> Of the sages;

And make your heart leap with the
Rhythm of a hora;
I will flood your soul with the flaming radiance
Of the sunrise,
And bring you peace in the tender rose and gold
Of the after-sunset.
All these have made me happy.
They are a part of me;
I shall become a part of them.

Author unknown

May our lives be worthy of remembrance and provide sustenance and purpose to others after we die. Thus the lives of those before us, ourselves, and those who live to continue the work will be linked for all time.

KADDISH

It is an ancient custom to kindle a *yahrzeit* candle and recite kaddish for the departed. We rise to say the "Kaddish."

The Mourner's Kaddish

MOURNERS

יִתְגַּדַּל וְיִתְקַדַּשׁ שְׁמֵהּ רַבָּא בְּעָלְמָא דִּי־בְרָא
כִרְעוּתֵהּ. וְיַמְלִיךְ מַלְכוּתֵהּ בְּחַיֵּיכוֹן וּבְיוֹמֵיכוֹן וּבְחַיֵּי
דְכָל בֵּית יִשְׂרָאֵל בַּעֲגָלָא וּבִזְמַן קָרִיב וְאִמְרוּ אָמֵן:

CONGREGATION AND MOURNERS

יְהֵא שְׁמֵהּ רַבָּא מְבָרַךְ לְעָלֵם וּלְעָלְמֵי עָלְמַיָּא:

MOURNERS

יִתְבָּרַךְ וְיִשְׁתַּבַּח וְיִתְפָּאַר וְיִתְרוֹמַם וְיִתְנַשֵּׂא וְיִתְהַדָּר
וְיִתְעַלֶּה וְיִתְהַלָּל שְׁמֵהּ דְּקוּדְשָׁא בְּרִיךְ הוּא. לְעֵלָּא מִן־
כָּל־בִּרְכָתָא וְשִׁירָתָא תֻּשְׁבְּחָתָא וְנֶחֱמָתָא דַּאֲמִירָן
בְּעָלְמָא וְאִמְרוּ אָמֵן:

MOURNERS

יְהֵא שְׁלָמָא רַבָּא מִן שְׁמַיָּא וְחַיִּים עָלֵינוּ וְעַל כָּל
יִשְׂרָאֵל וְאִמְרוּ אָמֵן:

MOURNERS

עֹשֶׂה שָׁלוֹם בִּמְרוֹמָיו הוּא יַעֲשֶׂה שָׁלוֹם עָלֵינוּ וְעַל־
כָּל יִשְׂרָאֵל. וְאִמְרוּ אָמַן:

The Mourner's Kaddish

READER AND MOURNERS

Yisgadal v'yiskadash sh'me rabbo, b'olmo deevro chiruseh v'yamlich mal-
chuseh, b'chayechon uvyo-mechon, uv'chayey d'chol beys yisroel, baagolo
uvizman koreev, v'imru omen.

CONGREGATION

Y'he sh'meh rabbo m'vorach l'olam ulolmey olmayo.

READER AND MOURNERS

Yisborach v'yishtabach v'yispo-ar v'yisromam v'yisnasch v'yis-hador v'yisa-
ley v'yishal-lol sh'meh d'kud-sho b'reech hu, l'elo min col birchoso v'shiroso
tushb'choso v'nechemoso daamiron b'olmo, v'imru omen.

Y'he sh'lomo rabbo min sh'mayo v'chayim olenu v'al col yisroel, v'imru
omen.

Oseh sholom bimromov, hu ya-aseh sholom olenu v'al col yisroel, v'imru
omen.

THEIR MEMORIES ILLUMINE OUR WORLD

There are stars whose light reaches the earth only after they themselves have
disintegrated. And there are individuals whose memory lights the world after
they have passed from it. These lights shine in the darkest night and illumine
for us the path.

-Hannah Senesch

At this point in the service, the congregation sings Phil Ochs's "When I'm
Gone."

THIS IS THE BEGINNING OF THE NEW YEAR

Read together:

This is the beginning of the New Year.
We are given this year
    to use as we will.
We can waste it,

or grow in its light
and be of service to others.
But what we do
with this year is important
because we will have exchanged
a year of our lives for it.
The last year is now.
May we not regret the price paid for it.
May we create for ourselves, our family, friends, and community a
year of health,
happiness, and peace. We especially take this time to welcome our new
shule members.

Shalom Chaverim
(Greetings of Peace to Our Friends)
Shalom chaverim, shalom chaverim, shalom, shalom
L'hit ray-ot, l'hit ray-ot, shalom, shalom.

At the end of the service we will eat apples and honey. The honey symbolizes our hope for sweetness in the year ahead. We shall then walk to the pond to perform Tashlikh. And now we say:

לשנה טובה תכתבו

L'Shana Tova Tikateivu
May you be written down for a good year.

Tashlikh

On the first day or Rosh Hashanah, Jews throw bread into water, preferably moving water, that contains fish. The tradition derives from the Book of Micah, where is is written: "And You [God] shall throw their sins into the depth of the sea." It is preferable that there be fish in the moving water into which we throw Tashlikh, since the "evil eye" supposedly cannot penetrate deeply enough to reach the fish.

Other customs from Jewish literature and folklore have contributed additional elements to the Tashlikh traditions. Often, people shake their clothes to symbolically shake out their sins. In some places, Jews even jump into the water to cleanse themselves.

Commentators have written about many symbolic themes in the Tashlikh ceremony: Water takes on many shapes, allowing our sins to float away. Water also represents purity, the purity we aspire to when we seek to turn and change our lives. When the world was created, before the land, plants, animals, and people inhabited it, it consisted only of water. So Tashlikh brings us full circle to the creation, the birthday and new year of the world.

In recent years, the Tashlikh ceremony has become a very public gathering, a social event in which people from various congregations and homes come together to share in the spirit of seeking forgiveness for wrongs they have committed. In this light, it is a fitting part of the *shule*'s tradition.

Read together:

> Let us think deeply, as deeply as the water
> As we throw out the actions we have done that we dislike,
> The actions we have done to hurt others.
>
> Let us watch the reflections of ourselves and the world
> Shimmering in the water, ever-changing,
> As we reflect on our year past and our year to come.
>
> Let us watch the bread drift on the currents,
> Swirling away that which we have cast out.
>
> The bread will fall apart and become part of the water,
> As we become part of the new year.
>
> Dear family, dear friends,
> We are sorry for the hurts we have caused.
> Let us all cleanse ourselves and start anew.

Read together:

> L'shana tova tikateivu. May you be written down for a good year.

Only parts of the Yom Kippur service used at the Brookline Workmen's Circle Shule are reproduced below.

Selections from a Secular Yom Kippur Service

Greetings. Welcome to the Yom Kippur service. Today we end the Ten Days of Awe, the period from Rosh Hashanah to Yom Kippur. This is the most important time in the Jewish calendar — a time for reflection, forgiveness, healing, and turning anew.

Kol Nidre

Erev Yom Kippur, the evening that starts the holiday, is often called *Kol Nidre Night*. For centuries, the chanting of the Kol Nidre service has been an intensely emotional experience. Composers, Jewish and non-Jewish, have been inspired to write musical settings for Kol Nidre. The words *Kol Nidre* mean "all vows." The Kol Nidre is actually not a prayer. Rather, it is a legal formula, whose purpose is to cancel vows of the past year that we have been unable to fulfill. As early as the eighth century, Jews sought to be absolved from vows they had made to God. As we so often hear, promises between people could not be absolved by asking God but only by consulting with the people involved.

It has often been said that the Kol Nidre was used to release Spanish Jews — who had been forced, under pain of death, to convert to Catholicism — from the vows they had been required to make as part of the conversion.

We can learn from Kol Nidre that it is a powerful thing to promise something and that we should live up to it. People depend on each other and need to be able to trust each other to follow through. Today, on Yom Kippur, we acknowledge the importance of keeping our promises.

Read together:

> All vows, promises, and commitments we made
> since last Yom Kippur and in the years before —
> May we be given strength to keep them
> But even as we vow next time
> We are conscious how last time
> We failed.

Kol Nidre reminds us that there are abiding values of the utmost importance to each of us, that sometimes we cannot maintain faithfulness to these values, and that we are not isolated and alone in this very human situation.

Rabbi Allen S. Maller

The Meaning of the Holiday

Leader: On Rosh Hashanah we began our celebration of the Days of Awe, ten days in which we reflect on the year we have just concluded and prepare for the year before us. For us, as for our ancestors, this ten-day period presents us with time and space for self-examination, personal judgment, and thoughtful reflection on the year to come. Yom Kippur concludes this very special period.

Children: What is Yom Kippur?

Leader: In ancient times, before the Babylonian exile, Rosh Hashanah, Yom Kippur, and Succot were all linked together as a harvest festival. In the Diaspora, there was a change in the observance of the holiday, and Rosh Hashanah and Yom Kippur took on separate roles.

Children: Why do we return ten days after Rosh Hashanah? Doesn't that holiday allow us enough time for reflection?

Leader: Reflection and change are lifelong endeavors. During the Ten Days of Awe, we repeat our lifelong commitment to making the world whole. Religious Jews believe that on Rosh Hashanah the book of life is opened and that on Yom Kippur it is sealed. As secular Jews, we may think of this as a period that requires us first to present a challenge and then gives us the time to reflect on how we can meet that challenge.

Children: But if this is about personal reflection and change, why do it in public?

Leader: There are many possible answers to this question. One is that it is not easy to make change and that we need to work together to do so.

One feature of the traditional Yom Kippur service is the public acknowledgment that we have sometimes missed the mark or fallen short. This embodies the recognition that it is hard to say that we need to turn. When we all say this together, it encourages us to heed that we are not alone. Together we can help one another find the courage and time to turn.

Also, by participating in a ceremony, we recognize that we are not only separate individuals. We become who we are in relation to others. The new directions we wish to take put us on a journey with others.

Children: Why do some people fast on Yom Kippur?

Leader: Observant Jews fast on Yom Kippur, neither eating nor drinking for one day. Although we might not do the same, it is worthwhile to consider the many meanings of fasting. First, by making a sacrifice, people can demonstrate that their repentance is deeply felt. Second, people may fast to remind themselves about self-control, thereby becoming better people in the year ahead. Third, fasting enables individuals to stop focusing on the needs of the body and instead to begin focusing the mind on the spiritual concerns of the holiday. Fourth, through fasting one is able to sense what hunger means and thus be more compassionate toward those who are always hungry.

Ashamnu and Al Chet

The "Ashamnu" and "Al Chet" are two confessional prayers that play a central role in the traditional Yom Kippur service; they are recited ten times. They were written as alphabetic acrostics, using all twenty-two letters of the Hebrew alphabet. "Ashamnu" lists "Of these things we have been guilty . . . " "Al Chet" lists "For the sins we have committed . . . " In these prayers, people seek forgiveness for a large number of actions, many of which they may not have even committed. For secular Jews, the "Ashamnu" and "Al Chet" remind us that we are fallible, and they invite us to reflect in honest self-judgment on the past year and to think seriously about how we will turn to hit the mark in the year to come. Even though we do not ask God for forgiveness, we, as secular Jews still ask for forgiveness from each other and ourselves.

The Meaning of Kippur

We should examine the meaning of another word that is central to this day. The word *kippur* is translated variously. We usually think of it as meaning "atonement." But a more literal translation is "covering sin." This means that there is no abstract forgiveness or absolution. Our actions cannot be undone. Instead, we repair or cover the action and begin afresh. We cannot remove the wrongdoing, but we can make amends, ask for and extend forgiveness, and seek to do better in the future.

We should also note that many of the transgressions listed in the "Ashamnu" and "Al Chet" are moral, not religious. They deal with the daily life of human beings. "Ashamnu" and "Al Chet" can remind Secular Jews that true forgiveness is between people.

It is significant that both of these listings are formulated in the first person plural — we. This reminds us that we are all in one community and responsible for each other.

YOM KIPPUR REFLECTIONS

Atonement, Judgment Day,
A Time of Reckoning,
Are too patriarchal for me,
The small child/person,
Humbled before her maker, father,
Hoping to be good enough,
For the Book of Life.

This metaphor
Does not inspire
The rebel, nonbeliever,
Reaching for empowerment and voice and place,
In this world.

So what does it mean
To have a conscience?
To be conscious and accountable?

What does it mean
To reflect on losses and celebrate victories,

With each other and our children,
Together?

Perhaps, to be held accountable
For my actions and the fate of my sisters and brothers,
Earns me the right
To be part of a community.

Perhaps, to be conscious
Earns me the task
Of sharing this awareness,
With my children

And yours.

Alice Rothchild

At this point in the service, the congregation sings Ruth Pelham's "Turning of the World."

What are all the blessings about in our prayers? What is the meaning of the "Kaddish" and other prayers, both religious originals and secular alternatives? They are about finding the good, the healthy, the holy in ourselves. We have created this world we live in. We are responsible for those around us. We make the lives we live. And thus, we need to discover what is holy in ourselves. Our self-reflection, our companionship with others, and our good deeds are ways that we can sanctify ourselves and our world.

Yussel's Prayer: A Yom Kippur Story

This is a slightly revised version of Barbara Cohen's retelling of a Yom Kippur story. Although it speaks about God, the lessons for secular Jews are clear.

In a small town in Poland, Yom Kippur was beginning. Everyone was on their way to temple, where they would pray all day, fasting and seeking forgiveness for things they had done wrong over the year. Actually, one person was not going to shul—Yussel, the orphan boy who worked in Reb Meir's dairy barn. He had never been taught anything, so he had little education, but he did know that this was a special day. Yussel stood in the courtyard, waiting for Reb Meir. Reb Meir came out with his sons; they were all wearing long black coats and large fur hats. Yussel tugged at Reb Meir's sleeve and asked, "Please, may I go to shul and pray with everyone else?"

"No," replied Reb Meir. "The cows must be tended. They don't know it's Yom Kippur. Besides, what good would it do you to go to shul? You can't read, so how could you understand the prayer book? How could you pray?"

So Yussel went off to the barn and called the cows, who came as they always did. He picked up his reed pipe and played so that the cows would follow him to the river. But Yussel did not stop at the kitchen, as usual, to beg for a piece of black bread from the cook. If he could not pray, at least he could fast.

Reb Meir and his sons, wealthy leaders of the community, sat in seats of honor by the eastern wall of the synagogue. They were nearest to the rabbi, who was widely respected and who, many felt, spoke directly with God. Reb Meir spoke the words of the prayers, but he was not really concentrating. His mind was on his business. He thought to himself. "If I can buy a thousand bushels of grain in Lublin next week, I can store it in my barns until deep winter sets in and then sell it at a great profit." Reb Meir's oldest son also mouthed the words, but he was daydreaming about asking his father to allow him to visit Warsaw. He thought to himself, "What a boring town this is. It will be so exciting to visit the theaters and restaurants of Warsaw."

All day Reb Meir and his sons prayed and fasted along with the rest of the congregation. The day seemed endless. There were many times when instead of praying for forgiveness of their sins, Reb Meir and his sons prayed only for darkness. When they saw the sun sinking in the west, they were sure that the closing prayers were near and that soon they would be finished and able to go home to eat. But the rabbi continued praying, reminding the people to listen to the words of all those celebrating Yom Kippur everywhere. Reb Meir began to think that if the rabbi did not begin the closing "Ne'lah" prayer in two minutes, he would leave anyway.

Yussel had also had a long day. His cows ate and drank, but Yussel did not even touch water to his lips. When the sun sank in the west, he picked up his reed pipe and cried out, "O God. I don't know any prayers. But I do know how to play the pipe. Since I can't give you my words, I give you this tune instead." On his pipe Yussel played a song of his own creation; it stemmed from deep inside him. He felt at peace with the earth, the stars, and the animals. Most of all, he felt at peace with himself.

At that very moment, the rabbi began to chant the "Ne'lah" prayers, asking God to seal the people in the Book of Life. He picked up the shofar and blew a long blast that echoed far out into the streets of the town. Yom Kippur was over. Reb Meir went to the rabbi and wished him *l'shana tova,* Happy New Year. "I have a question, Rabbi," Reb Meir said. "Why did you wait so long to begin "Ne'lah" and bring Yom Kippur to an end?" The rabbi looked into Reb Meir's eyes and replied, "I had a vision. In my vision I saw that the gates of heaven were closed. Our prayers weren't reaching God. They were not acceptable to Him."

"Why?" asked Reb Meir.

The rabbi shrugged. "I'm not sure," he said. "I think because they didn't come from the heart. And how could I end Yom Kippur when I felt that God wouldn't grant us forgiveness and mercy because he hadn't heard us ask for it?"

"But then you did," Reb Meir said. "Then you did end Yom Kippur."

The rabbi nodded. "I had another vision," he went on. "I heard a melody, a simple melody played on a reed pipe. I saw the gates of heaven open up. All our prayers went in to God, because he had opened the gates to admit that melody."

"But why?" asked Reb Meir. "Why just a tune on a reed pipe and not all the holy words we were saying?"

"Because," said the rabbi, "whoever sent that melody sent it with his whole heart. It was a true prayer."

Reb Meir left the shul with his head down and eyes thoughtful. On his way home he met Yussel, coming back from the pasture with the cows. By the light of the moon that shone above them, Reb Meir saw the little reed pipe in Yussel's hand.

"*L'shana tova*, Yussel," said Reb Meir.

"*L'shana tova*, Reb Meir," Yussel replied. He could hardly believe that this important man was wishing him a happy new year.

"Will you come into my house, Yussel?" asked Reb Meir. "Will you break the fast with me and my family?"

"Father!" exclaimed Reb Meir's eldest son. "He's so dirty and so ragged. How can you let him into the house?"

"Very easily," spoke Reb Meir. "Through the front door." He put his arm around Yussel's shoulders. Together they walked up the moonlit street, all of Reb Meir's sons and all of Yussel's cows trailing behind.

L'DOR V'ADOR
(From Generation to Generation)

Unto all generations, we remember.
We trace the names, shreds of books,
Faded Hebrew calligraphy on tombstones,
Marks of settlements,
Remnants to rebuild with.
In religious tradition, God writes our names in the Book of Life,
To determine our next year,
To number our days.
We may also think in another way
About the names in the Book of Life.
The Jewish people have much history to remember,
Many journeys to document, many relatives to locate,

As we have moved through the countries, empires, and epochs.
And so, we have always listed names,
From the Bible on forward,
To see where we have come from.
To know who we are, we must know where we come from.
It is our duty to mark and remember and tell.
Let us recount the stories of our ancestors and our families
We are a small part of a long journey
That we can tell to our children
To tell to theirs.

Phil Brown (October 1997)

KADDISH

Memories are the stones and mulch,
That shape the gardens of our lives.

Sophie, Hannah, Moishe, Gittel,
Susan, Harold, Miriam, Glen,
The naming of the dead
Wraps us in the shroud of their presence,
And the thread of memories
Binds our voices and visions together.

The gnarled, tremulous hand; the tight white bun, braided
    meticulously,
The angry yelling; the morning davening,
The proud face; the far away look of eyes that have long stopped
    seeing,
The defiant Communist; the suburbanite, two car garage and perfect
    50s lawn.

"It was his heart, it just gave out."
"Breast cancer, she was so young."
"His mind wandered and wandered until it just wandered away."
"My brother, he drowned, it was so terrible."
"The car swerved on the ice, they didn't have a chance."

We bear so many losses,
And each year there are more.
Some hacked abruptly from our lives.
Some fading away with the pain and infirmity that says, enough
    already, it's time to let go.

For some, the Kaddish holds us and rocks us with a sound and comfort
that is hundreds of years old.
For some, the bearing of witness amongst friends, the communal
shedding of tears,
Floats us in the sea of grief and survival.

And as we look up,
We see the faces of our lost ones,
Twinkling in the eyes of our children.

Alice Rothchild

Vine and Fig Tree

And everyone 'neath their vine and fig tree
Shall live in peace and unafraid.
And everyone 'neath their vine and fig tree
Shall live in peace and unafraid.

And into ploughshares beat their swords
Nations shall learn war no more.
And into ploughshares beat their swords
Nations shall learn war no more.

Lo yisa goy el goy cherev
Lo yilmadu od milchama

Lo yisa goy el goy cherev
Lo yilmadu od milchama

The Tradition of the Shofar

Read together:

On Rosh Hashanah Day
We listened
And we heard
The sounds of the shofar
Calling to us,
To listen!
To remember!
To think and dream
Of all that we have done,
And of things we might do.

Now, we hear again
The sounds of the shofar
This time telling us
To go from these holiday services
Into the days of the New Year.
With love in our hearts,
Understanding in our thoughts,
And a promise and a wish
To make each day of the New Year
One of challenge and growth.

A time for bringing
Hope into our lives,
Brightness into the lives of
Those we love,
And pleasantness into the lives
Of friends, strangers,
And people everywhere.

We again blow the shofar to awaken ourselves to the tasks facing us.
Tekiah
Shevarim
Teruah
Tekiah

With the sound of the shofar, we take with us the memories and hopes
we have spoken of and enter the new year.

Gut Yontif. Gut Yahr.

Works Cited

Adorno, Theodor. 1967. *Prisms.* Translated by Sam and Sherry Weber. London: Neville Spearman Ltd.

Appiah, Anthony. 1994. "Reflections on Taylor." In *Multiculturalism.* Edited by Amy Gutterman. Princeton: Princeton University Press.

Berger, Peter. 1995. *A Far Glory: The Quest for Faith in the Age of Credulity.* New York: Free Press.

Berkovits, Eliezer. 1973. *Faith after the Holocaust.* New York: Ktav.

Berlin, Isaiah. 1965. *Against the Current.* New York: Viking.

———. 1996. "On Political Judgment." *New York Review of Books* 43 (15).

Bershtel, Sara, and Allen Graubard. 1992. *Saving Remnants.* Berkeley: University of California Press.

Blum, Lawrence, 1995. "The Holocaust and Moral Education." *Philosophy and Public Policy* (Spring/Summer).

Brenner, Robert. 1980. *The Faith and Doubt of Holocaust Survivors.* New York: Free Press.

Bush, Larry. 1986. Address to Camp Kinderland Conference on "Secular Jewish Rituals." Tolland, Massachusetts.

Camus, Albert. 1942. *The Myth of Sisyphus.* Translated by Justin O'Brien (1955). New York: Alfred Knopf.

Cantor, Norman. 1994. *The Sacred Chain.* New York: Harper Collins.

Comte, Auguste. 1853. *System of Positive Philosophy.* Translated by Henry Martineau (1853). London: Brown.

Curtain, H. 1994. *Language and Children, Making the Match.* White Plains, N.Y.: Longman.

Diamant, Anita. 1988. *Jewish Baby Book.* New York: Summit.

Dostoyevsky, Fyodor. 1880. *The Brothers Karamazov.* Translated by Andrew McAndrews (1977). New York: Bantam.

Dubnow, Shimon. 1903. *Jewish History.* New York: Books for Libraries Press [1972].

Fackenheim, Emil. 1970. *God's Presence in History.* New York: New York University Press.

Falk, Marcia. 1989. "Toward a Feminist Reconstruction of Monotheism." *Tikkun* 3 (4).

Fein, Leonard. 1994. *Smashing Idols and Other Prescriptions for Jewish Continuity.* New York: Cumming Foundation Press.

Feld, Edward. 1995. "Beyond Silence." *Tikkun* 10 (4).

Fishman, Jacob. 1981. *Never Say Die.* The Hague: Mouton Publishers.

Gavison, Ruth. 1996. "Values of the State of Israel as a Democratic and a Jewish State." Public lecture delivered at the Shalom Hartman Institute, 24 October. Jerusalem.

Geertz, Clifford. 1973. *The Interpretation of Cultures.* New York: Basic Books.

Goodman, Saul. 1976. *The Faith of Secular Jews.* New York: Ktav.

Gottlieb, Roger. 1990. *Thinking the Unthinkable.* Mahwah, N.J.: Paulist Press.

Gramsci, Antonio. 1975. *Selections from the Prison Notebooks.* New York: International Press.

Haack, Susan. 1995. *Evidence and Inquiry.* London: Blackwell.

Habermas, Jurgen. 1992. *Faktizitaet und Geltung.* Frankfurt am Main: Suhrkamp.

Heschel, Susannah. 1983. *On Being a Jewish Feminist.* New York: Schocken.

Hobsbawm, Eric. 1994. *The Age of Extremes.* New York: Pantheon Books.

Howe, Irving. 1976. *The World of Our Fathers.* New York: Simon and Schuster.

Hume, David. 1779. *The Dialogues on Natural Religion* (published posthumously). Edited by Henry Aiken (1948). London: Hafner edition.

Johnson, Barbara. 1993. *Psychiatric Mental Health Nursing.* 3d ed. Philadelphia: J. P. Lippincott.

Jospe, A., and L. Yahil. 1972. In *The Encyclopedia Judaica.* Edited by Cecil Roth. Jerusalem: Keter Publishing Co.

Kaplan, Mordecai. 1934. *Judaism as Civilization.* New York: Macmillan Press.

Kennedy, D. F. 1985. *Complete Guide to Exploratory Foreign Language Programs.* Chicago: National Textbooks.

Kierkegaard, Søren. 1843. *Fear and Trembling.* Translated by Walter Lowrie (1941). Princeton: Princeton University Press.

Kymlicka, William. 1989. *Liberalism, Community and Culture.* Oxford: Oxford University Press.

Landis, John. 1981. "Who Needs Yiddish." In Fishman, *Never Say Die.*

Langer, Lawrence. 1995a. *Admitting the Holocaust.* Oxford: Oxford University Press.

———. 1995b. "No Cause for Celebration." *Tikkun* 10 (3).

Lerner, Michael. 1996. "The Rabin Assassination," *Tikkun* 11 (1).

Liebman, Charles. 1972. "Reconstruction." In *The Encyclopedia Judaica*. Edited by Cecil Roth. Jerusalem: Keter Publishing Co.

Lind, Michael. 1995. *The Next American Nation*. New York: Free Press.

Liptzin, Saul. 1972. "Czernowitz." In *The Encyclopedia Judaica*. Edited by Cecil Roth. Jerusalem: Keter Publishing Co.

MacIntyre, Alastair. 1984. *After Virtue*. South Bend: Notre Dame University Press.

Marx, Karl. 1845. *Theses on Feuerbach*. Translated by David McClellan (1977). Oxford: Oxford University Press.

———. 1977. *Selected Writings*. Translated by David McClellan. Oxford: Oxford University Press.

Moore, Thomas. 1992. *The Care of the Soul*. New York: HarperCollins.

Nagel, Thomas. 1986. *The View from Nowhere*. New York: Oxford University Press.

Netanyahu, Benzion. 1995. *The Origins of the Inquisition in 15th Century Spain*. New York: Random House.

Nietzsche, Friedrich. 1886. *Beyond Good and Evil*. Translated by Walter Kaufman (1966). New York: Vintage.

Nozick, Robert. 1974. *Anarchy, State and Utopia*. New York: Basic Books.

Nussbaum, Martha. 1994. "The Fall." *Boston Review*.

Parker, Susan. 1981. "An Educational Assessment of the Yiddish Secular School Movement in the United States." In Fishman, *Never Say Die*.

Petuchowski, J. 1972. "Reform." In *The Encyclopedia Judaica*. Edited by Cecil Roth. Jerusalem: Keter Publishing Co.

Pinsker, Leon. 1881. *Autoemancipation*.

Plaskow, Judith. 1990. *Standing at Sinai*. New York: Harper and Row.

Pogrebin, Letty Cotton. 1991. *Deborah, Golda and Me*. New York: Crown.

Popper, Karl. 1962. *The Open Society and Its Enemies*. Princeton: Princeton University Press.

Rawls, John. 1993. *Political Liberalism*. New York: Columbia University Press.

Riskin, Shlomo. 1996. "Aliyah and Jewish Identity Go Together." *Jerusalem Post* 6 September 6.

Roth, Cecil, ed. 1972. "Reform." In *The Encyclopedia Judaica*. Jerusalem: Keter Publishing Co.

Roth, Philip. 1967. *Portnoy's Complaint*. New York: Random House.

———. 1993. *Operation Shylock*. New York: Simon and Schuster.

Rubinoff, Lionel. 1993. "The Challenge of Auschwitz." In *Jewish Identity*. Edited by David Theo Goldberg and Michael Krausz. Philadelphia: Temple University Press.

Rudavsky, David. 1967. *Modern Jewish Religious Movements*. New York: Behrman House.

Sachar, Howard Morley. 1979. *A History of Israel*. New York: Alfred Knopf.

Sartre, Jean Paul. 1943. *Being and Nothingness*. Translated by Hazel Barnes (1956). New York: Washington Square Press.

Sayles, John. 1996. *Lone Star*. A film written and directed by John Sayles.

Schwartz, Sidney. 1994. "Students' Ideas of God." *The Reconstructionist* 59 (1).

Seeskin, Kenneth. 1995. "Jewish Philosophy—a Persuasive Definition." American Philosophical Association address, New York.

Silver, Mitchell. 1993. "Reply to Goldman." *Friends of Massachusetts Midwives* (Winter).

Steiner, George. 1995. *Perspectives in the Holocaust*. Boulder: Westview Press.

Taylor, Charles. 1994. "The Politics of Recognition." In *Multiculturalism*. Edited by Amy Gutterman. Princeton: Princeton University Press.

Trunk, Isaiah. 1976. "The Cultural Dimension of the Yiddish Labor Movement." *Yearbook of YIVO Institute for Jewish Research*. Vol. 16. New York: Yivo Books.

Wittgenstein, Ludwig. 1953. *Philosophical Investigations*. Translated by G. E. Anscombe. New York: Macmillan.

Zemach, Eddy. 1993. "Custodians." In *Jewish Identity*. Edited by David Theo Goldberg and Michael Krausz. Philadelphia: Temple University Press.

Zhitlowsky, Chaim. 1904. *Two Lectures on Yid and Mentsh*. Translated by Jonathan Boyarin. Edited by Marc Kaminsky. 1994. Unpublished.

Index

MITCHELL SILVER was born and raised in New York City and received his Ph.D. from the University of Connecticut. He has been teaching philosophy at the University of Massachusetts Boston since 1982. He is a contributor to *Defending Diversity: Contemporary Philosophical Perspectives on Pluralism and Multiculturalism* (University of Massachusetts Press, 1994) and has also written on health-care ethics. He is currently the cultural director of Camp Kinderland and the educational director of the Brookline, Massachusetts, I. L. Peretz School of the Workmen's Circle. He lives in West Newton with his wife, Ora, and his children, Isaac and Hadass.